Digital Economics

The Commerce of Information in the 21st Century

First Edition

Edited by Dave Seng
University of Arizona

cognella
SAN DIEGO

Bassim Hamadeh, CEO and Publisher
Jennifer McCarthy, Field Acquisitions Editor
Amy Smith, Project Editor
Abbey Hastings, Associate Production Editor
Jess Estrella, Senior Graphic Designer
Stephanie Kohl, Licensing Coordinator
Natalie Piccotti, Director of Marketing
Kassie Graves, Vice President of Editorial
Jamie Giganti, Director of Academic Publishing

Printed in the United States of America.

cognella® | CUSTOM
3970 Sorrento Valley Blvd., Ste. 500, San Diego, CA 9212

To my father, who once told a younger and more foolish version of myself,
"You can't survive without money."

Contents

Introduction vii

Unit I The Information Economy 2

1 Information and Markets 4
J. Edward Taylor and Travis J. Lybbert

2 A Renaissance of the Commons: How the New Sciences and Internet are Framing a New Global Identity and Order 32
John Clippinger and David Bollier

3 Digitalized Business Models for Pipeline Ecosystems 56
Vallabh Sambamurthy and Robert W. Zmud

Post-Reading Questions 74

Unit II Specific Issues Within the Information Economy 76

4 Digitalized Business Models for Network Ecosystems 78
Vallabh Sambamurthy and Robert W. Zmud

5 Preannouncing Information Goods 96
Jay Pil Choi, Eirik Gaard Kristiansen, and Jae Nahm

6 Versioning Information Goods 115
Paul Belleflamme

Post-Reading Questions 144

Unit III	Digital Currency: Bitcoin and Blockchain	146
7	Global Virtual Currency—Brief Overview Suhail Abboushi	148
8	The Bitcoin Revolution Bennett T. McCallum	158
9	The Market for Cryptocurrencies Lawrence H. White	166
10	An Introduction to Blockchain George (Yiorgos) Allayannis and Aaron Fernstrom	182
11	Blockchain Economies: The Crowd as the Market Maker Arun Sundararajan	200
	Post-Reading Questions	217

Introduction

SURPRISINGLY, THERE ARE VERY FEW BOOKS that explore the intersection of economics and the current digital reality that impacts each of our lives. This is especially remarkable when one realizes that all of the members that make up the Group of Seven (G7)—the seven largest advanced economies in the world—rely on nontangible information goods to such an extent that digital information makes up 70% of each country's GDP.[1] Usually, when one tries to explore the question of digital information and its economic implications on the economy, one notices that that the literature collects around three topics:

- The role of consumer information in the economy, which in the online world reduces to the role of network effects in the economy.
- The role of e-commerce in the economy, which amounts to digital or online marketing.
- The role of information and communication technology (ICT), which focuses on the technological side and emphasizes the role of computer science and the Internet of things (IOT) in the economy.

While these topics are very important, few books exist that bring them together and explore the overall impact digital information goods have on the economic situation we now find ourselves in the twenty-first century. This volume seeks to fill this absence, which is especially needed at the undergraduate level, by providing some of the most important readings in the field.

But what exactly is information, and what kind of impact does it have on the science of economics? For the purpose of this book, *information* is defined as anything that can be reduced to bits, digitally. The world now runs on the production, dissemination, and consumption of digital information. All of us constantly access all sorts of information, through all sorts of devices, from all sorts of providers. We read and interact with websites, we query databases, and we communicate with each other via social media. These sorts of activities permeate both our personal and professional lives. In order to successfully navigate this digital world, information consumers, information producers, and information policymakers need to understand what sorts of *information goods* are likely to be available and how much they are likely to cost.

1 Luciano Floridi, *Information: A Very Short Introduction* (Oxford: Oxford University Press, 2010).

In their book, Shapiro and Varian remind us that while technology changes, economic laws do not.[2] Economics will always be the study of how limited resources are used and the social cooperation that motivates individuals to produce and distribute goods in markets. The basic tools of economics—demand, supply, marginal cost, opportunity cost, and marginal benefit will still be used to guide the financial and policy decisions of information producers. At the same time, however, information goods have unique properties that physical goods do not. For instance, while only one person at a time can drive a particular car or eat a particular hamburger, millions of people can simultaneously read the same book, listen to the same song, and use the same software. Economists call these properties *nonrivalrous* and *nonexcludable* (which is why copyright law is such an important topic these days). In addition, once information is produced the cost of copying it is negligible (what economists call *zero marginal costs*). These are issues that are part and parcel to living, working, purchasing, and being entertained in an information society; these are the issues addressed in this book.

The intersection of economics and the information society is complicated. Nonetheless, by examining the overall economic structure in which the commerce of information exists, exploring important issues regarding digitized business models, and specific current trends such as Bitcoin and blockchain techniques, this book will further clarify how digital commerce functions in the twenty-first century.

2 Carl Shapiro and Hal R. Varian, *Information Rules: A Strategic Guide to the Network Economy* (Boston, Harvard Business School Press, 1999).

UNIT I

The Information Economy

This unit focuses on the nature of information in the digital economy, the unique properties of information goods, and the market structures of information producers. Information, of course, has always been important in economics. In the digital economy we find ourselves in today, information is now seen as a particular kind of good in the marketplace. Information goods are different from physical goods and have their own unique economic properties. For the purposes of this book, we use the definition of *information* as anything that has been digitized and commoditized (either as a good or service). Information goods, then, are simply the digital products we use every day, such as software, operating systems, digital books, or digitized movies, and the digital platforms we utilize to access them. Today, information producers have become the dominant firms in the economic marketplace (think of the enormous roles that Amazon, Facebook, and Google play in bringing you information products). In addition to e-commerce, nearly every level of business, education, entertainment, health care, finance, and banking rely on the exchange of information products and the networked communications technology that provides these services. This is why information goods have become so important to the information economy and why digital information has become the dominant driver of economics globally. Furthermore, there are many processes in the information market. These processes center around the occurrence (the creation or authoring), transmission (networking, distributing, access), processing and management (collecting, validating, indexing, and filtering), and usage (monitoring, modeling, analyzing) of information goods. These are central operations of every business and firm in the information economy. Without them, networked economics will not function, and firms spend bounteously to make sure these processes work seamlessly.

Unlike physical goods, information has particular properties. Information goods are both nonrivalrous and nonexclusive. While many people can enjoy a digitized song, movie, or book, only one person at a time can enjoy a hamburger or drive a car. This points to the nonexclusive character of digital information. It is very hard to prevent someone from using or gaining access to digital information. On the other hand, when an information good becomes inaccessible or corrupted for some reason, it has the potential to affect a very large number of people. Information goods are considered nonrivalrous because more than one person can share the benefit of the consumption of the same information product.

Another significant fact that distinguishes information goods from physical goods is that nearly all the costs are on the production side of the information good, and there are almost no costs at the reproduction and distribution side of the information good. What economists call "sunk costs" all occur at the production of the information good. Information goods can be very expensive to produce. However, the marginal costs of digital duplication and distribution are nearly zero. This increases the overall profitability of information goods and creates an interesting phenomenon among competitors in the digital marketplace. The competition among many information producers has made information cost less and less, sometimes even becoming free. Economists call this phenomenon *zero marginal cost* because the lowest marginal cost of most information goods on the Internet is free.

This condition of such freely available information has set up interesting new market structures. The main market structures we see today are the dominant firm, product differentiation, and cost leadership. For good or bad, digital network economies tend toward monopolies, which is why Facebook, Amazon, and Google and a few others have become dominant firms in the information economy. If an information producer wants to compete against monopolies, then it must either differentiate its product by adding unique value to its information good or service or by achieving cost leadership through network effects and scale. To compete in the information market, it is important to understand the market structure an information good falls into. These are the important themes that will be explored in this unit.

Reading 1

Information and Markets

J. Edward Taylor and Travis J. Lybbert

INTERNATIONAL DEVELOPMENT DEBATES, JUST LIKE DOMESTIC policy debates in most countries, often reveal how much we trust markets, on the one hand, and governments, on the other, to improve society. Framing these debates as either–or may be good political strategy, but it is often a false dichotomy that is ultimately not very helpful. To function efficiently, markets rely on a host of institutions, many of which require some form of government intervention to offset basic market failures. Conditions in developing countries frequently magnify these market failures. Development economists must appreciate how markets function in practice in poor countries and where they fail to function well, because these market failures can prevent the poor from reaping the big benefits markets can bring—benefits that planning without markets could never match.

Essentials

- Specialization and diversification
- Market integration and efficiency
- Institutions and transaction costs
- Market failures: asymmetric information
- Subsistence goods and shadow values
- Market failures: externalities and public goods
- The "knowledge problem"

Imagine you wake up one day and there are no markets. Not for food or other stuff. No credit, either—not that it would matter, without access to goods to spend money on. You'd eat whatever your plot of land gave you—no more, no less. You would be *your own* market; your internal balance of supply and demand would determine how much you consume and produce.

It also would determine how much you value things. If you're running low on food, you'd value it highly. In economics jargon, your "shadow price" of food would be high. If your plot produces too many tomatoes, your shadow price of tomatoes will be low.

I don't know about you, but I'd be in serious trouble without a food market. When people in Tigray province, Ethiopia, lost their access to food markets in 1983, the result was catastrophic (see sidebar 1.1).

Things would be better if we could get everyone in town together and form a market. You grow food, we do something else (like teach economics!). Someone else could make us candles, and others could bake us bread (assuming there's wax and wheat around), fire bricks, or carve furniture (assuming there's wood to be had). Having a local market, we could all begin to specialize.

With more far-flung markets, we'd get access to stuff we couldn't possibly produce locally and be able to sell stuff we produce best or have too much of. Tomatoes could be rotting

Sidebar 1.1 Famine and Missing Markets in Tigray

Between 1983 and 1985 a widespread famine took more than four hundred thousand lives in northern Ethiopia. The blame for the famine often is put on drought. However, the drought did not strike until months after the famine was already under way. In fact, as northern Ethiopia suffered famine, record harvests were reported in other parts of the country. Civil conflict against the Derg government and repressive policies shut down rural markets, forcing peasant households into self-sufficiency. When record low rainfall hit, markets could not function to fill the region's food deficit, and the rural population was left without access to food.

In January 2012 Ed visited a village in Tigray, the hardest hit province. The village had only a few hundred inhabitants, but this was market day. Thirty thousand people filed in from smaller villages as far away as twenty miles, all on foot. The line of people coming and going stretched off into the distance as far as he could see. Some hoisted bags of grain over their shoulders, others carried bags of produce or bunches of live chickens bound at their feet, and a few led goats on leashes fashioned from rope.

Ed asked his guide, an official in the state government, what this market looked like during the famine years. He sighed and said, "You do not understand. The soldiers would not let anyone walk the roads then. There was no market."

Alex de Waal, *Evil Days: Thirty Years of War and Famine in Ethiopia* (New York and London: Human Rights Watch, 1991), and personal interviews in Tigray province.

on the vine in your yard, but in a mill town in the next valley over there might be a tomato shortage. They'd pay dearly for your tomatoes and you for their wood, if only the two of you could discover one another, get together, and trade.

These insights about how the size of a market shapes incentives to specialize is a fundamental economic truth, but markets demand more than just buyers and sellers. Markets are based on specialization and trade, which require coordination and information. Buyers and sellers need to know about each other. If your "thing" is doing carpentry, you need to know where your buyers are and, in turn, where to get the food you'll need to eat.

One way to coordinate production across space is through centralized planning, as in the former Soviet Union and pre-reform China. Central planners faced an enormous task: coordinating production and demand across millions of producers and consumers and typically very large spaces (those countries were big!). They turned out not to be very good at it, as evidenced by their persistent use of rationing (exemplified by the long bread lines in Moscow in the 1960s), their inefficiency, and ultimately the demise of large centrally planned economies altogether.

Interestingly, large corporations in the world today face serious coordination challenges reminiscent in some ways of the ones faced by centrally planned economies. (Imagine the coordination it takes to make a Boeing 747!) Over the years, corporations have tended to oscillate between having highly centralized and decentralized decision models. They have come up with innovations to deal with their information and coordination demands, including structures that mimic markets and, of course, extensive use of computers and the Internet to track and coordinate activities.

Since ancient times, markets have been the answer to overcoming local resource constraints and gaining access to new goods. Archeologists have uncovered prolific evidence of ancient trade. For example, ceramic pottery and silver coins from fifth-century Athens are still being unearthed all around the Mediterranean Sea, from Egypt to Sicily. In ancient Athens, the Long Walls connected the city to its port, Pireaus, so that citizens would never be cut off from trade by sea, which provided most of the Athenians' food supplies. When Athens did lose control of the sea in the Peloponnesian War (404 BC), it quickly fell to Sparta and its allies—a vivid illustration of how critical access to markets is.

Today, markets are seen as the key to economic efficiency even in the world's former centrally planned economies. Why is this?

The Nobel laureate economist Friedrich August von Hayek had a simple answer to this question. He argued that markets effectively pool information from many different sources—more than any single person could easily understand—into a convenient measure of market conditions: a price (see sidebar 1.2). To most people, a price is nothing more than what you pay to buy something or what you get from selling it. To an economist, prices aggregate and

Sidebar 1.2 All in One Price

As a number of countries were experimenting with centrally planned economies, Friedrich von Hayek was looking "inside" prices. What he found there can tell us a lot about why centrally planned economies failed and why, without well-functioning markets, the economic prospects for poor societies are dim.

Think of anything that can shift around a supply or demand curve: changing technology, population, ethnicity of consumers, people's expectations, government policies, the weather, a war, the Internet, whatever. So many things that it's impossible to keep track of them all. Yet in a market, the intersection of supply and demand determines the price. If any of the multitude of things affecting supply or demand changes, we see it in the price. The Beatles said, "All you need is love." Economists say, "All you need is price." That's why market economies are better coordinated than centrally planned economies.

The price system, Hayek argued, is a "communications network" and the most efficient means of making use of economic information. It transmits information from one part of the market to another. For example, a drought might cause a grain-crop failure in one region, pushing up the grain price there. The higher price immediately communicates information to *other* regions where prices are lower. Astute traders see an opportunity to *arbitrage* (buy cheaply in one region and sell dearly in the other). In so doing, they resolve the excess-demand problem in the drought region while driving down prices there. If the market works very efficiently, a local drought will have almost no effect at all on local grain prices—the minute the price goes up, grain will rush in from other regions, driving it back down again. All because of the way prices convey information. The key to making prices play this valuable economic role is the rough-and-tumble process of market agitation that Hayek called "market competition."

Even well-developed market economies sometimes experience system-wide coordination failures leading to artificial booms and busts and even collapse into economic depression. These failures, Hayek argued, stem from coordination problems. Coordinating activities over time is more difficult than coordinating them at a given point in time. For example, producers have to make decisions today anticipating what other producers and consumers will do in the future. It turns out that prices are better at conveying information at a single point in time than through time. [...]

(*continued*)

Hayek's work changed the way we think about prices and the critical role that markets play in both developing and developed economies.

Roger W. Garrison and Israel Kirzner, "Friedrich August von Hayek," in *The New Palgrave: A Dictionary of Economics* (London: Macmillan, 1987), 609–14 (www.auburn.edu/~garriro/e4hayek.htm).

Friedrich A. von Hayek, "The Use of Knowledge in Society," *American Economic Review* 35 (September 1945):519–30 (www.econlib.org/library/Essays/hykKnw1.html).

convey information more effectively than any one person (or computer for that matter) could. A high price tells producers there is excess demand for their good, so they should produce more, and it tells consumers to cut back and seek out consumption substitutes. High input prices tell producers to seek out input substitutes while creating incentives for others to develop these substitutes. As we will see, this insight about markets has important implications for development policy and practice.

Markets are critical to economic welfare because they bring together sellers and buyers, integrate vast amounts of information, and distill that information into prices. In rich countries life would be unimaginable without access to a wide array of reasonably well functioning markets, from food to credit and insurance. It is almost never the case that a rich-country household has to produce something in order to consume it, or that its members cannot sell their labor for a salary or wage. Credit markets function for small businesses and farms to finance their investment projects. People pop out credit cards for convenience, to get through a tough time, or to buy things they can't afford at the moment. Insurance markets help protect people from unexpected income and health shocks. Every day more and more people interact in "virtual marketplaces," where buyers and sellers find each other and transact online, like on eBay and Amazon.com.

Missing markets create inefficiency. When markets don't work, prices vary from one place to another. Wages are high in my town but low in yours; food prices are low in my town but outrageously high in yours; I lack a forest but you have cheap wood. Almost nothing catches an economist's eye more quickly than price differences across space, because of the obvious efficiency implications. Widely varying prices for the same goods suggest that there is poor market integration and an opportunity to increase the economic pie for everyone.

Access to markets is just as compelling for a poor rural household in Rwanda, India, or Peru as for someone in a high-income country. Without good access to markets, a poor household cannot market its produce, obtain inputs, sell labor, obtain credit, learn about or adopt new technologies, insure against risks, or obtain consumption goods at low prices.

Equally important, it cannot use its scarce resources like land and labor efficiently. Its decision making is constrained.

Tradables, Nontradables, and Shadow Prices

When an economy does not have access to outside markets for a good, the good is called a "nontradable" for that economy, and the economy is called a "closed economy" for that good. The economy in question could be of a country, village, or even a household. The price of a non-tradable is determined by the intersection of demand and supply within the economy, as in an Econ 1 graph of market equilibrium; that is, it is *endogenous* to the economy.

When the economy is integrated with outside markets for a good, the good is said to be a "tradable," and the economy is called "open" for that good. The price of a tradable is determined outside the economy; that is, it is *exogenous*. At that price, if there is excess demand for the tradable, the difference is purchased in outside markets (imported). If there is excess supply, the surplus is sold in those markets (exported).

The notions of tradables, nontradables, and where prices come from apply to *any* economy—whether of a country, region, village, or household.

> *For a nation:* The minute a country opens up to international trade, world prices replace internal equilibrium prices for tradables. The world price is what people must pay for what they buy, or what they get for what they sell, on the world market.
>
> *For a village:* When a new road or communications network links a remote village up with a regional commercial center, goods that once were nontradable can become tradable. Village prices get replaced by prices determined in the outside market.
>
> *For a household:* A subsistence household—one that consumes what it produces and has to produce what it consumes—is a very small closed economy with respect to the subsistence good. The subsistence good has a price, which we call a "shadow price." You can think of it as being what the subsistence household would be willing to pay in order to have a little more of the subsistence good. We cannot see this price, because there is no market to show it to us, but it is there, and we can see its shadow (hence the name) and infer something about it if the right data are available (see sidebar 1.3). Keep this in mind as you read this chapter; it is fundamental to understanding trade and economic development. This shadow price gets replaced by an exogenous

Sidebar 1.3 Estimating the Shadow Price of Corn

You know what a shadow price is—you've surely "felt" one before. Imagine you're backpacking in a remote part of the Sierras and a bear gets your food. (That happened to one of us once, sad to say.) What you would pay for a freeze-dried pack of lasagna then! That's a shadow price. If you were standing in a backpacking shop, your shadow price would be the same as the price on the shelf. Hungry, isolated, and foodless in the mountains, *where there is no market,* you'd almost certainly be willing to pay more.

We can't see shadow prices, but sometimes we can estimate them. Consider a subsistence corn farmer in a remote village in southern Mexico. Assuming he follows basic economic precepts of optimizing behavior, he will produce at the point where the price just equals the marginal cost, as we saw in chapter 7. If we can estimate the marginal cost, then, we'll know what price the farmer is using to value his crop, whether it's for the market or for his family's own consumption.

A recent study used this approach to estimate the shadow price of maize for Mexican farmers. For commercial farmers, who are integrated with markets, the shadow price was found to be not significantly different from the market price. For subsistence farmers growing traditional maize varieties, though, it was significantly higher. The more remote the farmer was from markets, the higher his shadow price. Indigenous farmers were found to place a particularly high value on their traditional corn varieties.

This study showed how to estimate the shadow price of a subsistence crop, and it offered an explanation for why small farmers seem to produce corn at a loss: they put a higher value on their corn than the market does. Friedrich von Hayek would not be happy about that!

Aslihan Arslan and J. Edward Taylor, "Farmers' Subjective Valuation of Subsistence Crops: The Case of Traditional Maize in Mexico," *American Journal of Agricultural Economics* 91, no. 4 (2009):895–909.

market price if the subsistence household becomes connected with village markets or markets outside the village.

Some goods by their very nature tend to be nontradables. Haircuts are an example: it's hard to buy them from somewhere else unless you travel to wherever the hairdresser is. (Ed "imported" a pretty good haircut from Paris last year, but that's because he happened to be there for a workshop.) Lodging and restaurant food are other examples of nontradables. Sometimes, goods that are nontradable can become tradable. Highly perishable foods, like fish, are nontradables if they have to be carried by hand or on a donkey's back over long distances in the heat. They can become tradables if traders have trucks and ice boxes, public transport becomes available, or the fisherman gets a motorcycle.

When goods and services that *could* be tradable *are not,* two important questions arise. First, "Why not?" And second, "What are the consequences for economic welfare, particularly of the poor?"

What Makes Tradables Nontradables?

The explanations for why things that *could* be tradable are *not* tradable fall mostly into two categories: transaction costs and trade policies. High transaction costs can inhibit trade within as well as among countries. Trade policies almost always have to do with trade among countries; it is rare for a country to regulate trade within its own borders. In the rest of this chapter we will learn the essentials of understanding transaction costs and how they can limit or shut down markets within countries. In the next chapter we will learn about international trade and trade policies.

Transaction Costs

Usually government policies do not limit trade within countries. However, *transaction costs* can turn tradables into nontradables within countries in much the same way that restrictive trade policies cut countries off from international markets.

The market price is what a buyer pays or a seller receives as a result of a transaction, like the ones that happen billions of times a day in marketplaces and stores around the globe. Transacting is not free, though. Buyers and sellers have to know where to find one another. Both have to know the specifics of what is being transacted, including its quality. When you sell something to me, property rights change hands. What was yours becomes mine. We both need to be convinced that you had the right to sell it and I have secure rights to the thing once I buy it. All of these things have to happen every time we buy or sell anything: a potato, a day's work, a piece of property, a loan, or an insurance policy.

Simply put, there are three kinds of transaction costs:

1. The costs of searching out buyers or sellers and discovering or signaling the quality of the good or service being bought or sold.
2. The costs of negotiating deals and setting up contracts.
3. The costs of enforcing contracts once the deal has been made.

For a potato, (2) and (3) would probably be too small to even think about, but (1) might be important. For property, credit, insurance, labor, and many other goods and services, all three are likely to be considerable. In developed countries, institutions [...] evolve to deal with these, but in poor economies, the institutions needed to lower these costs enough so that transactions actually occur are often weak or nonexistent. The result is market failure.

Many of the institutions [...] have big economic effects because they determine the transaction costs involved in these market transactions. For many transactions, like buying a lemon, transaction costs might be trivial. But what if the lemon is an old car?

The Power of Information

In 1970, UC Berkeley economist George Akerlof published a revolutionary paper called "The Market for 'Lemons.'"[1] The paper was so novel that it got rejected by three top economics journals before eventually winning Akerlof the Nobel Prize. It was about the power of information to make—or break—markets. Its argument goes something like this:

You want to sell your used car. After taking good care of it all these years, you know it's in top shape, and you want to get a good price for it. But what do the potential buyers know? Only what they can see. There is *asymmetric information:* you know more about your car's quality than they do. Unless you can persuade them otherwise, the most they'll be willing to pay will be the price of the average-quality car out there.

So what do you do? Unless you can figure out a way to resolve this information asymmetry, you either sell below what you know your car is worth, or else you pull your car off the market. If you decide not to offer your car for sale, the average quality of cars on the market falls. Over time, this lowers used car prices. Other people with high-quality used cars leave the market, quality and prices fall further, and before you know it, only low-quality cars are left. This is what Akerlof calls "The Market for Lemons."[2] In the extreme case, the market collapses.

When the *Journal of Political Economy* rejected this paper, the editor informed Akerlof that "if this paper was correct, economics would be different."

It was correct, and economics is different.

Today we understand that information is the lubricant that makes markets work. Yet information asymmetries abound, especially in poor countries. Because of them, markets can fail. Surrounded by market failures, poor people's prospects of escaping from poverty are grim.

Food export markets provide a classic example of information asymmetries that make markets fail—for small producers, at least. Diversifying into high-value export crops is critical if poor countries wish to increase their foreign exchange and raise farm incomes. Some African countries, such as Ethiopia, Kenya, and Uganda, are well positioned to supply crops year-round to developed countries, particularly in Europe. However, without the right information this trade cannot happen.

Take food safety, for example. High-income countries have stringent food safety standards. The United States inspects food imports to make sure they comply with food safety rules, even inspecting foreign food facilities.[3] The European Union, the world's biggest food importer, requires that all imported food meet the same level of food safety as food produced within the EU.[4]

Food safety concerns are understandable, of course. But even if a small African farmer can meet the EU's food safety requirements, how will she convince the EU that she has done so? The cost of many small producers complying with these requirements is likely to be significantly higher than the cost for a few big producers. Certifying food safety is a transaction cost of selling food to high-income countries, and it can impose high costs on poor countries (sidebar 1.4).

Sidebar 1.4 The High Cost of Saving Two in a Billion

If countries wish to export food to developed countries, they have to meet food safety standards concerning pesticide residues, harvesting and packing operations, and a means to trace back to their source any food safety problems that do arise. In 1997, the European Union set new, stringent limits on aflatoxins, which are toxic compounds that contaminate certain foods and can result in the production of acute liver carcinogens. The proposed limits were far below the limits that some individual EU countries had previously adopted. A number of food-exporting countries, including Bolivia, Brazil, Peru, India, Argentina, Canada, Mexico, Uruguay, Australia, and Pakistan, raised concerns that the new standards were unnecessary and overly restrictive.

What effect would this new food safety standard have on developing countries? Three World Bank economists estimated the impact on African food exports, using a gravity model [...]. They found that the new standard would reduce health risk by approximately 1.4 deaths per billion a year, but it would cut African exports by 64%, or US$ 670 million, compared with existing international food safety standards. Their findings illustrate the trade-off between health risks and the high transaction costs rich-country food standards impose on poor-country producers.

Tsunehiro Otsuki, John S. Wilson, and Mirvat Sewadeh, "Saving Two in a Billion: Quantifying the Trade Effect of European Food Safety Standards on African Exports," *Food Policy* 26, no. 5 (2001):495–514.

Another example involving certification is titling [...]. A formal title provides security that the seller really owns the property being sold. Without it, a potential buyer would face risks that easily could kill the deal. Around the globe, governments keep public records of land and building titles and histories of sales, which permits "title searches." In the United States, you cannot get a loan to buy a house without a title search; this information creates the credit. That's why land titling has been a focus of development projects by international development banks.

Information is critical to making other markets work. Without the certification that a fruit or vegetable was organically grown, who would pay the price to "buy organic"? Certification is the key to green, eco-friendly labeling. The same goes for any quality standard. The US Department of Agriculture enforces quality standards for agricultural products; no meat packing plant is without its USDA inspector and inspection stamps. These activities not only protect consumer health but also create information vital to making markets work.

In a striking example of the power of information and uncertainty, beef consumption in Japan fell 60% after the first case of mad cow disease was reported there in 2001. The vast majority of beef in Japan was free of the disease, of course, but without access to information about *which* meat was mad-cow free, the market reeled. The Japanese beef market recovered once the country began testing *all* of its cows.

How Markets Can Lower Transaction Costs

What exactly is a market? When you think of a market you might conjure up images of a grocery store or a mall, or perhaps a marketplace like the one in Tigray, Ethiopia, to which we linked up earlier in this chapter. Markets do not have to be physical places, though. If you bought this book, there's a good chance you did it online, without going to a bookstore. More and more, commerce within and among countries is conducted online, thanks to the likes of Amazon, eBay, and many other companies. eBay is a prime example of a virtual marketplace. It brings buyers and sellers together without ever having them at the same location. People use it for one simple reason: it dramatically lowers transaction costs. Sellers can easily make their wares available for the whole world to see, and buyers can search these goods out effortlessly. The transaction can happen with the click of a mouse. What's someone else's becomes yours instantly. There are still transaction costs. Sellers have to make an effort to list their goods and describe them adequately so that prospective buyers can learn about them. Buyers have to sit down and search out what is available online. And information asymmetries have to be dealt with. Buyers need assurances that they will get what they think they are paying for, and sellers have to be sure that the buyer's money is good. Online marketplaces have solutions for these information problems. They track the reputation of buyers and sellers, facilitate the transaction by letting people pay with secure electronic wallets (like PayPal), and even provide quality guarantees and easy returns should a transaction not turn out right. These services are all about reducing transaction costs in online markets.

So what is a market, then? Here are some definitions taken from well-known dictionaries:

mar·ket \ˈmärkət\

An open place or a covered building where buyers and sellers convene for the sale of goods. (Dictionary.com)

A meeting together of people for the purpose of trade ... a public place where a market is held. *(Merriam-Webster)*[5]

A regular gathering of people for the purchase and sale of provisions, livestock, and other commodities. *(Oxford)*[6]

None of these captures what economists really mean when they talk about markets. Here's a more comprehensive definition, which encompasses virtual as well as physical markets:

A market is where

- buyers and sellers find one another and their wares,
- price discovery happens, and
- an infrastructure and set of institutions facilitate the transfer of property rights from one person to another.

The third function of markets above—facilitating the transfer of property rights—is fairly simple for a persimmon or laptop. However, it can be very complicated indeed for a loan or an insurance policy, which is why we have a special chapter in this book dedicated to credit and risk. The notion of information is central to all three aspects of our definition of markets. Buyers and sellers have to learn about each other and the true nature of the goods or services to be transacted. Prices have to convey information in order for the market to work properly, as we saw in sidebar 1.2. Buyers and sellers have to be reasonably sure of who holds the property rights before and after a transaction is made—and how these rights will be protected. If any bit of this information is missing, the transaction is likely to fall apart.

Information asymmetries can easily shut small farmers out of domestic as well as international markets. Consider a poor farmer who can produce high-quality berries at a low price. In town, exporters are willing to pay 20 cents a basket for berries like the ones he can grow. Poor roads and communications, however, cut the farmer off from information about buyers: where to sell, when to sell, how to ensure quality, and the price the farmer might get once he transports his berries to the market. This makes marketing a perishable crop too expensive and risky. So the farmer produces a few baskets for his family's and maybe a few neighbors' consumption, and he spends the rest of his time doing low-wage work, when available, on a nearby ranch. A basket of berries costs him 10 cents to produce (including the cost of his time). Implicitly, then, this is his decision price, or the price at which he is willing to produce berries. If he could become part of the export supply chain, his decision price would instantly rise to the market price. He could be more efficient, shifting some or all of his time from low-wage work to berry production, and he would have an incentive to invest in his farm. Most importantly, he could generate badly needed cash for his family.

We can illustrate the welfare loss from high transaction costs using the concepts of producer and consumer surplus. Let's begin by seeing what the producer and consumer surplus are without village-town trade, and then we'll see what trade does to them.

Producer Surplus

Without trade, village supply and demand determine the village equilibrium price and quantity of berries, as shown in figure 1.1. Following the basic rule for profit maximization, the quantity of berries supplied in the village is given by the point where $p_v = MC$, that is, where the village price line hits the supply curve. You can see in figure 1.1 that, at the equilibrium price, the optimal output is Q_v. Producers make no profit on the last unit supplied (because its MC just equals the price). However, they *do* make a profit on all the other units ($Q < Q_v$), because on those units the price exceeds the MC. Total profits are given by the area of triangle B, which is the sum of the difference between price and MC for all of the units supplied, up to Q_v. (In calculus terms, in case that's how you like to think, it's the integral from zero to Q_v of the function $p - MC(Q)$.)

This is the *producer surplus*. For all units from zero to Q_v, producers get a price higher than the minimum they would require in order to supply the goods. The producer surplus is our measure of producers' economic welfare.

Consumer Surplus

There is an analogue to the producer surplus for consumers. Not surprisingly, it is called the "consumer surplus." Have you ever paid less for something than you would have been willing to pay? Maybe picked up what you want on sale, surprised by how cheap it was, and then asked yourself what you'll do with all the money you saved? That difference between what you would have been willing to pay and what you did pay is your consumer surplus.

Look at the market demand curve in figure 1.1. It represents consumers' willingness to pay for each quantity of the good. The quantity demanded in the market is given by the point where the village price line hits this demand curve; in this figure it is Q_v. For all the quantities from zero to Q_v, consumers would have been willing to pay more than the village price. The sum of differences between consumers' willingness to pay and the village price, then, is the total consumer surplus in this market. It is shown as triangle A in the figure. It will be our measure of consumers' economic welfare.

Total economic welfare is the sum of producer surplus and consumer surplus. It is the sum of these two triangles.

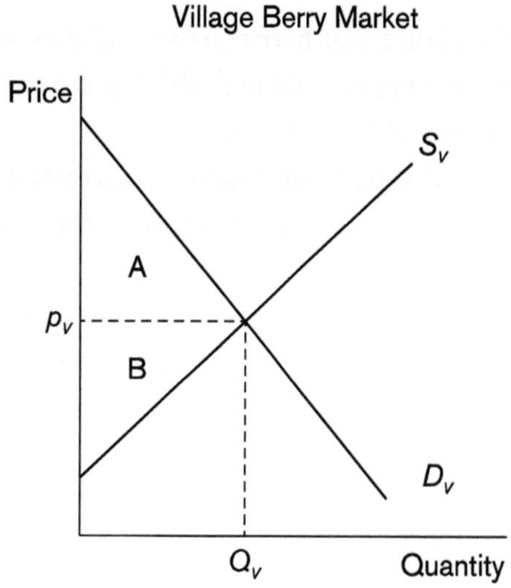

FIGURE 1.1 Equilibrium in the Village Berry Market without Trade.

Trade and Economic Welfare

What does village-town trade in berries do to villagers' economic welfare? Suppose that in town, our berry producer could sell his berries at a regional price equal to p_r. This price might be determined by supply and demand in the regional berry market, or it might even come from the world market, if town traders export the berries they buy from local farmers. The right side of figure 1.2 illustrates the case in which the price is determined by equilibrium in the regional berry market.

On the left side of figure 1.2 we see the village berry market again. The way we drew this figure, the regional price, p_r, is higher than the village equilibrium price, p_v. Naturally, given

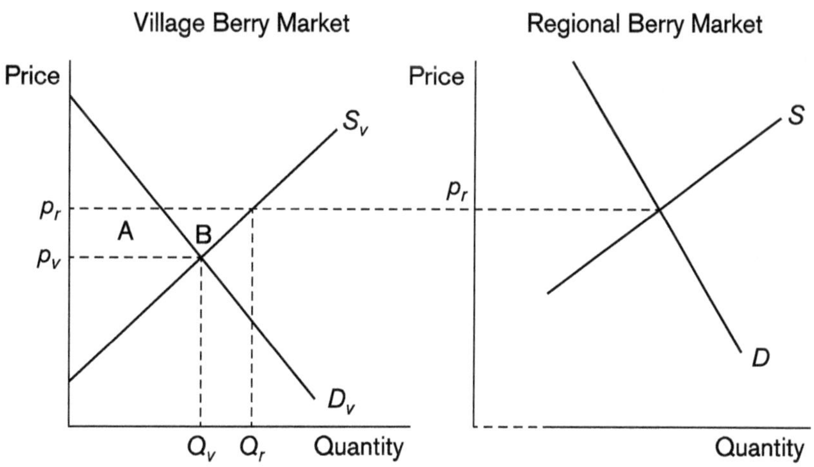

FIGURE 1.2 If the Regional Price is higher than the Village Price, trade increases the Producer Surplus more than it Decreases the Consumer Surplus. Thus, the total Economic Surplus Rises.

the choice, our berry farmer will choose to sell in the town, at the higher price. That's the price village consumers will have to pay the farmer if they want him to sell berries to them instead of to the town.

In this particular example, farmers gain from trade, but consumers lose. Consumer surplus falls by an amount equal to the trapezoidal area A in figure 1.2. That's the decrease in the size of the triangle underneath the demand curve when the price rises from p_v to p_r. Producer surplus, however, increases by an amount equal to areas A plus B. The gain to farmers exceeds the loss to consumers, and total economic welfare increases. In theory, producers could fully compensate consumers and still have higher profits than without trade. (Whether they will or not is another question. It underlies controversies about free trade, which we will consider in chapter 12.)

You might wonder what happens if the regional price is *lower* than the village price. We leave it as an exercise to show that the total economic surplus still increases from trade. If $p_r < p_v$, producer surplus decreases, but consumer surplus rises more than enough to compensate.

How Transaction Costs Can Kill Trade

In order to sell in the regional market, though, the farmer will have to incur a transaction cost equivalent to $\$t$ per unit sold. You can imagine the high cost of transporting the berries over bad roads, and before that, whatever costs in money and time she has to incur to travel to town, find out about prices there, and arrange the sale (a cell phone might help). Then there's always a risk that, once she delivers the berries to the market, the buyer will change his mind and decide not to buy (an enforceable contract would help). Market uncertainty adds what economists call a "risk premium" to t. You can think of it as the amount the farmer would be willing to pay to insure against the possibility of the sale falling through. When you talk to farmers in poor villages, these are the sorts of things they mention when explaining why they do not sell in outside markets.

Given these transaction costs, the farmer's net price will be $(1 - t)p_r$. Figure 1.3 shows the case where the price the farmer gets by selling in town, net of transaction costs, is less than the village price. Faced by high transaction costs, the farmer is better off selling only in the village, at the village price p_v. In doing so, he produces less and loses profit (producer's surplus) equal to the areas A + B in figure 1.3. Consumers gain by being able to buy berries at the lower village price, but their gain (area A) is not enough to make up for the producer's loss.

In this age of the supermarket revolution, getting small farmers into the Walmart supply chain can be the key to raising agricultural incomes and reducing poverty. But transaction costs can make Walmart shut its doors to small farmers (see sidebar 1.5).

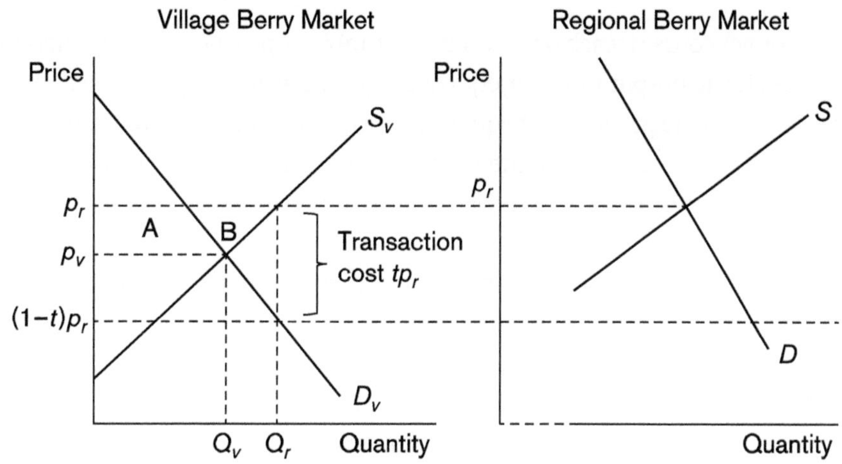

FIGURE 1.3 **When Transaction Costs cut Producers off from Higher Prices in Outside Markets, Producer Surplus Falls (area A + B). Consumer Surplus Increases (area A), but not by Enough to Compensate for the fall in Producer Surplus.**

Sidebar 1.5 Walmart in Nicaragua

Many people think of supermarkets as the rich world's place to shop, but the rapid rise of supermarkets is transforming agricultural supply chains in Africa, Asia, and Latin America. The supermarket explosion leaves development economists with big new questions. Can poor farmers make their way into the supply chains of Walmart and other major players in the supermarket space, given the exacting standards they face? Or will the supermarket revolution pass them by and possibly leave them more marginalized than before?

An economist at Columbia University's Earth Institute set out to answer these questions by asking what determines whether small farmers become suppliers of food to Walmart in Nicaragua. This is a tricky question, because as in program evaluation (chapter 2), unobservable variables may determine whether farmers participate in the Walmart supply chain, and they can easily confound estimates of how other things affect participation.

This study followed the same farmers over time. It found that only farmers with advantageous access to roads and water are likely to participate in the Walmart supply chain. The study is important because it identifies obstacles to small-farmer participation in the Walmart supply chain, including factors related to transaction costs.

Hope C. Michelson, "Small Farmers, NGOs, and a Walmart World: Welfare Effects of Supermarkets Operating in Nicaragua," *American Journal of Agricultural Economics* 95, no. 3 (2013).

Microeconomics courses teach us that firms optimize by producing where their marginal cost (MC) equals the output price, or equivalently, where each input is used at the point where its marginal value product just equals its price. Consumers do something similar by demanding goods at the level where their marginal rate of substitution (MRS, the slope of the indifference curve or ratio of marginal utilities any two goods create) just equals the ratio of prices.

If everyone bases decisions on the same prices, things cannot be any more efficient. The MC will be the same for all producers (and equal to the output price). The marginal rate of substitution will be the same for all consumers (equal to the ratio of prices).

As you can see in figure 1.3, though, when there are high transaction costs, different producers (for example, near or far from markets) may face different prices and thus produce at different MCs. Recall that the supply curve *is* the marginal cost curve. The farmers who supply the regional market produce at an MC equal to p_r, whereas the village farmer produces at an MC equal to p_v. The same thing happens to consumers: they equate their marginal rates of substitution with the ratio of the prices they face, which may be very different from the prices others face.

When this happens, efficiency could be increased—dramatically, perhaps—by reducing or eliminating transaction costs, so that trade can equalize prices across markets. Remember this—it is the fundamental problem that high transaction costs create in poor economies: market failure occurs when economic actors are unable to get together to make efficiency-enhancing trades. Transaction costs resulting from imperfect information are a major reason why this happens. (Another is civil strife, as in the example from Tigray at the start of this chapter.) In fact, billions of people—particularly poor people—opt out of markets, apparently because the transaction costs of using markets are too high.

When transaction costs cause prices to vary across space, a cell phone can literally keep food from rotting on the vine—or fish from rotting on the beach (see sidebar 1.6).

Transaction Costs In Input Markets

So far we've focused on the effects of transaction costs in output markets. Asymmetric information and high transaction costs can also shut farmers out of input markets. When a farmer cannot get fertilizer or hire labor at the times needed, or cannot be sure of input quality, he may sow less land or not adopt more productive technologies, and his output may fall as a result. Efficiency is critical because even a small income gain can make a huge difference for an impoverished household—particularly if that gain can be sustained month after month, year after year.

Sidebar 1.6 Saving Fish with Cell Phones

People need price information in order to trade efficiently. In Kerala, India, more than 1 million people fish. While at sea, fishermen can't observe prices at markets along the coast. Transportation costs are high, and fish are perishable. This keeps fishermen from moving from port to port looking for the best price once their boats are full. Thus, almost all fishermen sell their catch locally, and this can create a surplus of fish in some places—in fact, the price of fish can drop all the way to zero. When that happens, fish literally are left to rot. Meanwhile, just down the coast, people in other towns might be happy to pay a good price for this fish. If only the fishermen had known—they could have chosen to put in their boats down the coast, instead.

Between 1997 and 2001, mobile phone service was introduced in Kerala. Robert Jensen hypothesized that this could be very good for fishermen and consumers—not to mention the fish. He gathered data on the ups and downs of fish prices along the coast both before and after the introduction of cell phones. His analysis found that mobile phones dramatically reduced price variability and waste and raised fishermen's profits as well as consumers' welfare. Since improvements in market efficiency can benefit all market participants, even fishermen without cell phones were better off when some of their fellow fishermen started using them.

This study is a dramatic illustration of how the exchange of information via cell phones enabled fishermen to sell their catch where prices are high, leveling out price variability along the Kerala coast. Cell phones made the fish market work, and the market made people better off—while saving a whole lot of fish. And obviously, this effect is not unique to fish markets: development economists have found similar dramatic market effects due to the introduction of cell phones. Jenny Aker, for example, found that the arrival of mobile phones in Niger between 2001 and 2006 substantially reduced the variation in grain prices across rural markets, bringing big benefits to the hardest-to-reach markets.

Robert Jensen, "The Digital Provide: Information (Technology), Market Performance, and Welfare in the South Indian Fisheries Sector," *Quarterly Journal of Economics* 122, no. 3 (August 2007):879–924.

Jenny C. Aker, "Information from Markets Near and Far: Mobile Phones and Agricultural Markets in Niger," *American Economic Journal: Applied Economics* 2, no. 3 (July 2010):46–59.

Labor Markets

Anyone who has taken microeconomics knows the textbook solution to the labor-hiring problem: employers should hire workers up to the point where their marginal value product (MVP) just equals the wage. The MVP is how much value (gross revenue) the last (marginal) worker will create. The wage is how much it will cost to hire him.

But how can we be sure that that last worker will really produce that MVP? Or the worker before him, for that matter? What if you hire him and he doesn't work hard, generating less revenue than the wage you have to pay him? This is called "shirking," and it is a form of moral hazard. Employers can deal with this problem by monitoring the workers they hire, just like a bank can monitor borrowers, but that's expensive.

There is also the possibility of adverse selection. Some workers are more productive than others. How do you know you'll end up with a "good" one—that is, a worker who produces an MVP higher than the wage? If the worker is a member of your own family, you'll have good information about him. If not, information may be asymmetric—the worker knows how good he is, but you do not. It might be possible to overcome adverse selection by offering a wage higher than the going market wage in order to attract more productive workers. But this, like monitoring, is costly.

The costs of monitoring and screening workers are transaction costs in labor markets. The true cost of hiring a worker is the wage plus these transaction costs. If the transaction costs are high enough, the labor market will fail: no workers will be hired. Then producers are forced to use their own labor. If you can hire workers, it doesn't matter how big your family's labor endowment is—you simply hire up to the point where the MVP equals the market wage. If you can't, then how much you produce depends on how much family labor you have.

In a labor-constrained household, the "family shadow wage," or opportunity cost of family time, is high. (The family shadow wage is the wage you would be willing to pay if you could hire workers.) In a labor-abundant household, the family wage is low; the market failure traps labor in the household. In that case, you would be willing to work for a relatively low wage, but no one will hire you because of the asymmetric information problem: employers are not sure how productive you'll be.

If my shadow wage is low and yours is high, we might both be better off if I worked for you. You'd pay a wage lower than your reservation wage, and I'd get a wage higher than my reservation wage. If transaction costs in the labor market are too high, though, the labor exchange won't take place.

There is a simple solution to the adverse selection and moral hazard problems in labor markets: pay workers a piece rate. It is common in both poor and rich countries to pay farmworkers a flat cash amount per unit harvested: box, kilo, bundle, and so forth. Harvest workers in Mexico often are paid a share of the corn crop. Fishermen often pay their crew a share of the catch. California farmers pay strawberry pickers a piece rate per twelve-pint tray during peak harvest periods.[7]

Piece rates have advantages and disadvantages. From the producer's point of view, they have the advantage of shifting all the risk associated with adverse selection and moral hazard onto the workers. Farmers know exactly how much it will cost to pick, say, a ton of peaches if they pay a piece rate, but not if they pay a wage. Piece rates have the disadvantage of encouraging workers to focus on quantity, not quality, for example, to pick as many peaches as possible but not worry about bruising them. Employers who pay piece rates thus have to be extra careful about monitoring quality, for example, by checking the fruit and docking workers for poor quality.

The piece-rate system ensures that workers get paid according to their productivity. Pick fast and your day's pay will be higher. Pick too slowly and you might not have enough food to eat. This is good news for highly productive workers, but it obviously is a disadvantage for less-productive ones. Less-productive workers may not be able to pick enough to cover their subsistence (or the minimum wage, if there is one). In California, farmers are required by law to pay all workers at least the minimum wage, even if they are not productive enough to "pick" the minimum wage. This shifts some of the risk associated with adverse selection and moral hazard back onto employers. While some kinds of work lend themselves to piece rates, others do not. It's easy to pay a piece rate to strawberry pickers, but what about workers in soil preparation, planting, or weeding?

Other Inputs

When people face transaction costs in input markets, the price they pay for their inputs includes the cost of making the transaction. Adverse selection and moral hazard are not so much problems in the case of purchased inputs; the quality of fertilizer usually is pretty much known by everyone, and fertilizer—unlike workers—does not have a mind of its own or need to be monitored.

Other problems can create transaction costs and make input markets fail, though. Foremost among them is timing. Not having an input at the time it is needed often is as bad as not having it at all. Seed, fertilizer, insecticides, and herbicides all must be applied at just the right time or the farmer will risk losing his crop. Input markets have to work efficiently to make sure this happens, yet often they do not.

Poorly functioning input markets can even keep people from adopting more productive technologies. The Green Revolution (high-yielding) seeds [...] were engineered to give high yields as long as complementary inputs, particularly fertilizer, are applied in a timely fashion. If a farmer is unsure that he'll be able to buy fertilizer at the moment it has to be applied, he may be better off not planting the high-yielding variety.

Sidebar 1.7 Nudging Poor Farmers to Use Fertilizer

Poor farmers in Africa do not use nearly enough fertilizer. For example, fertilizer use in sub-Saharan Africa was only 8 kg/ha in 2002, compared with 101 kg/ha in South Asia. Such massive disparities in fertilizer use between Africa and the rest of the world suggest that there are structural impediments limiting fertilizer availability and demand. It is very unlikely that African farmers are applying fertilizer at a level that equates its marginal value product with the world price. They act as though the price of fertilizer is much higher than the price in the market. Why the disparity?

One possibility is that poor farmers simply don't have the cash. Three economists offered a different explanation: timing. Even poor farmers who are willing to pay the market price for fertilizer cannot be sure they'll be able to get the fertilizer they need when they need it.

In a clever experimental study in Kenya, some farmers were offered free fertilizer delivery early in the season and others not, while still others were offered a fertilizer subsidy. The study found that offering delivery early was more effective at increasing fertilizer use than was a subsidy—not to mention cheaper.

Esther Duflo, Michael Kremer, and Jonathan Robinson, "Nudging Farmers to Use Fertilizer: Evidence from Kenya," *American Economic Review* 101, no. 6 (2011):2350–90.

People could take measures to ensure that they have the inputs they need at the time they need them. For example, instead of investing their scarce cash in more productive activities, they could use it to stockpile fertilizer when they can get it, then let the fertilizer sit there until the time comes to apply it. Or they could invest time and money into searching out sources of inputs, from distant cities if needed. By taking steps like these, farmers could make sure they have the inputs they need at the time they are needed, but obviously these steps are costly. In the end, the effective price of fertilizer is the market price plus the transaction cost the farmer incurs to make sure he has the fertilizer when he needs it. That transaction cost may make all the difference (see sidebar 1.7).

Transaction Costs and Spatial Market Integration

So far, we have discussed participation in either output or input markets as a binary variable. That is, a given farm household either sells its maize in the local market or it does not; it either hires labor or it does not. As we've already explored, transaction costs can have a big influence on this decision, and the decision can, in turn, have a big effect on household efficiency and welfare. Because they affect these decisions, transaction costs can have a big impact on how markets in one location are related to other markets. This is what economists call "spatial market integration," which is often a key determinant of how and how well markets in developing countries function.

While potential buyers and sellers typically face a binary decision to participate in a market or not, spatial market integration is measured as a continuous variable. If a wheat market in Meknès, Morocco, is unintegrated with the other wheat markets in Morocco (much less international wheat markets), then wheat prices in Meknès will be completely determined by local supply and demand. In the case of drought, wheat prices will skyrocket. If instead the Meknès wheat market is fully integrated with the world wheat market, a local drought will not affect local prices because any local shortfall will be filled by the world wheat supply.

Most input and output markets in developing countries fall somewhere between these two market integration extremes. Whether a given market is poorly integrated or well integrated depends on many of the sources of transaction costs we have already encountered: information, transportation, contracts, tariffs and other barriers to trade, and so on. This degree of market integration can directly affect welfare outcomes.

In addition to subjecting households to greater price volatility—and, in the case of food markets, greater vulnerability to food insecurity—poor market integration can constrain local productivity by directly affecting production decisions. For example, a few years ago Travis was conducting focus group discussions with wheat farmers in Meknès. It was March, and it was shaping up to be a perfect rainfall year—the wheat looked beautiful. But the farmers were intentionally getting lower yields than they could have. Why? Because nearly all the farmers had decided not to use fertilizer once they realized how good the rainfall would be. This was especially perplexing to agronomists because fertilizer dramatically increases yields when rainfall is good. What then was holding back these farmers?

As the farmers explained (with impressive economic intuition), "We know fertilizer could really increase our yields this year because of the rainfall, but even without fertilizer everyone's yield will be high and wheat prices will collapse at harvest. With lower prices, we might not even cover the cost of the fertilizer!" This is what poorly integrated markets look like to poor farmers.

The Role of Government

We conclude this chapter with some thoughts about the role of government in a world of asymmetric information and market failures.

Economists almost uniformly agree that markets are crucial to people's welfare. Free-market economists believe that the free functioning of markets, without government intervention, leads to the greatest common good, often citing Adam Smith's reference to "an invisible hand." This belief is an underpinning of free-trade agreements among nations and market reforms within them. The Fundamental Theorem of Welfare Economics states that competitive markets lead to a "first best" allocation of resources that is *Pareto efficient;* that is, nobody can be made better off without someone else being made worse off.

The fundamental theorem does not necessarily hold when markets are incomplete or information is imperfect—two common features of poor economies. We have seen that there are many cases in which there is no market, and we will see still others in the chapter on credit and risk. In such an environment, there is no first-best outcome, and a government hands-off or laissez-faire approach to markets is not likely to be optimal. As the Nobel laureate economist Joseph Stiglitz explained it, "The theories that said that markets work perfectly were all based on very simplistic models of perfect competition, perfect markets, and perfect information ... The reason that the invisible hand often seemed invisible was that it wasn't there."[8]

The question today is no longer whether governments should be involved in markets, but how much—that is, finding the right balance between the market and government.

Grounds for Government Intervention in Markets

One does not have to reject market economics to recognize situations in which governments should become involved in markets. One of these is the provision of information, which can lower transaction costs for everyone. Governments around the world have statistical bureaus that gather information and make it publicly available.

There are other instances in which a strong case can be made for government intervention in markets:

> *Externalities:* The actions of an individual have bad (or good) impacts on others for which the individual doesn't pay (or get compensated). Externalities are crucial in environmental economics, from pollution to biodiversity. Markets, left to themselves, produce too much air and water pollution (which harms people who breathe the air or drink the water), too little research (which creates public benefits), too little education (my education can make other workers more productive), too few beehives (bees pollinate peach orchards),

Sidebar 1.8 Which Seeds to Save?

Plant breeders have been remarkably successful at creating new high-yielding seeds to meet the growing global food demand. Green Revolution seed varieties were engineered from traditional varieties with the characteristics agronomists wish to breed into the new varieties. But what if the traditional varieties weren't there anymore?

To reap the benefits of high-yielding varieties, farmers have to plant them. But to create new seed varieties in the future, scientists need the genetic diversity found in traditional seed varieties. What if the new seeds are so superior that farmers stop growing traditional varieties altogether? What if other forces at work, like the spread of markets, lead farmers to stop growing traditional varieties, which then go extinct? How would scientists get the genetic resources they need to continue breeding new crop varieties—whether to increase yields or to breed in resistance to new diseases and pests?

There is not a market for biodiversity, so when farmers decide to stop growing traditional varieties, they do not take into account the costs to society of losing valuable crop genetic resources. Researchers have found evidence that traditional seed varieties are disappearing, a process called "genetic erosion."

Some research suggests that high transaction costs and marginal environments may slow crop genetic erosion. Studies of wheat in Turkey, potatoes in Peru, and maize in Mexico find that isolation from markets limits the spread of high-yielding varieties. When people face high transaction costs and must produce what they consume, they are much more likely to plant traditional varieties—because they taste better. Most high-yielding varieties were engineered to outperform traditional varieties, but only in high-quality environments with fertile, level land and access to water. Farmers are more likely to plant traditional seeds on marginal lands. Transaction costs and marginal environments, then, seem to be friends of crop genetic diversity.

This raises an important question: As rural markets become better integrated with national markets and new seeds are engineered to do well in marginal environments, how will we make sure that we have the genetic resources we need for agricultural research?

Stephen B. Brush and Erika Meng, "Farmers' Valuation and Conservation of Crop Genetic Resources," *Genetic Resources and Crop Evolution* 45, no. 2 (1998):139–50.

Stephen B. Brush, J. Edward Taylor, and Mauricio Bellon, "Technology Adoption and Biological Diversity in Andean Potato Agriculture," *Journal of Development Economics* 39, no. 2 (1992):365–87.

M. Van Dusen and J. E. Taylor, "Missing Markets and Crop Diversity: Evidence from Mexico," *Environment and Development Economics* 10, no. 4 (2005):513–31.

too much global warming (how much carbon did you put into the atmosphere today?), too little information (how do you turn a profit selling information in a poor village?), and too little biodiversity (sidebar 1.8). Yet another negative externality is trash, which sadly is a pervasive feature of developing-country landscapes.

Public goods: Roads, marketing infrastructure, communications, police, and firefighting are public goods that create benefits for society that are difficult for private investors to capture; thus, there are not likely to be enough of them unless governments get involved. A classic case is firefighting. If fire departments were private, I might pay for fire protection but my neighbor might not. Yet if her house catches fire, the firefighters will have to put it out in order to save my house—a classic free-rider problem.

Market power: The welfare gains from markets depend on competition. When someone gains too much market power, either as a seller or buyer, the fundamental theorem breaks down. This is the justification for antitrust legislation.

Resolving the information problems and providing the infrastructure needed to make markets function properly involves classic problems of increasing returns to scale and public goods. [...] Let's review them here.

Creating an information system involves high (fixed) setup costs of gathering the information and making it available in a form that people can use. However, once an information system is in place, the cost of providing the information to an additional person is negligible or zero. Marginal cost pricing is not feasible, as in the case of a bridge. You can put information online and it can spread like wildfire. It's difficult to exclude people from having information once it is available. There's a natural free-rider problem here. Once new information gets out, no one can control where it goes, particularly in a world of online news, social media, and e-mail. Information creates important externalities, too. The positive spillovers from information were central to the endogenous growth model [...].

These characteristics of information have advantages and disadvantages. A big advantage is that once information gets out there, it can spread and create benefits widely. A disadvantage, though, is that there is little or no private incentive to invest in information systems, because it is hard for private investors to make money by producing something over which they have little control. These are problems similar to what we came across with regard to education and health investments. Left to their own devices, people will underinvest in information—and health and education, and roads and bridges. The same arguments apply to communications and marketing systems.

This is why Cornell economist Chris Barrett writes: "The institutional and physical infrastructure necessary to ensure broad-based, low-cost access to competitive, well-functioning markets" requires "significant investment, typically by the public sector, paid for out of tax revenues or aid flows. One has to get institutions and endowments, as well as prices, 'right' in order to induce market-based development" (p. 300).[9]

But, just because a market doesn't work well does not mean the government should fix it. There are many problems out there competing for scarce public funds. Is fixing a particular market failure the best use of scarce public resources? Picture a poor isolated village facing high transaction costs. The government could build a new road there and put in a cell phone tower, but the same money could be used to provide credit to poor farmers or schools or health care for their children. Policy makers, like poor people, often face cruel trade-offs.

Markets and the "Knowledge Problem"

Understanding how markets work and where they work well can provide a yet deeper perspective on the role of governments in economic development. Hayek, who—as we learned at the beginning of this chapter—thought a lot about how markets work, was convinced that despite their potential flaws markets do something no individual, no committee, no team of experts, and no government agency could. Markets collect little bits of information from those choosing to transact in markets as well as from those choosing not to participate in markets. When they are able to adjust to changing conditions, prices convey extremely valuable information about the underlying conditions as experienced by individuals.

Hayek's insights about markets set the stage for what he called the "knowledge problem": we are quick to formulate big plans to directly improve society, but rarely possess the knowledge of current circumstances required to make these big plans succeed. No one person or committee possesses this knowledge because it "is not given to anyone in its totality" (p. 76).[10] But markets can aggregate this diffused knowledge—that is, if they function well enough.

[...] This "knowledge problem" appears often in international development dilemmas. Big development plans and projects often fall far short of expectations because of this problem. According to Hayek, appreciating the nature of this knowledge problem and what it implies for program and policy design is fundamental to economics because it relates directly to markets: "The curious task of economics is to demonstrate to men [and women] how little they really know about what they imagine they can design" (p. 76).[11]

www.rebeltext.org/development/qr11.html
Learn more about information and markets by exploring multimedia resources while you read.

Appendix
The Math of Lemons

In his award-winning paper, George Akerlof gave a simple example to show how asymmetric information can lead to a market failure. Here's how it goes:

Everyone knows that used cars vary in quality. Imagine an index of quality such that the worst quality car gets a "0" and the best quality car gets a "1." We do not know how the quality of used cars out there is distributed across the [0,1] quality interval, so we'll assume it's even, or uniform. That means the average quality equals ½.

Sellers and buyers both value cars based on their quality. Again, to make things simple, suppose sellers value cars identically to their quality, so that a car with quality equal to q is worth $\$q$. This might sound strange, since q is always between 0 and 1, but if you're thinking in, say, tens of thousands of dollars, a car worth \$1/2 on the q scale would cost \$5,000, and so on.

To make this example interesting, buyers have to value cars differently than sellers. It makes sense to imagine that cars are worth more to buyers than sellers in terms of the utility or satisfaction an additional car would bring. Akerlof assumed that a car of quality q is worth $\$3/2q$ to a buyer. (Actually, buyers routinely seem willing to spend more than sellers are willing to accept. Farm-gate prices are far lower than what consumers pay for food at a grocery store, and anyone who buys something at auction has to pay a buyer's fee, which makes the price paid higher than the price received by the seller.)

In theory, then, it seems like the price for a used car will end up somewhere between $\$q$ and $\$3/2q$, depending on the bargaining power of the buyer and seller. Both buyer and seller would be better off if a transaction in this price range happened.

Now here's the catch: Only sellers know the quality of their car; in other words, information about car quality is asymmetric. The buyer's best guess is that a given car's quality is average—that is, $q = ½$. If this is the case, the buyer won't be willing to pay $\$3/2q$; she'll only be willing to pay half that, or $½ \times 3/2\$q = 3/4\$q$. But the seller won't sell a car of quality q at a price less than $\$q$. The market fails; the high-quality cars get pulled off the market, and only the worst cars ("lemons") are left.

The "market for lemons" problem can arise in any situation in which sellers have better information about the quality of a good or service than buyers do. The thing being traded (or not) could be a commodity. (Does your produce meet food safety standards? Is it organic?). As we'll see in the next chapter, it could also be a service. (Will you be a productive worker if I hire you? Will you pay me back if I loan you some money?)

End Notes

1. George A. Akerlof, "The Market for 'Lemons': Quality Uncertainty and the Market Mechanism," *Quarterly Journal of Economics* 84, no. 3 (1970):488–500.
2. George A. Akerlof, "Writing the 'The Market for "Lemons"': A Personal and Interpretive Essay" (www.nobelprize.org/nobel_prizes/economics/laureates/2001/akerlof-article.htm).
3. United States Food and Drug Administration (www.fda.gov/Food/InternationalInteragency Coordination/default.htm).
4. European Commission, "Health and Consumers" (http://ec.europa.eu/food/food/chemicalsafety/residues/third_countries_en.htm).
5. www2.merriam-webster.com/cgi-bin/mwthesadu?book=Dictionary&va=market.
6. www.oxforddictionaries.com/us/definition/american_english/market.
7. "Labor: U.S. Fruits and Vegetables," *Rural Migration News* 17, no. 1 (January 2011) (http://migration.ucdavis.edu/rmn/more.php?id = 1596_0_5_0).
8. Joseph E. Stiglitz, "Smith's 'Invisible Hand' a Myth?" Address to the Commonwealth Club of San Francisco (February 22, 2010; www.youtube.com/watch?v=9qjvwQrZmpk).
9. Christopher B. Barrett, "Smallholder Market Participation: Concepts and Evidence from Eastern and Southern Africa," *Food Policy* 33, no. 4 (2008): 299–317.
10. Friedrich August Hayek, *The Fatal Conceit: The Errors of Socialism* (Chicago: University of Chicago Press, 2011).
11. Ibid.

Reading 2

A Renaissance of the Commons

How the New Sciences and Internet are Framing a New Global Identity and Order

John Clippinger and David Bollier

Cultures, like people, can run out of ideas. They can exhaust themselves in the face of events and ideas they can no longer predict, explain, or control. When they do, they revert to the repetitive assertion of the simplest and most soothing of their founding ideas. These attempts to ward off the unknown through the ritualized assertion of familiar core beliefs are what anthropologists call a "ghost dance." The name is taken from a Sioux Indian ritual dance designed to resurrect ancestors. Sioux warriors believed the dance made them impervious to the bullets of the U.S. Cavalry in the 1870s.

What may seem to be a bizarre ritual is in fact a well-documented practice of all cultures, traditional and modern. Many events in contemporary American life can be understood as a ghost dance of denial: ritualistic behavior that people hope will ward off unpleasant social and economic realities, ecological perils, and new global interdependencies that are profoundly threatening to established cultural norms. The ghost dance desperately repeats unexamined, unquestioned "truths" despite contrary evidence.

In our time, the ghost dance can be seen in a celebration of laissez-faire capitalism, radical individualism, and the alienability of all human activity and nature for market consumption. In their time, these myths were invaluable. They helped emancipate the "common man" from ancient obligations to feudal overlords by giving individuals the power not only to elect their own representatives, but to freely sell their labor in open markets. Civil freedoms would henceforth be linked with market freedoms.

Adam Smith and the American Founding Fathers were not championing a "market absolutism"; they realized that both commercial interests and individual rights depended critically upon the integrity of a shared moral and civic order. This was the idea of the "commonwealth," now a little-used term in public life. The essential principle of the commonwealth, as John Adams once put it, is that "no man, nor corporation or association of men have any other title to obtain advantage or particular and exclusive privileges distinct from those of the community, than what arises from the consideration of services rendered to the public."[1]

What was originally seen as a common-sense curtailment of the absolute powers of monarchs (read governments) and the vested rights of a ruling class, has today morphed into an all-embracing economic, cultural, and political dogma. The subtle arguments about inalienable rights and common obligations made by Jefferson, Madison, Smith and other seventeenth- and eighteenth-century philosophers, have congealed into a self-contained, ritualized belief system.

Without limitation, today's doctrine of "free markets" righteously insists that markets should govern virtually all aspects of civic, cultural and economic life. In fact, this doctrine dominates our politics, economics and public policy. Because it has become universalized, unassailable, unarguable and closed, free-market doctrine has become a dogma, or what we have called "FMD."

FMD declares that individuals maximize their self-interest by buying and selling in the "free market," and that the renowned Invisible Hand—the aggregation of these transactions—advances the public good. Believers in FMD see market activity as the supreme expression of "freedom." Any collective alternatives to the "free choices" offered by the market, especially government action, are seen as coercive and benighted.

Since FMD regards individuals as the sole originators of wealth, it follows that they alone should be entitled to own and control wealth. Government action to control property is considered inherently suspect because government is bureaucratic and wasteful, goes the thinking, while "free" individuals acting through the market are far more intelligent and innovative. Because the market is presumed to be more efficient than government, the default strategy for managing public resources is to privatize and marketize them. Attempts by government to restrict the prerogatives of ownership are often blasted as confiscatory, punitive, or unconstitutional "takings."

As for the social disruptions and environmental harms caused by market activity, FMD regards them as aberrations that markets will ameliorate over the long-term. The churn of "creative destruction"—the phrase coined by economist Joseph Schumpeter and much-touted by the *Wall Street Journal*—is said to be our best assurance of social equity and accountability. This faith is reflected in such "common sense" as "a rising tide raises all boats" and "progress through economic growth."

FMD is far more than a matter of economics, however. It is a moral calculus and foundational set of social norms. It declares price to be the best indicator of value and that market principles as the fairest way to allocate wealth and other rewards. In this sense, FMD is not just the centerpiece of conventional economics, but a catechism of our politics, economics, and culture—our American creed.

An Insurgent New Worldview

Yet even as FMD orthodoxy dictates the scope of permissible discussion in American life, a powerful new tide is rushing in to batter the citadel. Dissenting critiques are emanating from a variety of improbable sources—the hard sciences, behavioral economics, and complexity theory, robust new types of Internet-based communities, and startling new transnational social movements.

These eclectic and evolving insurgencies do not constitute a coherent response to FMD—yet. But look more closely, and with an open mind, and begin to connect the dots. A remarkable array of scientific discoveries, academic conceptualizations, and social practices are converging around some common principles. One can discern, in fact, some deep and disruptive challenges to conventional notions of property rights, free markets, organizational hierarchy, national sovereignty, and human nature.

Surely a primary exhibit is the startling growth of free and open source software, especially as exemplified by Linux. It seems nothing short of miraculous that a global network of thousands of volunteers operating via the Internet could build a highly complex operating system that could out-perform Microsoft's products. Our surprise merely suggests the limits of our mental categories, which cannot fathom how online communities harness personal identity and collaboration to produce such a sophisticated product. A number of major companies such as IBM and Hewlett-Packard, however, understand that open source is a serious business proposition, not mere idealism, and have made it a core part of their competitive market strategies.

Equally astonishing are the varieties of Internet-based networking communities that are outflanking commercial venues. Collaborative Web sites, listservs, peer-to-peer file sharing, weblogs, institutional repositories at universities, new content licensing schemes and "tagging" protocols for digital content: such tools are giving rise to entirely new sorts of creative genres, research literature, and cultural platforms. In turn, these online platforms are propelling the growth of many powerful social movements of global scope—sustainable environmentalism, human rights, socially responsible trade, affordable AIDS drugs, peace.

Within the academy, meanwhile, genetics, evolutionary biology, and brain neuroscience are challenging classical models of human brain functioning and cognitive processes. Comparative anthropologists and evolutionary psychologists are making breakthrough findings about our species' deeply embedded instincts for social cooperation. A new generation of economists is finding that neoclassical economic theories are just too rigid and abstract to do justice to the empirical realities of modern economic life. Behavioral economics is building a new intellectual edifice to explain how personal and social factors affect economic activity. Complexity theory is providing new conceptual tools for understanding the nonlinear, dynamic flows of natural and economic systems.

Predictably, the Guardians of our traditional order—neoclassical economists, the scientific establishment, the major political parties, Washington policy elite, the corporate media, and business leadership—generally have little interest in the dissenting critiques. FMD creed is, after all, comfortably entrenched and seamlessly comprehensive. Its defenders do not "need" to explain disturbances on the periphery. FMD provides a "good enough" template for explaining how things "really" work.

And in truth, most of us have so internalized the cognitive universe of FMD that it seems a bit disingenuous to rail against some external villains. The perceptual myopia that afflicts our culture—let's be frank—lies within ourselves. It is not easy to change one's sense of identity and cultural outlook, let alone cognitive habits. Psychology experiments have shown that the more a belief system fails, the more tenaciously its adherents cling to it.

This may help explain why American culture seems caught in some sort of Groundhog Day, senselessly forced to repeat the same cycles of the past ad infinitum. In our fixation on free-market dogma, we are enacting our very own ghost dance. We are stuck in an interregnum. An aging corpus of free-market dogma maintains a tight stranglehold on American life even as its explanatory power wanes in the face of new realities.

As the ghost dance intensifies, it is worth asking: Why is the old order imperiled, and how is it incompatible with emerging trends? Based on the fragmentary evidence now emerging, what are the key features of the new worldview? How might we begin to embrace a more realistic understanding the human condition and social structures in the twenty-first century?

A Renaissance of the Commons

The emerging paradigm that we see, based on the dispersed insurgencies bursting out, is the renaissance of the commons. The commons is a social regime for managing shared resources and forging a community of shared values and purpose. Unlike markets, which rely upon price as the sole dimension of value, a commons is organized around a richer blend of human needs—for identity, community, fame, and honor—which are indivisible and inalienable, as well as more "tangible" rewards.

In a commons, transactions are based on ongoing moral, social, and personal relationships, not episodic, impersonal exchanges of money. A commons is also marked by openness. This helps assure that developments affecting the community's interests can be scrutinized by all. It also helps the commoners identify and punish free-riders, preventing the so-called tragedy of the commons. (This term is actually a misnomer because it describes an open-access regime of private appropriation; a commons, by contrast, is managed by consensual rules, membership, limits on alienability, transparency, etc.)

Human societies need markets for their ability to stimulate innovation, efficiency, and growth. Price is a powerful organizing tool in this respect, facilitated by the division of resources into private property. But human societies also need things that are indivisible and inalienable, which is the essence of the commons. If the social relationships and values that constitute a commons can be bought and sold—made alienable—they are destroyed. It is hard to trust someone whose loyalty and judgment can be bought, just as we lose respect for a government corrupted by bribery and corruption. Similarly, many shared resources—parks, libraries, ecosystems, democracy—can only be sustained if they are held "in common." Their organic integrity must be protected against private exploitation, lest the shared resource be converted into a market and destroyed.

While the champions of FMD regard markets as the universal, default norm of human social organization, recent developments seem to be refuting that. Evolutionary scientists are coming to believe that many social behaviors that are crucial to the commons—social reciprocity, trust, shared values—have played a vital practical role in assuring human survival and adaptation. These human behaviors have been at least as important as the more familiar economic notions of competition and alienability.

Now, with the rise of the Internet, we are seeing a strangely appropriate convergence of the future and the past: A lightweight, high-tech infrastructure, the Internet, is enabling some primordial human impulses to come to the fore in powerful new ways. Fundamental truths that FMD has always denied—that human cooperation comes naturally, that collective action can be more efficient than markets, that the gift economy is a potent source of value-creation and human satisfaction—are being vindicated. It is still quite early in the game, but the commons may be the critical matrix for understanding many of the rebellions now underway.

It is foolish to think that the new commons will (or should) replace markets. Markets are far too necessary to human welfare to disappear. But what is likely to emerge—indeed, what is already occurring—is the rise of a hybrid without a name that will complement, and mitigate free-market dogma. This new path, the commons template, is neither laissez-faire capitalism nor state-managed collectivism. It moves beyond the antimonies of "free" versus "regulated" markets and seeks to resolve the intensifying contradictions of market capitalism. Through the commons template, one can imagine having the efficiency, flexibility, and freedom of markets on the one hand, and preserving and advancing the common good on the other.

The following sections explore the remarkable renaissance of the commons as reflected in new academic approaches, economic schools of thought, social practices, and global movements.

New Scientific Evidence vs. Homo economicus

One of the most potent challenges to free-market dogma—and affirmations of the commons—is coming from new scientific findings about human nature. Thanks to recent research into brain functioning, genetics, developmental and evolutionary psychology and biology, and comparative anthropology, we need no longer accept the armchair speculations of seventeenth-century philosophers such as David Hume, John Locke, and Thomas Hobbes about the actual propensities and capacities of human beings.

Although our understanding is by no means complete, recent research points to a coherent new understanding of basic aspects of human nature. The research—which is inherently nonideological and eminently testable—is almost a point-for-point refutation of the premises of free-market dogma. The implications are enormous. If the different strands of the emerging sciences could be woven together and popularized, the resulting synthesis could catalyze a sea change in our images of ourselves and human society.

While FMD conveniently offers an antiquated, highly simplified model of human nature and economic behavior, a new, more dynamic model of human agency and social identity is starting to emerge. Our history as a species reveals that social cooperation, not just brutal competition, has been a critical evolutionary factor in the survival of the human species. Unfortunately, the story of human nature continues to be told in the sound bites of seventeenth-century philosophers. A more balanced, subtle, and realistic account is long overdue.

The skeptic might ask, Why should we bother to address the vision of human nature put forward by free-market dogma? Why does it matter? Such an inquiry might be interesting and diverting, but so what if *homo economicus* is an agreed-upon fable, an abstract ideal? Isn't that more or less how the world works?

That is precisely the point: the world does not work according to the conventional representations of FMD, and those representations have incalculable sway over economics, politics, public policy, and culture. To be sure, nasty, brutish behavior still exists and flourishes. But the new sciences are showing that social reciprocity and trust are deeply engrained—indeed, biologically encoded—principles of our humanity. They are a precondition even for markets.

As Karl Polanyi (1957) described in his landmark book, *The Great Transformation*, no "free market" can survive very long without extensive social institutions and shared ethical norms. A lot of cooperation and trust is needed to devise legal regimes, establish regulatory agencies, administer a judicial system and maintain consumer confidence in markets. FMD is notably deficient in recognizing this fact, however. This was vividly demonstrated when free marketeers tried to introduce market competition to the former Soviet Union. Predictably, the experiments floundered because the necessary institutions of civil society and cultural norms simply did not exist.

This very blind spot in the epistemology of the market has long been at work in the West as well. Without outside intervention, FMD generally doesn't recognize that social ethics, a healthy environment, product safety, and community well-being are important to the long-term vitality of markets. Its economic theories see them as distracting sideshows to the main action, market exchange. Without collective oversight (which defenders of FMD constantly seek to undermine), scandals such as Enron, Global Crossing, WorldCom, and Arthur Andersen are, sadly, inevitable.

It is here that the new insurgencies are making remarkable headway against FMD. Ingeniously, they are harnessing the forces that FMD dismisses as "exogenous variables" and leveraging them to maximum advantage. This is the most significant (and unacknowledged) achievement of the Internet—the empowerment of countless new forms of social communion, creativity, and knowledge without the ministrations of the market. The powerful psychic and social energies driving the growth of the Internet are quite inexplicable—and invisible—by the terms of FMD.

Consider it the revenge of the commons: the social context that FMD has long regarded as incidental is now surging forward as a powerful force in its own right. The emergence of the commons in cyberspace has a tantalizing correspondence with new scientific findings about the evolutionary character of the human species.

The Scientific Case for the Commons

A growing body of evidence suggests that social trust and cooperation has been the enduring theme of human evolution. The FMD model of *homo economicus*, which purports to be a universal norm, actually has very little basis in fact or history. There are three general lines of evidence.

1. ***Social exchange is an "evolutionarily stable strategy" (ESS) and thus the critical platform for cognitive development in humans.***

In evaluating the "fitness" of an adaptation or mutation, geneticists, evolutionary biologists, and mathematical game theorists often look for evidence of an "evolutionarily stable strategy," or ESS. Such strategies are noteworthy because they are powerfully adaptive and stable; in effect they cannot be displaced by any other evolutionary strategy—or mutation or phenotype—because there is no advantage in doing so. If an evolutionary trait can be considered an ESS by the lights of genetics or evolutionary biology, therefore, it constitutes powerful evidence that it is a deep aspect of human nature.

Recent studies have argued that the notion of "reciprocal altruism" is an ESS. So are many innate "social contracting algorithms" of the human brain.[2] What makes this evidence

especially compelling is that the ESS approach can successfully predict what kind of "strategies" and even special competences will emerge in different social exchange networks. For example, many different species—vampire bats, wolves, ravens, baboons, and chimpanzees—exhibit similar social behaviors and emotions such as sympathy, attachment, embarrassment, dominant pride, and humble submission. Both ravens and vampire bats can detect cheaters and punish them accordingly—a skill needed to thwart free-riders and maintain the integrity of the group.

This indicates that "cooperative strategies" have evolved in different species and, because of the evolutionary advantages that they offer, become encoded in their genome. While much more needs to be learned in this area, evolutionary sciences appear to be identifying some of the basic principles animating the "social physics" of human behavior.[3] When different species independently "arrive at" the same ESS, it suggests that there is a unifying social physics governing complex forms of behaviors regardless of the species.

2. ***Reciprocal social exchange is a highly specialized brain function critical to the rise of identity, community and culture.***

The fact that humans can communicate, coordinate, and carry out social exchanges so effectively stems from uniquely human social "algorithms" for doing so—patterns of instinctive response that are genetically encoded. Social contract algorithms are those innate capacities of individuals that enable human societies to function as communities. Such algorithms include a person's sense of justice and guilt, social reciprocity through gift-giving, and an ability to read social cues.

While earlier sociobiologists believed that natural selection worked almost exclusively at the individual level of gene mutation, it has become increasingly clear that many social algorithms also coevolve at the "group" level.[4] David Sloan Wilson, an evolutionary biologist who has written extensively on natural selection and cooperation, writes that "social groups become so functionally integrated that they become higher-level organisms in their own right."[5] At such a point, evolutionary pressures appear to play out at the collective level, not just at the genetic and individual level. (There is a spectrum of views about the level at which natural selection is most influential—group or individual—but not even Darwin was as radical an individualist as many contemporary scientists such as Richard Dawkins, author of *The Selfish Gene.*)[6]

Historically, many scientists and economists have relied upon rational models of self-interest to explain how organisms evolve. Game theory and "prisoner's dilemma" scenarios are often used to explore how people really behave. The presumption is that people's natural inclination is to win at the expense of their opponent or their neighbor. But neuroscientists are discovering that rational-actor models grossly misrepresent how the human organism actually functions. It seems that we as species are neurologically hardwired to be empathic and cooperative, and to connect emotionally with what is occurring in the world in general. Moreover, this occurs at a species level, not at an individual level.[7]

A species sustains itself through such cooperation. In this sense, the idea of the commons is not a cultural artifact of English history. It is a driving principle of natural selection that is literally manifested in the architecture and physiology of the brains of *homo sapiens*. It reveals itself in the kinds of effective group cooperation that humans have shown throughout two millions years, and in the development of language itself, which is thought to serve important social-bonding purposes.

Brain neuroscience is starting to confirm that we may be hardwired to empathize and cooperate. A group of neuroscientists in Parma led by Giovannia Rizzolatti and Vittorio Gallese studied how brain neurons responded in the prefrontal cortex of macaque monkeys. Scientists found that when a monkey performed a complex motor action, the same neurons would fire in other monkeys who were merely watching.[8] These neurons—"mirror neurons"—are complemented by "canonical neurons" in adjacent brain tissue, which fire when an animal sees an object of the kind normally involved in a given action. All these neurons, in turn, are connected to the portions of the brain that process emotions and govern empathy.

As linguist George Lakoff explains,

"We know from psychology professor Paul Ekman's research that configurations of facial muscles express certain emotions. Presumably, our mirror neurons fire when we see the same configurations of facial muscles on someone else that our facial muscles would make. And that firing can activate our own emotional centers. In short, that allows us to empathize—to feel someone else's pain or joy. ... We have evolved to be empathetic (via mirror neurons and connections to the emotional centers of the brain) and to be connected to the world (via canonical neurons). Empathy and connection to the other and to the physical environment are central aspects of human nature!"[9]

Altruism is not limited to human beings, but is typical of many different social species. Experiments with monkeys have shown that monkeys would refrain from pulling a chain to deliver food if it would result in shocking other monkeys. This suggests that ethics—a sense of compassion and reciprocity—is not some kind of softheaded, idealistic, and therefore untenable evolutionary strategy of the sort dismissed by tough realists. It is, rather, a well-established fitness strategy that seems to be encoded in the behaviors of many species. The highly respected neurologist Antonio Damasio has argued in his recent book, *Looking for Spinoza*, that social emotions have an identifiable physiology and measurable role in the behavior of the human brain. Anger, fear, shame, indignation, jealousy, pride, compassion, gratitude, sorrow, and joy appear to be part of "an overall program of bioregulation."[10]

Damasio writes: "The biological reality of self-preservation leads to virtue because in our inalienable need to maintain ourselves we must, of necessity, help preserve other selves. If we fail to do so so, we perish and are thus violating the foundational principle, and relinquishing the virtue that lies in self-preservation. The secondary foundation of virtue then is the reality of a social structure and the presence of other livings organisms in a complex system of interdependence with our own organism."[11]

Evolutionary biologists have also discovered that, contrary to the precepts of free-market doctrine, people tend to act in ways that express and reinforce the social exchange rules of their group, which typically follow principles of reciprocal exchange. Social exchange—"I'll scratch your back if you scratch mine"—is the process of cooperating for mutual benefit. Sometimes called "reciprocal altruism," it is an adaptive trait that is a deeply rooted product of natural selection that benefits the collective. The history of cultures shows that social exchange is in fact a human universal; it is not a recent cultural invention.

"This mutual provisioning of benefits, each conditional on the others' compliance, is rare in the animal kingdom," write evolutionary psychologists Leda Cosmides and John Tooby (2002). "Social exchange cannot be generated by a simple general learning mechanism, such as classical or operant conditioning. ... This strongly suggests that engaging in social exchange requires specific cognitive machinery, which some species have and others lack."[12]

Cross-cultural analysis has verified the neurobiological evidence. In a survey of fifteen very different societies, economist Samuel Bowles has shown that the celebrated *homo economicus* invoked by neoclassical economists does not exist in any recognizable form. He simply could not be found.[13]

3. *The rational "free choices" that FMD considers a primary justification are in many instances reflexive social "flocking."*

One of the central premises of FMD is that individuals consciously make rational choices to advance their self-interests, which a responsive market then actualizes to achieve the public good. But new findings in brain neurology are showing that a great deal of human behavior is not a matter of conscious deliberation and rationality, but of physiological and social instinct. New discoveries about cognition and thought suggest that humans are patently not "rational actors" who approach every situation free of deeply ingrained genetic predilections and cultural habits. As a species, we act in species-symptomatic ways—ways that define and perpetuate the collective (the species), not the individual. Moreover, "rationality" is but one of many capacities of the brain. Some of the most influential forces driving human behavior are autonomic reflexes that are independent, highly localized, and fragmented in the brain.

Cognitive scientists are now realizing that it is too parochial to focus exclusively on the brain if we wish to understand human intelligence. Cognition does not take place in brain tissue alone. It takes place in the context of our bodies and the external environment, both of which we constantly use to gather information, draw upon as memory aids, and conduct computations. Patients with Alzheimer's Disease, for example, rely heavily upon a highly structured environment, much of it self-created, in order to recognize things, make mental associations, and reason. Change the patients' physical environment—move them to another location—and they lose large portions of their memory and cognitive capacity. In a similar way, all of us rely critically upon an external "scaffolding" of cognitive aids—books, newspapers, computers, other people, telephones, symbols, etc.—to "think" and function intelligently.

FMD is therefore incorrect to depict conscious and rational thought as a sovereign, independent force residing within individuals. The mind is deeply intermingled with its external environment, and is particularly influenced by the cultural milieu that it inhabits. "Individual brains should not take all the credit for the flow of thoughts or the generation of reasoned responses," writes cognitive scientist and philosopher Andy Clarke. "Brain and world collaborate in ways that are richer and more clearly driven by computational and informational needs than was previously suspected."[14] Without abstract metarepresentations of language, ritual, social cues, and so forth, "rational choice" is literally impossible.

Contrary to FMD view of independent choice, human beings seem to be neurologically and genetically hardwired with many innate routines and protocols, most of which help social groups to coordinate their actions. These routines and protocols are essentially social in nature and driven more by instinct than by rationality. Because these evolutionary features of the human brain seem so deeply rooted and enduring, evolutionary game theorists believe they reflect an "equilibrium selection"—i.e., an Evolutionary Stable Strategy for human survival. At heart, we are social creatures, not rational automatons.

Beyond Determinism: A Constructivist Human Nature

The empirical findings of the new sciences do not suggest a reductionist notion of a fixed and universal "human nature" of the sort portrayed in countless "nature/nurture" arguments. Rather, they suggest a far more "spacious" model of human nature. Human nature is not "determined" by genes, as popular mythology often seems to hold. It consists of shared and specific competencies that are expressed in different ways by different societies. It is not a reductionist model, but a profoundly constructivist model. Innate propensities coevolve over time with a wide range of social and physical conditions.[15]

Seen from this perspective, we can see that FMD is a highly artificial, if not fictional, notion of humanity. The free-market dogma worldview systematically, ideologically, privileges certain attributes of human beings while disregarding other innate propensities. It ignores the crucial interdependencies that individuals have with each other, with other cultures, and with nature. It validates a normative universe of cognition that is at odds with our genetic, neurological, psychological, and social history as a species. It should not be surprising that FMD is also proving to be highly destructive of the natural environment.

It is time to recognize that our "neurocognitive architecture" has coevolved with the natural environment over millions of years, predisposing us toward certain baseline psychological, social, and cognitive behaviors. In the long sweep of human history, the values and behaviors that we take as normative in our high-technology, market-driven, media-saturated environment, are, in fact, profoundly aberrational.

The new scientific findings are not merely parlor-room curiosities. As we will see next, they could be the foundation for more enlightened public policies. Rather than privilege the unexamined tenets of free-market individualism, we could get better and more humane results if we began to leverage our deeply engrained social tendencies.

New Economic Challenges to FMD

Just as the evolutionary sciences are contesting FMD schema of human nature, so behavioral economics is questioning its core economic assumptions. Over the past generation, consumer activists and environmentalists have amassed a considerable literature documenting the chasm that separates market theory and realities.[16] A handful of prominent economists—John Kenneth Galbraith, Kenneth Arrow, and Vernon Smith come to mind—have dwelt on the serious contradictions of FMD. But now a new generation of economists is beginning to fashion a coherent alternative set of theoretical principles for understanding how markets actually work. Free-market dogma may never be the same.

The standard modus operandi for many economists is to traffic in theoretical abstractions and give short shrift to on-the-ground realities. An old joke has two economists on a desert island when a soda bottle washes ashore. One declares, "Assume a bottle opener. ..." New schools of economic thought—especially behavioral economics and complexity theory—are moving beyond this widely accepted cop-out. While they emphasize different sets of principles, the new approaches share a contempt for three primary tenets of free-market economics—the notions of unbounded rationality, unbounded selfishness, and unbounded willpower.

The first presumes that economic actors can be perfectly informed in all their economic choices. The second presumes that economic actors necessarily act to maximize their personal and material gain. And the third presumes that economic actors have limitless determination to achieve these objectives. These axioms supposedly combine to animate the Invisible Hand, the familiar principle of Economics 101, which holds that each individual and corporation will generate the optimum public good by pursuing its own narrow self-interests without impediment. The confluence of private capital, private property, and private self-interests are said to drive us, efficiently and effectively, to new levels of innovation, wealth creation, and progress.

But this idealized model of human economic behavior is plausible only if one discounts or ignores the "externalities" that usually accompany market behavior—the social disruptions, ecological damage, health and safety hazards, and deferred costs. It is easy to understand why we might collude in overlooking these costs. Many are hard to measure and are speculative in nature. (What are the real costs of driving the snail darter into extinction?) The chief beneficiaries of FMD, investors, are usually not eager to document the full breadth of market externalities lest they be required to pay for them.

Finally, the actual inequities and costs of FMD have been tolerated for so long because the only other coherent method of wealth-creation—the centralized command-and-control system typified by the former Soviet Union—was so notoriously wasteful and inefficient. The standards for judging the success of FMD are singularly low.

And so FMD, despite its patent deficiencies, continues to be accepted as a virtual natural law of economics and the fundamental model for wealth creation and development throughout the world. Social inequities, environmental degradation, cultural homogenization, and wealth concentration are accepted with a shrug as tragic yet necessary costs of achieving "progress." Tom Friedman of *The New York Times* has approvingly called this Faustian bargain the "golden straightjacket."[17]

Behavioral economics is beginning to open up new vistas of possibility, however. By developing rigorous empirical models of the ways that markets actually behave, and by bringing market "externalities" back into the discussion, behavioral economists are pioneering radically different metrics for understanding the supposed efficiency and rationality of free markets. Their findings are undermining the largely unexamined assumption that markets are the most effective and legitimate mechanisms for collecting and allocating public resources. Using new types of on-the-ground research, behavioral economists are validating that humans actually exhibit a "bounded rationality" in their market choices. They often exhibit trust and reciprocity towards other economic players rather than selfishness. They exhibit limited motivation to maximize their "rationality" and personal gain. Social exchange theory is beginning to describe how people naturally make decisions and cooperate.

One must emphasize, again, that market activity is not going to become obsolete any time soon. It not only produces negative externalities (events beyond the market transaction itself) such as pollution and social disruption; it often produces positive externalities. Much of the story of the transition from feudalism to mercantilism, indeed, is about how popular access to capital undermined the power and privilege of landed and titled elites, and opened the door for broader participation in the economy. The market system created new jobs, new wealth based on merit, and new economic and political freedoms.

From the vantage point of the twenty-first century, however, we can now see that there are inherent limitations to what eighteenth-century price mechanisms and property conventions can achieve. While FMD declares that the price mechanism makes all resources substitutable, for example, the real world of human beings, nature, and public resources is not always so tractable. Not all resources are, or should be, indivisible and inalienable, as FMD presumes. Progress may not really be served by letting markets decide which new species should be invented; by promoting incessant television-watching among young children; and by building functional substitutes for the melting polar ice caps. FMD is also ill-equipped to allocate resources and incentives in fair and humane ways.

Yet just as the Enlightenment and market capitalism lifted the yoke of feudalism and unleashed unimagined forms of creativity, prosperity, and civic participation, so the renaissance of the commons offers new strategies for resolving many of the paralyzing conundrums of market capitalism. The new sciences and commons-based social regimes point to new principles for coping with issues—externalities, market failure, irrational behaviors, agency costs, and public goods—that otherwise cannot be easily addressed within the terms of market theory.

Behavioral economists are not the only ones looking for new theoretical principles; others are using complexity theory to help explain nonlinear behaviors and the importance of social context in markets, among other real-life dynamics. This still-emerging critique is far more humanistic and socially oriented than the rigid, quantitative models of conventional economics. Instead of trying to come up with tidy mathematical formalities that depict a specious market equilibria, complexity theorists are far more concerned with understanding the importance of singular evolutionary pathways (for individuals, companies, and economies), the properties of self-organizing systems, and the patterns of nonlinear, dynamic change.

Taken together, these new types of economic thought are subverting some core principles of an earlier economic worldview and striding toward a post-market economics that has yet to be named or fully described. This novel but highly cogent worldview is all but incomprehensible to mainstream economic models of the world that derive, let us recall, from the simplistic, static and mechanical concepts of seventeenth-century thought. Not surprisingly, the guardians of FMD and their critics have yet to engage in a frank, direct dialogue; their categories of understanding are so radically incommensurate!

The new sciences are attracting increasing attention, however, and for a simple reason. They are better able to explain contemporary economic phenomena. They make more sense. The growing maturity of behavioral economics can be seen in the recent Nobel Laureates given to Professor Vernon Smith of George Mason University and Professor Daniel Kahneman of Princeton University, both of whom are behavioral economists. Similarly, since its founding in 1994, the Santa Fe Institute, the leading outpost of complexity theorists, has steadily gained in stature among innovative, forward-thinking economists.

The Rise of the Internet and Global Culture

If the latest advances in evolutionary sciences and economics remain unknown to most of the public, the impact of the Internet is another matter. Its social, economic, and political repercussions are one of the most stunning developments of recent history. Here, too, the story is mostly about the surge of the commons and the limits of free-market dogma.

"We share a collective blind spot to the possibility that human beings can act together to create real value, without relying either on selfish exploitation of private property (or markets or firms) or top-down governmental action," write Internet law scholars David Johnson and Susan Crawford. "Today's political conversation ignores the potential for emergent, networked collective action. But right in front of our noses is a living example of a system that is working to produce value without visible control or rent-seeking behavior."[18]

This living system is, of course, the Internet. But because its dynamics do not fit easily into current political and economic categories, its powerful role in creating value through social collaboration remains largely unseen. Many modes of interaction occur over the Internet, but the most robust ones tend to leverage our social desires to share and collaborate. Listservs, collaborative Web sites, open source software, and peer-to-peer (P2P) file sharing technologies are among the ways that a dispersed, decentralized collective of people are coming together to create value. Scientists use P2P networks to collectively advance their research; thousands of online self-help groups host everything from genealogical research to child-adoption guidance to volunteer mapping of the craters of Mars.

Not only do these new self-organizing, "bottom-up" networks of individuals arise spontaneously without the customary "top-down" organizing apparatus of a corporation, government agency, or nonprofit, they tend to be much more innovative and efficient than market mechanisms. The kinds of leadership and coordination that once required a business enterprise—as economist Nobel Laureate Ronald Coase declared in his famous 1934 essay on the rationale for forming corporations—can now take place outside of formal boundaries of a corporation with greater efficiency and creativity.[19] This is powerfully confirmed by the flourishing open-source software movement and explained in theoretical detail by

NYU law professor Yochai Benkler in his essay, "Coase's Penguin."[20] (The penguin is in the logo for Linux software.)

The efficiency claims for the commons are supported by conventional economic analysis. "The laws of network topology dictate that the more people can be connected, and the more easily those connected people can form into value-creating groups, the more easily value will be created," write Johnson and Crawford (2003).

The resulting conversation creates immense value that is not counted in economic terms nor treated as part of any governmental/political system. Yet this interwoven tapestry of collective conversation provides a large and growing percentage of the value humans collectively seek: our education, our decisions about what to do with our privately owned resources (our capital, our time, our products and services), our decisions regarding what government should do, and our social and family relationships. This new "commonwealth" has flourished precisely because, having gone unnoticed, it has had a chance to thrive.

Because FMD systematically fails to recognize the powerful influence of social context, it fails to appreciate that its own structure of property rights, contracts, enforcement, profit incentives, and so forth, are sustained by a vast social apparatus and cultural norms which entail huge agency and transaction costs. It is very expensive for a company to offer high salaries to top management, hire attorneys to draft contracts, go to court to enforce violators, and so forth. But when leadership, coordination and motivation can be achieved easily through self-synchronizing, self-enforcing means, gracefully leveraging our natural social tendencies, why should anyone be surprised that such a system of exchange will be more efficient, effective and equitable than a market system? Communities of trust and transparency can be fantastically efficient! The rise of the Internet and various software systems are so powerful precisely because they leverage people's natural desire for meaning, trust, and social belonging—traits that FMD cannot understand, but which are deeply embedded in our evolutionary history.

This is the as-yet-untold story of the commons. In the commons, price alone is not the sole arbitrator of value and property rights may actually impede the creation of value. A larger set of human values, embodied in historically unique communities, determines the meaning of value. Money is not the only meaningful currency.

Such concepts are difficult for people steeped in our current property-bounded traditions to accept. How can we collectively create valuable resources that are not owned by anyone (or that are owned by everyone, by way of government)? We assume that resources must be treated as property to make sure they are distributed, by way of the market, to those who can exploit them most efficiently. We believe that we should create "public goods" by means of government. But in the age of the Internet, these obvious propositions are not necessarily true. Intangible resources that we often treat as intellectual property increase in value as they are made available to the Internet, where others can easily find them and add value. (The rub: private companies may or may not be able to capture that increase in value for themselves alone.)

Significantly, this commons perspective is entirely supported by the findings of the evolutionary sciences. Human beings share a common genetic heritage with all forms of life, and we are therefore indivisible and interdependent with other species. Far from evolving as independent, self-actualizing, and materialistic actors, human beings emerged as a relatively small and vulnerable species 150,000 years ago because we developed a unique set of social contract algorithms based on language and cooperation. How oddly appropriate: the Internet and related technologies are simply allowing us to give fuller expression to our evolutionary legacy!

This helps account for the fledgling new forms of global culture that are coalescing around issues that must be addressed if we are going to survive as a species: preservation of ecological systems, international cooperation to assure world peace and human rights, and more socially constructive forms of global commerce. By empowering our social natures at a grassroots level, beneath the power of market institutions and nation-states, a new citizen-driven ethic is emerging on the global stage.

As David Bollier describes in his 2003 Aspen Institute report, *The Rise of Netpolitik*, the Internet is giving new global platforms to diasporic ethnic communities such as dispersed populations of emigrant Chinese and exiles from Ghana and Zimbabwe.[21] It is enabling international political movements to coordinate the work of thousands of citizens, leading to impressive public agitation to ban land mines, and clean up the Bhopal chemical disaster. Millions of citizens are bypassing the corporate media and converging around personal Web logs and independent Web sites to find information they consider more reliable or at least more overt about their biases.

In short, the commons is growing rapidly. As it becomes a less exotic and more familiar cultural category, so there is a greater prospect of creating more transparent, accountable, ecologically benign, and humane institutions. Just as the environmental movement introduced a new kind of framing rhetoric into public dialogue, so "the commons" opens up new opportunities to reframe issues. It asks us to move beyond conventional dualities of private versus public, market versus state, individual versus the group, consumer versus seller. Such dichotomies become less relevant as the new models of commons-exchange take root and proliferate.

But what might these models look like? We conclude by offering a speculative preview of how the commons perspective might alter our approach to numerous public policy questions.

Public Policy in the Age of the Commons

The resurgent notion of the commons may be most valuable in helping us reconceptualize approaches to public policy and localized modes of self-governance. One of its signal strengths is its capacity to combine social, moral, and ecological choices with serious economics in a coherent theoretical framework. The concepts that describe the commons, if elaborated, could serve as valuable building blocks for a kind of postmarket critique. Precisely because it approaches economic questions in a holistic, long-term way, it embodies a more humane and sustainable vision.

The worldview implied by the commons opens up fresh new avenues for the imagination and institutional innovation. One promising idea is a new conception of ownership rights and decision-making authority. Collective action can often lower "agency costs" within organizations through greater efficiencies of trust, reciprocity, and self-enforcing social contracts. They also tend to result in more equitable outcomes.

One way to facilitate the creation of organized commons is to develop new forms of "tags" that can "mark off" work that is developed through a commons, as opposed to a market. This is essentially what the General Public License, or GPL, does for products of free software communities. It sets the work product off from the standard market products and identifies it as legally "belonging" to the commons. This ensures that no free riders can "take private" the code that the members of the commons have created.[22]

One can also imagine new public policy vehicles for asserting direct and responsible stewardship of collective resources. Already there is a burgeoning movement seeking to use certain segments of the public's electromagnetic spectrum as a commons (instead of assigning exclusive control to commercial licensees). The State of Alaska has pioneered the use of a stakeholder trust, the Alaska Permanent Fund, to share oil revenues from drilling on state land, with all Alaskan citizens.[23] This model has inspired a Sky Trust proposal to give all citizens an equity stake in the atmosphere, so that they can reap the financial benefits of selling "pollution rights" to corporations (instead of giving away those rights for free).[24]

The essential point of such commons vehicles is to bypass the bloated overhead of traditional corporations and government bureaucracies, and to more directly empower citizens in the stewardship of resources that they legally or morally own.

The commons approach to policymaking has some deep implications for how we reconcile market activity with the natural environment. By recognizing that human beings are interdependent with all of life—rather than somehow apart, as FMD holds—we can begin to craft institutions that are more compatible with life systems. Amory Lovins and his colleagues have developed this perspective in their book, *Natural Capitalism*.[25]

Embracing the principles of the commons can also yield greater efficiencies and sustainable wealth-creation opportunities. Market theory holds that creating private property rights gives people indispensable incentives to produce new wealth. But the empirical evidence of this framework is being refuted in a growing number of wealth-creating realms. Software development, natural resource management, and online knowledge, among other areas, are showing that a commons stewardship can be more efficient, sustainable and feasible over the long-term. It turns out that the much-vaunted efficiency of material self-interest, as advanced through property rights, is often an illusion because the markets/property/contracts framework structurally ignores the significant externalized costs it displaces onto other people and nature. A commons critique also helps us get beyond some fatally deceptive assumptions of market theory, which holds that all inputs are essentially fungible and substitutable.

But this logic has catastrophic results when applied to nature—for good reason. Ecological areas tend to be unique and indivisible. FMD makes a "category mistake" in applying false analytic terms onto natural systems that are organic and interconnected. FMD presumes that parts of nature can be divided, monetized and traded without harm to the whole. The past half-century of pell-mell economic development has vividly demonstrated the ecological fallacy of this doctrine.[26]

In a similar fashion, a commons critique can help expose the dangers of surrendering the social order and its values to commercial forces. Major corporations are now exploiting brain and anthropological research to explore how humans make affective attachments from childhood through adulthood.[27] Sony's highly successful Aibo robotic dog is an early prototype of such emotionally designed products. Disney has similar aspirations in designing animation and theme-park characters.

This intent of such research is to develop emotionally irresistible products and experiences, and to intensify brand loyalties and product dependencies. The market logic is impeccable and ingenious. But the morality and cultural wisdom of exploiting children's "Darwinian buttons" in order to open up new market opportunities is dubious. The commons perspective gives one a philosophical vantage point from which to confront the problematic behavior of markets.

Yet another realm that may be invigorated by a commons perspective is international relations and globalization. Throughout most of history, human beings have divided themselves into separate tribes and relied upon force to preserve their tribal differences. But as the once-separated segments of the "family of man" inexorably comes together on the global stage, more people are beginning to realize that we must either learn to coexist with nature and with each other—or destroy nature and humanity itself.

Rather than accept our past identity as controlling and immutable, the human species must somehow, as a matter of survival, engineer a new leap in our cultural and moral evolution. We must own up to our atavisms, our propensity for reflexive, violent flocking behavior in the face of uncertainty and threat. The Holocaust, Rwanda, Kosovo, and other pogroms against The Other are not the exception but the rule of human history. But if, in the past, these were evolutionary stable strategies and contributed to the overall evolutionary success of the species, they are patently lethal in the context of a globally integrated humanity.

Neurologist Antonio Damasio has noted that innate human propensities for cooperation and trust have a dark side as well. "The nice emotions can easily turn nasty and brutish when the are aimed outside the inner circles towards which they are naturally targeted. The result is anger, resentment, and violence, all of which we can easily recognize as a possible embryo of tribal hatred, racism and war. This is the time to introduce the reminder that the best of human behavior is not necessarily wired under the control of the genome. The history of our civilization is, to some extent, the history of a persuasive effort to extend the nest of "moral sentiments" to wider and wider circles of humanity, beyond the restrictions of the inner groups, eventually encompassing the whole of humanity."[28]

This may be the story of the new global culture that seems to be emerging—a fitful movement, it would appear, that aspires to cultivate new values and social protocols. At this point, no one can simply declare anything so grand as a new identity and ethos for the emerging global culture. Yet we can start to realize that the either/or, us/them perspective that pits one closed worldview against another is a relic of the Pleistocene era. There is a dawning awareness that it is seriously maladaptive in today's highly integrated, technologically potent global culture. As weapons of mass destruction have grown smaller, cheaper and more available to everyone, we are facing a threat to humanity that is utterly unprecedented.

What may seem like a moral or cultural crusade of utopian dimensions may in fact be a pragmatic necessity, even to those with the most callous notions of self-interest. Recognizing our identity as a species and our fragile place in evolutionary history may be the first, indispensable step toward saving ourselves.

Such a collective revelation is becoming even more urgent as the lines between what is natural and humanly constructed blur. Various new technologies are enabling unprecedented comingling of biological life forms with human design—genetic manipulations of agricultural seedlines, genetic engineering of human beings and animals, and irreversible manipulations of ecological systems and the global atmosphere. These developments signal a new era in human history. Human beings are no longer the children and adversaries of nature, the abject subjects of the gods. We are nature's stewards; we have become our parents. Nature is not something outside ourselves; it is something that we are constructing—cocreating—with all forms of technology, resulting in new forms of coevolution between ourselves and nature.

Even though we are totally unprepared for this responsibility, within the next decade human societies will somehow have to confront—or evade—the inevitable problems that ensue. To the extent that many problems stem from our overweening faith in FMD, a critique that acknowledges our common humanity—and not just the competitive pursuit of private gain—could help us chart a new course.

It's Time to Start a New Conversation

It is time to get beyond the ghost dance that afflicts this moment in our history. We desperately need a new humanistic vision, one that gets us past the large flaws and dated assumptions of FMD. The archetype of the commons may provide just such a platform for building such a vision. It complements the findings of the new sciences, it cogently deconstructs free-market ideology, and it offers its own feasible alternatives.

There could not be a more apt moment for ambitious, imaginative thinking. The new sciences are yielding a rich harvest of new insights into our contemporary circumstances. The Internet is enabling rich new forms of value-creation and social exchange. Many old models of economic life and human nature, relics of the eighteenth century, are crumbling. The rudiments of a new citizen-based global culture are sprouting up.

But we must remember that the old rarely yields to the new without a struggle. The new must be actively and imaginatively built. That will require forging new networks of visionary thinkers and bringing disparate disciplines together into new conversations. It will require challenging the comfortable shibboleths of FMD and taking new risks to develop a more accurate understanding of the human species.

Could there be a more urgent task for the twenty-first century? It is a daunting challenge, to be sure, but the long-term transformations—for economics, politics, policy, and culture—could not be more needed.

Notes

1. See McCullough (2001, 222).
2. See Cosmides and Tooby (2002).
3. John H. Clippinger, "Why Routing is Better Than Sharing," November 2002 (work in progress, on file with author).
4. See Durham (1991).
5. See Sober and Wilson (1998, 176).
6. See Dawkins (1976).
7. One compelling bit of evidence that social exchange is a universal trait for all human societies is a study that compared the ability to detect deceit among the Shiwiar, a nonliterate, isolated Amazonian tribe of hunter-horticulturalists, and Harvard undergraduates. If the ability to identify cheating were the product of culture or economic development, clear differences in competence

would be discernible. But the study found that "cheater detection reasoning" has been found in every developed and developing country that has been studied. See Sugiyama, Tooby, and Cosmides (2000).

8. See Rizzolatti, Fadiga, Fogassi, and Gallese (1999).
9. George Lakoff, personal communication, 2003.
10. See Damasio (2003, 162).
11. See Damasio (2003, 171).
12. See Cosmides and Tooby 2002.
13. A cross-cultural survey of fifteen societies by economist Samuel Bowles has shown that the celebrated *homo economicus* that neoclassical economists routinely invoke does not exist in any recognizable form. See Henrich, Boyd, Bowles, Camerer, Fehr, Gintis, and McElreath (2001).
14. See Clark (1997, 69).
15. The fact that there are genetically encoded innate mechanisms that predispose or shape human thought and action should not come as a surprise. But this does not imply that there is strict determinism of human activity. If anything, the complexity sciences are especially respectful of the indeterminacy and indeed unpredictability of many of seemingly simple behaviors. Geneticists also recognize that genes are not literal blueprints that strictly determine morphological development or growth over time. Hence the so-called nature/nurture dichotomy—so often seized upon by the popular press—is a false one engendering much heat and little light. See, e.g., Pinker (2002).
16. See, e.g., Mullainathan and Thaler (2001).
17. See Friedman (1999, 83–92).
18. David Johnson and Susan Crawford, private correspondence.
19. See Coase (1937).
20. See Benkler (2002–2003).
21. See Bollier (2003).
22. The General Public License is a legal innovation of the Free Software Foundation, at <http://www.fsf.org>.
23. For more on the Alaska Permanent Fund, see <http://www.apfc.org>.
24. See Barnes (2001).
25. See Hawken, Lovins, and Lovins (1999).
26. See McNeill, McNeill, and Kennedy (2001) and Flannery (2001).
27. See Thompson (2003). See also, letter from Gary Ruskin (2001), of Commercial Alert, to Emory University President James Wagner, calling for a halt to all neuro-marketing experimentation on human subjects at Emory.
28. See Damasio (2003, 163).

References

Barnes, Peter. 2001. *Who owns the sky? Our common assets and the future of capitalism.* Washington, DC: Island Press.

Benkler, Yochai. 2002–2003. Coase's penguin, or Linux and the nature of the firm. *Yale Law Journal* 112(3): 369–446.

Bollier, David. 2003. *The rise of Netpolitique: How the Internet is changing international politics and diplomacy.* Washington, DC: Aspen Institute.

Clark, Andy. 1997. *Being there: Putting brain, body, and world together again.* Cambridge, MA: MIT Press.

Coase, Ronald H. 1937. The nature of the firm. *Economica* 4(NS) (16): 386–405.

Cosmides, Leda, and John Tooby. 2002. *Evolutionary psychology: A primer.* Santa Barbara: University of California, Center for Evolutionary Psychology.

Damasio, Antonio. 2003. *Looking for Spinoza: Joy, sorrow and the feeling brain.* New York: Harcourt.

Dawkins, Richard. 1976. *The selfish gene.* Oxford, UK: Oxford University Press.

Durham, William. 1991. *Coevolution: Genes, culture and human diversity.* Stanford, CA: Stanford University Press.

Flannery, Tim. 2001. *The eternal frontier: An ecological history of North America and its peoples.* Boston: Atlantic Monthly Press.

Friedman, Thomas L. 1999. *The Lexus and the olive tree.* New York: Farrar, Straus, and Giroux.

Hawken, Paul, Amory Lovins, and L. Hunter Lovins. 1999. *Natural capitalism: Creating the next industrial revolution.* Boston: Little, Brown.

Henrich, Joseph, Robert Boyd, Samuel Bowles, Colin Camerer, Emst Fehr, Herbert Gintis, and Richard McElreath. 2001. In search of *Homo economicus*: Behavioral experiments in fifteen small-scale societies. *American Economic Review* 91(2): 73–78.

Johnson, David, and Susan Crawford. 2003. The Commonwealth Project. Unpublished memo on file with authors, February 16.

McCullough, David. 2001. *John Adams.* New York: Simon and Schuster.

McNeill, J.R., John Robert McNeill, and Paul Kennedy. 2001. *Something new under the sun: An environmental history of the twentieth century.* New York: W.W. Norton.

Mullainathan, Sendhil, and Richard H. Thaler. 2001. Behavioral Economics. In *International Encyclopedia of Social Sciences*, New York: Pergamon.

Pinker, Stephen. 2002. *The blank slate: The modern denial of human nature.* New York: Viking.

Polanyi, Karl. 1957. *The great transformation: The political and economic origins of our time.* Boston, MA: Beacon Press.

Rizzolatti, Giacomo, Luciano Fadiga, Leonardo Fogassi, and Vittorio Gallese. 1999. Resonance behaviors and mirror neurons. *Archives Italiennes de Biologie* 137(2–3): 85–100.

Ruskin, Gary. 2001. Sell the naming rights to your suits, Councilman. News release Available at <http://www.commercialalert.org/index.php/category_id/1/subcategory_id/82/article_id/21>.
Sober, Elliot, and David Sloan Wilson. 1998. *Unto others: The evolution and psychology of unselfish behavior.* Cambridge, MA: Harvard University Press.
Sugiyama, Lawrence S., John Tooby, and Leda Cosmides. 2000 Cross-Cultural evidence of cognitive adaptations for social exchange among the Shiwiar of Ecuadorian Amazonia. *Proceedings of the National Academy of Science USA* 3529: 99(17): 11537–11542.
Thompson, Clive. 2003. There's a sucker born in every medial prefrontal cortex. *New York Times Magazine*, October 26, 2003.

Reading 3

Digitalized Business Models for Pipeline Ecosystems

Vallabh Sambamurthy and Robert W. Zmud

Over the last century, pipeline ecosystems have been the dominant organizing paradigm. In just about all *established* economic arenas, e.g., automotive, packaged foods, personal care goods, pharmaceuticals, smartphones, mobile communication services, healthcare services, big box retailers, etc., value-units are delivered to consumers through tightly-coordinated value streams. This chapter examines the nature of pipeline ecosystems by describing:

- Why Pipeline Ecosystems Exist
- Digitalizing Pipeline Ecosystems
- Disintermediation, Reintermediation and Intermediary Transformation

Why Pipeline Ecosystems Exist

Figure 3.1 depicts a simplified industry value stream for companies—like *Ben and Jerry's*, *Häagen-Dazs*, and *Baskin Robbins*—that produce ice cream (through a mix of upstream channels) and then market finished products to consumers (through a mix of downstream channels). In such a pipeline ecosystem, the ice cream producer determines which ice cream raw materials, flavors and delivery channels are likely to be most favored by consumers and fashions a value stream to produce and deliver ice cream products to these consumers. However, if one or more of the upstream/downstream participants does a poor job carrying out its responsibilities, or if the ice cream producer does a poor job anticipating the consumers' expectations or coordinating value stream work flows, then the consumers' expectations will not be met. Further, because of the complexities involved in coordinating value stream work flows, the producer could choose to perform all of the activities involved with the value stream, i.e., be fully *vertically integrated*. However, as explained below, it usually is neither economically nor operationally desirable for the producer to do so. Three concepts explain why this is the case: *economies of scale and scope*, *transaction costs*, and *intermediation*.

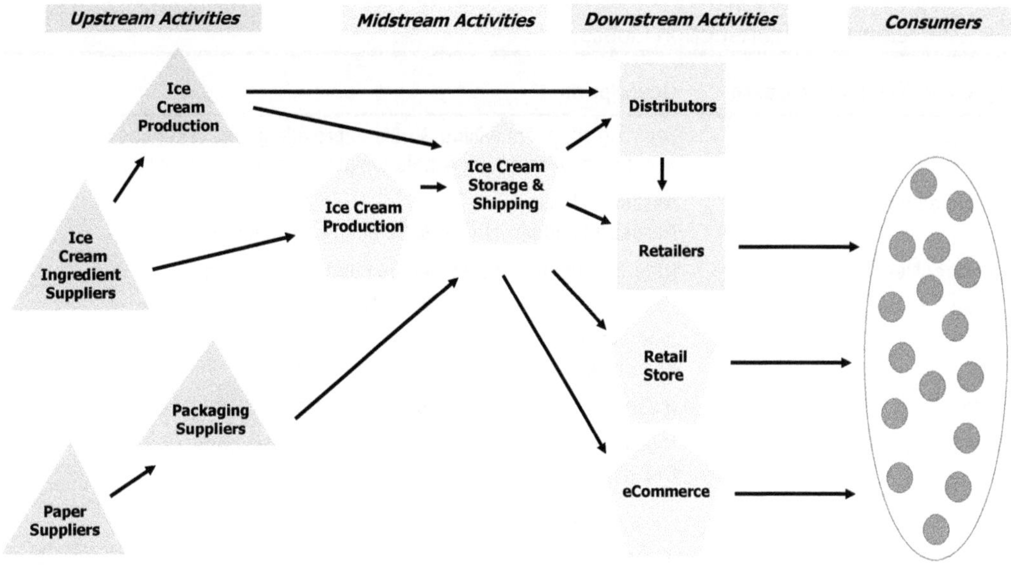

FIGURE 3.1 Ice Cream Industry Value Stream.

Economies of Scale and Scope

Economies of scale refers to the advantages that arise with increased volume of output, and ***economies of scope*** refers to the advantages that arise when a family of related goods are produced rather than a single good. Viewed most simplistically: by covering fixed costs with larger activity volume, the cost to execute the activity drops; by specializing in an activity, the activity's variable costs can be reduced through experience, analysis and training; by performing a set of similar activities, the fixed and variable costs of each activity can be reduced. It is the existence of economies of scale and scope that are at the basis of the consideration given by most producers to using the services of other organizations to carry out many, if not most, value stream work activities.

Transaction Costs

Transaction costs are involved with a fundamental market-related decision, generally referred to as the ***make-versus-buy decision***: when does a company (individual) decide to make an item or perform an activity itself (herself) rather than another company (person) make the item or perform the activity? Answering this question is intuitively simple: compare the total cost of doing it yourself against the total cost of having someone else doing it for you.

The total cost to produce an item or perform an activity can be represented as sum of associated *production* and *transaction costs*. ***Production costs*** are the direct costs to produce

TABLE 3.1 Common Transaction Costs.

Types of Transaction Costs	Description
Search	Locating suppliers willing & able to provide goods & services. Locating buyers willing & able to purchase good & services.
Bid Selection	Assessing bids. Assessing suppliers/buyers. Selecting a supplier/buyer.
Contract Negotiation	Determining mutually agreeable contract provisions. Renegotiating contract provisions.
Bonding	Insuring against failure to deliver/purchase. Insuring against substandard performance.
Legal	Insuring against inadequate contract provisions.
Monitoring	Monitoring ongoing supplier/customer performance. Deciding to terminate or renegotiate contract.

an item or perform an activity; ***transaction costs*** are the additional costs involved when an item or activity is acquired from someone else. Table 3.1 defines common transaction costs.

Because of economies of scale and scope, organizations specializing in producing a family of items or performing a family of activities have the potential to provide higher-quality, lower-cost goods and services than does a non-specialist. However, acquiring an item or a service from a specialist always involves transaction costs (refer back to Table 3.1). The key question, thus, becomes: "Overall, is it less expensive to do it myself or to have the specialist do it for me?" Often, the answer is to have the specialist do it for you.

Intermediation

Intermediation refers to an organization's choosing to reach suppliers or end consumers through another organization, an ***intermediary***, rather than directly. Say, for example, that you would like a dish of ice cream made by a specific ice cream producer. You could buy a pint directly from a retail store operated by the producer or from a nearby grocery store (who buys the ice cream directly from the producer or, more likely, from a distributor or wholesaler). Unless you live close to a producer retail outlet, the transaction costs (e.g., search, travel, etc.) you would experience are likely to be quite high. As a result, you would not buy a pint of ice cream directly from the ice cream producer; instead, you would buy a pint from a nearby grocery store. Because of such difficulties faced by producers in reaching consumers, most producers use downstream intermediaries in order to reach a large number of consumers. A similar logic can be applied in explaining the use of upstream intermediaries. Table 3.2 describes common activities undertaken by intermediaries.

Adding a new intermediary to an existing value stream always introduces additional costs, as each intermediary naturally wishes to make a profit from their involvement in the value stream. However, as these additional profits are spread across the large number of

TABLE 3.2 Common Intermediary Activities.

Types of Activities Performed by Intermediaries	Description
Search Efficiency	Locate & procure products/services/information. Locate suppliers.
Demand Aggregation	Gather orders from multiple consumers and negotiate prices & contracts with producers. Gather products/services/information from multiple suppliers and negotiate prices & contracts with producers.
Create Packages	Buy in bulk and reassemble into packages that meet the needs of specific consumers or producers.
Guarantee Transactions	Handle complex transactions. Insure payments & shipments.
Manage Logistics	Delivery of goods: upstream & downstream.

value-units moving through the value stream, it often proves to be the case that both producers and consumers ultimately benefit from the presence of the new intermediary.

Digitalizing Pipeline Ecosystems

The nature of market-focused ecosystems has evolved dramatically over the three eras of digital disruption, particularly with regard to the value-units delivered to consumers, the enabling digitization and digitalization, and the payment and trust systems employed. Table 3.3 provides an overview of the major changes that have occurred. The most significant of these changes for pipeline ecosystems are described below. Each one of the three eras of digital disruption within pipeline ecosystems is now described, with this section ending with a discussion of how these changes have resulted in the value streams associated with pipeline ecosystems being *disintermediated*, *reintermediated* and characterized by *intermediary transformation*.

Era 1

Leadership teams of organization-participants within pipeline ecosystems expect their operations, staff and managerial employees to be looking for ways to enhance value-units, cut costs, improve market responsiveness, and accelerate the development of new, revenue-generating value-units. These beneficial outcomes all derive from efforts taken to improve organizations' *internal* managerial and operational processes. Figure 3.2 provides a way to conceptualize these processes.[1] ***Primary processes*** refer to work activities directly involved

1 This conceptualization is derived from ideas introduced by: M. E. Porter, *Competitive Advantage: Creating and Sustaining Superior Performance*, New York: Free Press, 1998.

TABLE 3.3 Evolution of Pipeline Ecosystems.

Era	Value-Units	Digitization & Digitalization	Exchange Currency	Trust Systems
1	Digital complements	• Data/document standards • Point-to-point connectivity • Intra- and inter-organizational (managerial & operational) business process efficiencies	• Banking system • Credit/debit card systems	• Government & third-party institutions • Contracts • Brand • Social capital
2	Digital value-units	• Internet • One-to-many connectivity • Data, process, analytic & collaboration platforms • Social media • Omni-channel producer-consumer interaction	• Digitalized payment systems	• Third-party digital trust seals • Consumer monitoring (product & producer reviews)
3	Social complements	• Many-to-many connectivity • Smart devices • Big data platforms • Big data analytic platforms • Social messaging platforms	• Reputation • Social capital • Bitcoins	• Community monitoring • Peer-regulation • Self-regulation

FIGURE 3.2 A Pipeline Organization's Managerial and Operational Processes.

in delivering value-units to customers, and ***support processes*** refer to work activities that provide direction, resources and oversight for the primary processes. All too often, however, these work activities are hindered by constraints—both real (e.g., time, space, resource limitations, etc.) and imagined (i.e., ingrained in employees' thinking as a result of culture, history, inadequate supervisory direction, inadequate training, etc.).

The availability of new digital technologies, industry data/document standards and results from analyzing digitized transactional data proved instrumental in enabling value stream participants to overcome many of the constraints that otherwise were inhibiting efforts to improve internal processes and external workflows. ***Data/document standards*** allow data and documents to be accessed and used by value stream participants. For example, many industry groups developed data and document specifications as a means of facilitating B2B transaction flows. This was referred to as ***EDI*** (***Electronic Data Interchange***). As might be expected, EDI made it possible for value stream participants to interconnect their (increasingly-digitized) workflows. When operational processes improve within and across a value stream's participants, two things occur. First, the performance of the entire value stream improves—to the benefit of all participants, but especially for consumers. Second, as intermediaries are specialized to a greater extent than are producers, intermediaries are able to more-quickly apply process improvements to enhance their business models. As a result, intermediaries tended to gain increased influence in value streams and, correspondingly, to increase their relative shares of the value being created. However, such gains in the influence of intermediaries were somewhat attenuated by the abilities of creative producers to lower their cost structures and to attach digital complements (e.g., better and more information, information-based services, product/service migration paths, etc.) to the value-units being delivered to, thereby enhancing the producer's value-proposition and strengthening both the producer's market position and relative influence within the value stream.

For the most part, Era 1 pipeline ecosystems made use of well-established payment and trust systems. The only true innovation that occurred was the emergence of a digitally-enabled payment system: credit and debit card payment systems.

Era 2

The digital technology that ushered in Era 2 was the development and widespread adoption of the *World Wide Web*. At its core, the **WWW** (***World Wide Web***) serves as a one-to-many connectivity mechanism enabling organizations (and individuals) to store data and documents in an online space such that these data and documents can easily and inexpensively be accessed and used by other organizations (and individuals). The *WWW* (along with its enabling technologies) led to three digitalization innovations that irreversibly disrupted pipeline ecosystems: purely-digital value-units, platforms, and omni-channel promotion, ordering and delivery.

Purely-Digital Value-Units

Like their physical counterparts, purely-digital value-units do not exist in a vacuum but require a vast enabling-ecosystem. For example, consider a very familiar physical product—the automobile. In order for you to buy a car directly off of the sales lot and drive it, a huge number and variety of things must exist: automobile retailers, service/repair shops, insurance providers, fuel stations, roadways, traffic lights and signage, traffic laws and regulations, etc. Most important, a correspondingly huge number of standards need to have been established and need to be followed in order for the entire automobile ecosystem to operate seamlessly.

A similar enabling-ecosystem needs to exist for purely-digital value-units, such as digital books, mp3 audio tracks, navigation maps, and digital coupons. Devices must exist through which a purchased value-unit can be accessed and used, retailers must exist to offer the value-unit to a consumer and then deliver a purchased copy to the consumer's device, and payment systems must exist so that the exchange can take place between the retailer and the consumer. As with physical goods, many standards must be established and followed for the ecosystem to operate seamlessly.

Although physical and digital value-units both require enabling-ecosystems, the markets for physical and digital value-units differ in two major ways. First, the cost-structures of digital value-units tend to be much lower than the cost-structures of physical value-units. Second, *long-tail effects* characterize digital value-unit markets to a much greater extent than physical value-unit markets.

Relative to digital value-units, physical value units have moderate-to-high initial costs (e.g., design, testing and marketing) and moderate-to-high *variable* production costs (e.g., labor and materials). Let us compare the costs between manufacturing a car and developing a digital book. Car manufacturers incur high fixed costs (e.g., large plants, sophisticated manufacturing and design technologies, etc.) and high variable costs (e.g., parts and assembled components, labor). In contrast, while a digital book may have high initial costs (the labor costs involved in authoring, editing and formatting the book), a digital book has very low variable production costs—often approaching zero. This is because the costs of replicating digital goods are minimal, unlike most physical goods. For example, the 100th car coming off of an assembly line will cost essentially the same to produce as the first car off of said assembly line. However, the 100th digital copy of a text book costs only a minute fraction of the expense involved in producing the first digital version. The production costs associated with digital goods are dominated by the cost of producing a first copy, with few constraints limiting growth in demand. Simply put, digital goods have far more opportunities for large-scale growth than do physical goods.

The ***long-tail phenomenon*** refers to the ability of digital markets to offer a far broader variety of value-units than could be offered in comparable physical markets. Participants in physical markets are constrained in the breadth of value-units being offered because of the costs of holding inventory. Generally, firms strive to offer the 20% of value-units that generate 80% of sales. It simply is not economical to cater to the remaining 80%. Consider a hardcopy book that was a bestseller a year ago, but has since been displaced by more recent bestsellers. Even though a small demand for this hardcopy book is likely to persist over time, most hardcopy retailers will keep few, if any, copies of the book on hand due to acquisition costs and physical storage space constraints. Similarly, consider a book on hiking in the Andes mountain ranges written by an authoritative expert. While there might be a sizeable demand for such a book among hiking enthusiasts (especially those planning a near-term hiking expedition in the Andes), the book is unlikely to have the broad popularity needed to merit space on most hardcopy retailer's bookshelves (unless, perhaps, you walk into a bookstore in Cuzco, Peru).

On the other hand, digital retailers are finding it profitable to service the needs of customers whose tastes represent the more specialized products populating the *long-tail of the demand spectrum*. For example, an MIT study from the early 2000s found that nearly 30-40% of *Amazon's* book sales represent products in this long tail.[2] This ability of digital markets to service the long-tail of demand can be explained by a number of factors:

- Digital retailers experience lower costs of stocking inventory because they do not use physical shelf space to stock and display their products. Instead, they apply digitalized product inventories, often including products held by other ecosystem participants.
- Digital retailers experience lower costs of promotion and advertising via a proliferation of Internet and social media sites.
- Digital retailers experience lower acquisition costs.
- Digital markets are not constrained by geography. They can reach customers locally, regionally, nationally or globally. At that scale, digitized retailers can aggregate the demand for niche products to achieve dramatic scale economies.
- Digital consumers can make use of digitalized search mechanisms to locate digital retailers and specific digital value-units.

---

2 E. Brynjolfsson, Y. Hu, and M. D. Smith, "From Niches to Riches: Anatomy of the Long Tail," *Sloan Management Review*, Summer 2006, pp. 67–71.

- Digital consumers have access to massive amounts of value-unit-related information (e.g., reviews of specific value-units or of value-unit categories, such as lists of the best point-and-shoot cameras).

Platforms

Value streams in pipeline ecosystems become *longer* and *wider* each time another upstream or downstream intermediary is added. Although each added-participant offers new capabilities to be leveraged, the complexities involved in coordinating data, information and material flows between value stream participants increase as well.

Consider the value stream shown in Figure 3.3. Note that numerous data/information flows and material flows are involved, and that all of these flows occur between adjoining participants. Each participant determines demand forecasts from data and information provided by only the most adjacent participants. Without access to consolidated data from all participants in a value stream, these forecasts tend to be error-prone, erratic and worsen over time. Participants experiencing high levels of demand uncertainty often suffer late deliveries, overstocking, high expediting costs, stressed employees, dissatisfied customers, and lost revenue.

Value stream participants developed tactics to deal with demand uncertainty, the two most common being *vertical integration* and *stock holding.* With ***vertical integration***, an organization chooses to do more value stream activities itself, thus shortening and narrowing its value stream. But, in doing so, the advantages gained through specialization

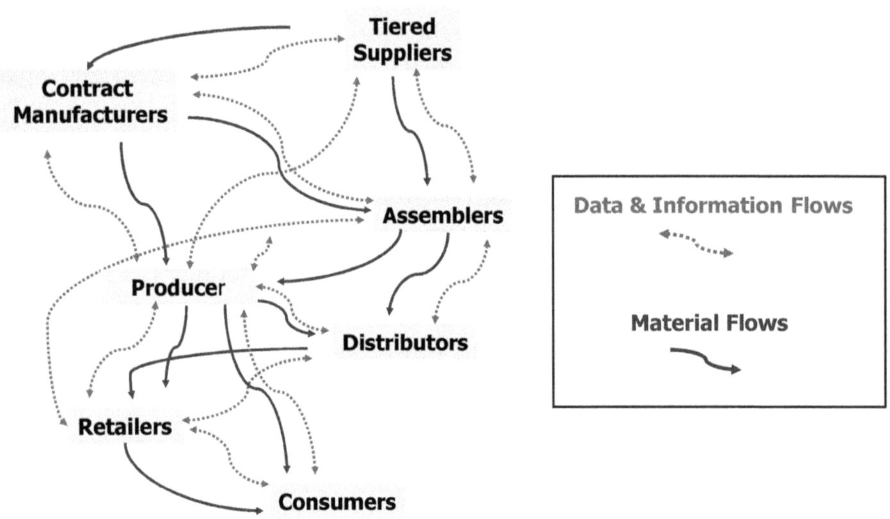

FIGURE 3.3 Conventional Value Stream.

and intermediation are lost. With ***stock holding***, an organization builds up various kinds of inventories, thus providing buffers that soften the effects of poor demand forecasts. But, in doing so, higher inventory costs arise that can lead to higher prices (stressing consumer demand) and/or lower profit margins.

Era 2 digitalization provided a much better way to cope with the challenges of long and wide industry value streams. Figure 3.4 depicts a platform-enabled value stream. In general terms, a ***platform*** uses digital technologies to host digital and digitally-enabled resources. In this case of a ***value stream platform***, these hosted resources are likely to include: digitized data and documents, digitalized managerial and operational processes that operate on these data/documents, tools for analyzing data, and tools enabling employees from participating organizations to interact and collaborate. By using the resources available through value stream platforms, value stream participants can: better plan their own work activities; better plan and then coordinate the data, information and material flows that permeate a value stream; and, collaborate to resolve problems that arise.

Many successful value stream platforms have been built, owned and managed by powerful value stream participants. Classic examples include *Dell*'s platform for executing its *build-to-order* business model (see Figure 3.5) and *Enterprise Rent-A-Car*'s platform for executing its *repair rental car* business model (see Figure 3.6). Considerable efforts have been taken by industry consortiums, (e.g., electronics manufacturing, automobile manufacturing,

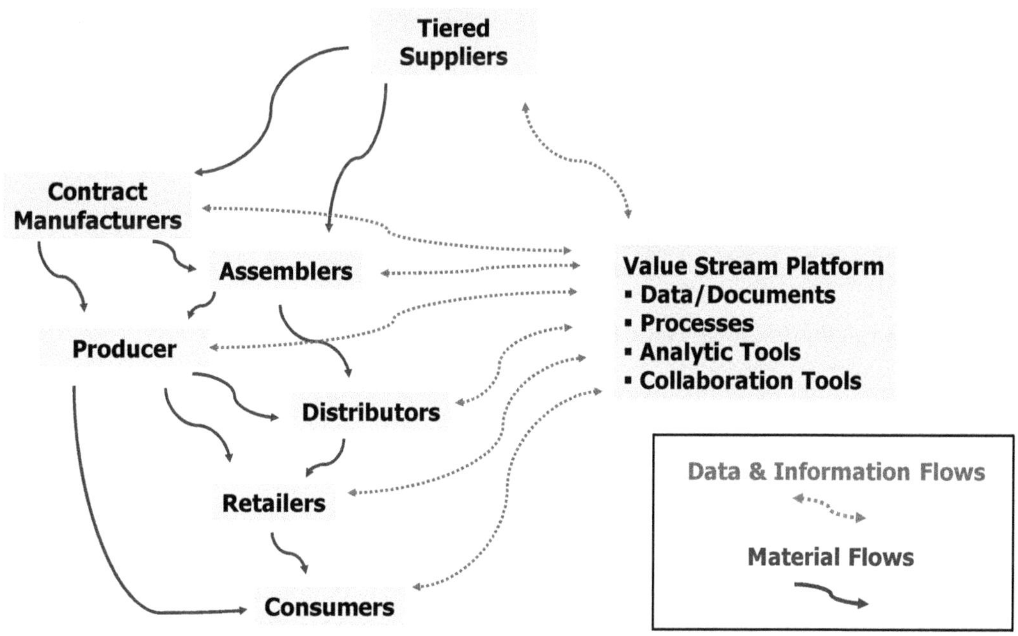

FIGURE 3.4 Platform-Enabled Value Stream.

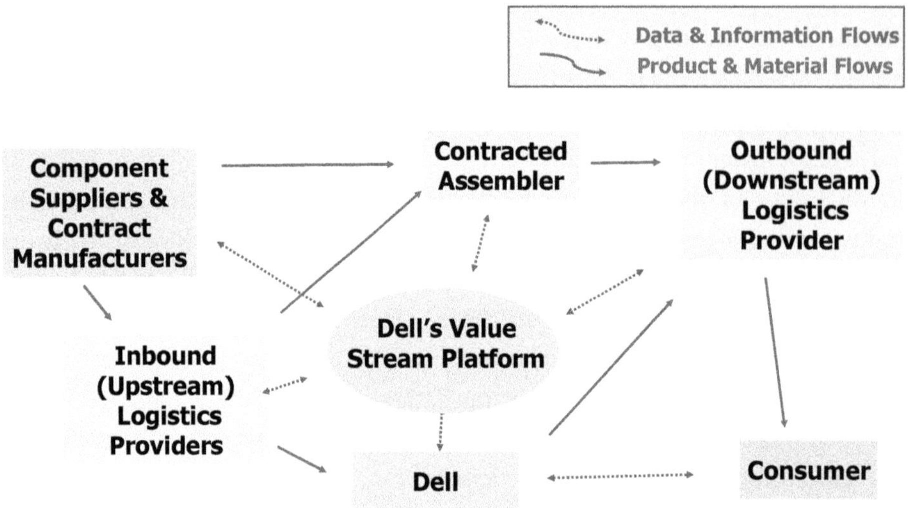

FIGURE 3.5 *Dell's* Value Stream Platform.

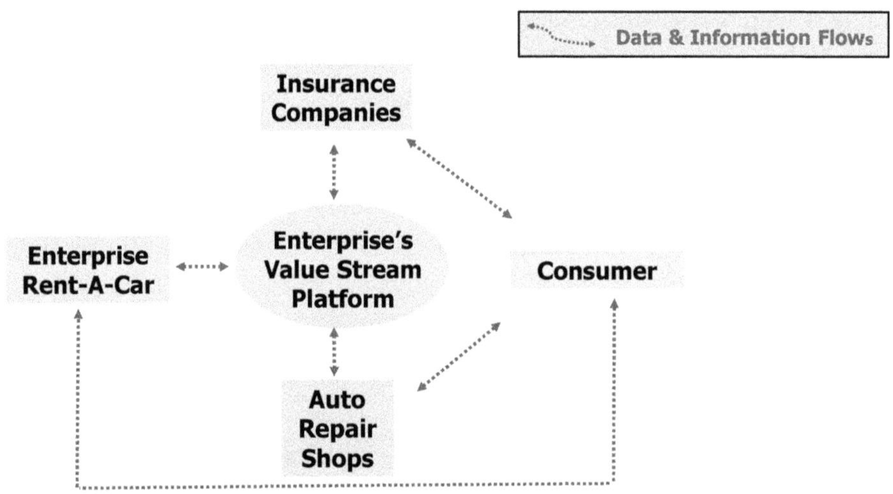

FIGURE 3.6 *Enterprise Rent-A-Car's* Value Stream Platform.

chemical production, etc.), to define and implement platforms to be used across the varied value streams that comprise these industries' market ecosystems.

Omni-Channel Promotion, Ordering and Delivery

As Era 2 progressed, advances with *WWW* technologies accelerated, increasing the functionality, ease-of-use and availability of value stream platforms. One of the key targets of platform enhancement involves the variety of channels used for promotion, ordering and

TABLE 3.4 Value Stream Participant Interaction Channels.

	Era 1 Channels		Era 2 Channels	
Medium	**Promotion**	**Ordering & Delivery**	**Promotion**	**Ordering & Delivery**
Mass	Radio Television Print Magazines Newspapers Catalogs Direct Mail	Retail Store	Internet Ads Producer Website Retailer Website Informational Websites Posted Reviews Messaging email/text	eCommerce B2C B2B
Personal	Telephone Face-to-Face	Mail Services Parcel Services Telephone Face-to-Face	Search-Targeted Ads Messaging email/text/chat	Messaging
Social	Group Event *Avon* *Tupperware*	Group Event	Social Media Groups Messaging Interactions Targeted Ads Blogs	

delivery activities (see Table 3.4). As a consequence, value stream participants enlarged the portfolio of channels through which participant interactions occurred. Such interactions involve data, information and/or material flows between:

- Participants' digitalized processes (e.g., a producer's component ordering system interacts with a supplier's sales order processing system).
- Participants' employees (e.g., a producer's purchasing clerk interacts with a supplier's customer support representative via a series of texts).
- A participant's digitalized process and another participant's employee (e.g., a producer's purchasing clerk interacts with a supplier's order tracking system).
- A participant's digitalized process and an individual consumer (e.g., a consumer interacts with a producer's online storefront).
- A participant's employee and an individual consumer (e.g., a consumer interacts with a producer's customer support representative via an online chat capability).
- Two (or more) individual consumers (e.g., two consumers interact through a producer's online customer forum).

Payment and Trust Systems

The accelerating growth of B2C e-commerce witnessed innovations in both payment systems and trust systems. Purely-digital alternatives, such as *PayPal* and *Amazon's 1-Click*, have emerged in response to consumers' desire for more accessible and convenient payment systems for online transactions. Similarly, innovations were targeted at increasing consumers' willingness to engage with e-commerce retailers (e.g., third-party institutions such as *VeriSign*) and to purchase products on a sight-unseen basis (e.g., consumer reviews). Consumer reviews, in particular, have become a culturally-accepted trust mechanism, despite concerns[3] about fake reviews and a tendency for contributed reviews to possess a socially-influenced bias toward positive ratings.

Era 3

Era 3 digitalization emerged largely as a consequence of the coming together of *smart devices*, value-unit *social media complements* and *pervasive connectivity*. A ***smart device*** refers to an assembled piece of digital technology (e.g., a product, a component, a tool, an accessory, etc.) that provides a digital capability to sense, analyze and act on environmental signals. Table 3.5 describes some familiar but, in contrast to what is happening today, *not-so-smart* smart devices. Value-unit ***social media complements*** refer to the opportunities made available to value-unit consumers to engage with the value-unit's producer and/or retailer and with other consumers via social media. ***Pervasive connectivity*** is a characteristic of an ecosystem where collections of smart devices across the ecosystem are interconnected, thus creating opportunities for anywhere, anytime interaction; these interactions contribute (e.g.,

TABLE 3.5 Some Familiar Smart Devices.

Device	What is Sensed	What Action is Taken
Smartphone	Screen icon touch	An app is launched
Home Thermostat	Ambient room temperature	Furnace (air conditioner) turned on when ambient temperature too low (high)
Tire Pressure Sensor	A tire's current air pressure	Dashboard icon lights up when the tire's air pressure is too low
Smart Refrigerator	The condition of a refrigerator's water filter	A display icon lights up when the water filter needs to be changed
Vehicle Navigation GPS Unit	Satellite signals indicating the coordinates of the unit's geographic location	An icon is positioned on a displayed digital map that indicates the vehicle's position, direction & speed
Shipment Unit Packaging Sensor	The force exerted on a shipped unit if and when the unit shifts or drops while in transit	If sufficient force is detected, the shipped unit is returned to the point of origination for damage assessment
Electronic Device Fault-Diagnosis	Temperature of the device	A series of pre-programmed tests are performed on the device's circuitry

3 S. Aral, "The Problem with Online Ratings," *Sloan Management Review*, Winter 2014, pp. 47–52.

sensed data, novel ideas, reviews, etc.) significantly to business model value propositions. How are individuals (typically, employees and/or consumers) motivated to contribute to the ecosystem? While (direct or indirect) monetary payment has traditionally been a dominant primary mechanism, alternative mechanisms—reputation and social capital—are proving to be equally, if not more, effective.

The pervasive connectivity of smart devices can produce huge volumes of streamed data, popularly referred to as ***Big Data***, to be captured, organized and analyzed. Era 3 digitalization enables value stream participants to: maintain an awareness of targeted events occurring across a value stream, as well as within adjacent value streams; to capture data about these events; and, to apply statistical and mathematical models to these data in developing deeper understandings of the competitive context, of value stream participants (e.g., raw material suppliers, component suppliers, services providers, downstream-consumers, etc.), and of specific competitive situations. Table 3.6 provides two relatively straightforward examples of the benefits obtainable from ***Big Data analytics***.

This capability to capture, archive and analyze large streams of transaction-related data has made viable a new trust mechanism: *self-regulation*. With ***self-regulation***, an organization captures data associated with critical market-related transactions, monitors these data for

TABLE 3.6 Big Data Analytics Examples.

Bicycle Pump Producer Buzz Analytics	***City of Boston Street Bump iPhone App***
Digitalization	
Captured consumers' messages on social media (*Facebook, Twitter*, etc.) about bicycle pumps.	Drivers turn on app and placed iPhone on car dashboard.
Analyzed messages to prioritize pump features and to identify the weaknesses of the producer's pump *vis-a-vis* competitors' pumps: less durable, hose harder to use, and contained a costly but low-ranked built-in gauge.	App captures data about potholes encountered (location, estimated depth/size, etc.) and transmits these data to a *City of Boston* data server.
Tearing down competitors' products revealed higher-quality components and less bulky packaging.	Captured data cleansed (e.g., non-pothole bumps filtered out) & analyzed to prepare listings of potential potholes to be filled.
Outcomes	
Removed pressure gauge and reduced packaging.	Potholes fixed before they become major road hazards and while repair costs are relatively low.
Applied cost savings to use higher-quality components.	Recurrent potholes can signal serious road management problems.
Source	
D. Fedewa, G. L. Velarde and B. O'Neill, "Using Buzz Analytics to Gain a Product and Marketing Edge," *McKinsey Quarterly*, Number 2, 2016, pp. 14–15.	D. O'Leary, "Exploiting Big Data from Mobile Device Sensor-Based Apps: Challenges and Benefits," *MIS Quarterly Executive*, December 2013, pp. 179–187.

problems, reacts responsively and responsibly if (and when) problems arise, and keeps (governmental or third-party) regulators and value stream participants aware of these activities.

The Promise of Car Data[4]

To catch a glimpse of what is on the horizon as Era 3 progresses and intensifies, let us take a not-so-futuristic look at how Big Data analytics is changing automotive-related competitive contexts.

During the coming decade, technology entrepreneurs and digital giants are expected to partner with incumbents in the automotive industry to exploit an expected surge in the availability of car data and to introduce innovative car-related features and services for which consumers are expected to be very willing to pay. What exactly is car data? A short list would include data about: the road and environmental conditions, the status of a car's various components (e.g., engine, battery, tires, etc.) and systems (e.g., power, steering, safety, etc.), vehicle usage history (e.g., speed, direction, location, past and current trips, etc.), driver/passenger personal data and preferences, and direct communications from the vehicle (e.g., phone, text, email, calendar, social media, etc.). At present, a key unknown is: "Will most people be willing to share this information for free?" Most observers feel the answer will be *Yes* given the immediate benefits to be derived by a vehicle's driver and passengers (see Table 3.7). What do you think?

Why is this scenario so appealing to ecosystem participants? The answer lies in both sides of the profit model component of a business model: generating revenue and reducing cost.

TABLE 3.7 Immediate Driver/Passenger Benefits from Sharing Car Data.

Safety	Time
• Real-time emergency calls • Early on-scene accident reporting • Information to support rescue services • Real-time road hazard warning	• Reduced travel time through optimized routing, navigation & traffic management systems • Reduced time to locate parking through connections with parking services
Convenience	**Cost**
• Reduced breakdown risk and vehicle downtime through predictive maintenance and connections with repair & spare parts service providers • Concierge services (refueling, carwash, in-trunk delivery) • Overall, a more-connected lifestyle	• Reduced insurance cost through pay-as-you-drive insurance schemes • Reduced toll/road tax rates through an automated payment infrastructure

4 This section is based on material from: D. Mohr, G. Camplone, D. Wee, T. Moller and M. Bertoncello, "Car data: Paving the Way to Value-Creating Mobility", *McKinsey Quarterly*, March 2016: https://www.mckinsey.de/files/mckinsey_car_data_march_2016.pdf

New sources of revenues include: selling or leasing new products and services to car owners, leveraging car data with other sources of data to push tailored advertisements to drivers and passengers, and selling/leasing curated car data to third-parties. New means of cutting costs involve creative uses of car data and car connectivity to reduce the R&D, production, delivery and marketing costs associated with automobile-related products and services. In essence, the *connected-car* is increasingly being seen as *the first step into the store* and, when combined with *autonomous driving*, as a prime space for retail where producers and retailers directly interact with a captive consumer.

Disintermediation, Reintermediation and Intermediary Transformation

Over the last two decades, digital disruption has introduced seemingly constant participant turnover into most pipeline ecosystems. Established organizations are frequently losing prominence in markets and, not infrequently, exiting markets—think *Borders*, *Blockbuster* and *Circuit City*. Simultaneously, scores of new, highly-digitalized entrants are participating in these same markets (as well as discovering new, profitable niches in existing markets or creating entirely new markets).

Today, the ever-accumulating stocks of digitalization capabilities arising from the three eras of digital disruption have seeded and continue to see radical structural changes in pipeline ecosystems. The primary drivers of these ecosystem structural changes are *disintermediation*, *reintermediation* and *intermediary transformation*. ***Disintermediation*** occurs when an intermediary is bypassed, thus shortening and narrowing a value stream. ***Reintermediation*** occurs with the appearance of a new intermediary, whose presence lengthens and broadens a value stream. ***Intermediary transformation*** occurs when an existing intermediary vertically integrates, thus becoming a producer. Table 3.8 describes these structural change-events for the upstream and downstream segments of pipeline ecosystems. Below, we provide examples of each type of change-event for the downstream context.

Almost all producers in consumer markets (e.g., clothing, shoes, digital devices, furniture, grocery products, art, music, etc.) are *disintermediating*, to varying extents, their downstream ecosystem via a B2C sales channel. B2C channels provide many benefits—most are obvious, but some are not-so-obvious—to producers and to consumers. Producers enjoy: a new revenue-generating sales channel complementing, rather than cannibalizing, existing sales channels; higher profit-margins on B2C sales, especially with overstocked items; the opportunity to directly touch and interact with consumers, building loyalty and engagement; and, the opportunity to indirectly and directly involve consumers in new product development activities. Consumers enjoy: access to a producer's entire product line and to

TABLE 3.8 Value Stream Structural Change-Events.

	Downstream
Disintermediation	Producer bypasses intermediaries to directly engage in market exchanges with consumers.
Reintermediation	Entry of digitalized retailer, whom facilitates market exchanges between producers & consumers. Entry of digitalized infomediary (an intermediary dealing solely with data & information), whom identifies sought value-units and/or producers to consumers.
Intermediary Transformation	Intermediary integrates backwards to become a producer creating & delivering value-units to consumers.
	Upstream
Disintermediation	Producer bypasses intermediaries to directly engage in market exchanges with raw material suppliers, component suppliers and/or service providers. Supplier bypasses intermediaries to directly engage in market exchanges with producers and/or bypasses producers to directly engage in market exchanges with consumers.
Reintermediation	Entry of digitalized distributor facilitating market exchanges between producers & raw material suppliers, component suppliers and/or service providers. Entry of digitalized infomediary identifying sought raw materials, components & services, as well as suppliers/providers, to producers.
Intermediary Transformation	Intermediary integrates backwards to become a producer, creating and delivering value-units to suppliers, intermediaries, producers and/or consumers.

product-support content; immediate, and often early, access to a producer's new and overstocked products; the ability to express feelings of satisfaction and dissatisfaction directly to a producer; opportunities to engage with the producer and with other consumers in learning about a product and product-related activities; and, opportunities to influence a producer's next generation of products. Who loses? Clearly, the intermediaries, i.e., distributors and retailers, who have been partially or fully disintermediated.

As described in Table 3.8, there are two primary *reintermediation* pathways with downstream ecosystems: the entry of a digitalized intermediary and the entry of a digitalized *infomediary*. An ***infomediary*** is a digitized intermediary that gathers content from across the *WWW*, curates the content and provides access to this curated content. *Amazon*'s foray into the retail marketplace for books is the iconic example of a digitalized entrant serving as disruptive intermediary, and *Google*'s reshaping of Internet search is the iconic example of a digitalized entrant serving as a disruptive infomediary.

Finally, highly-capable and influential intermediaries able to develop deep knowledge of a pipeline ecosystem may be able to exploit this knowledge to become a producer of the value-units being delivered to consumers. Two examples nicely illustrate the breadth of possibilities. *Netflix* successfully disrupted the pipeline ecosystem for film and television video not once, but twice: first as a partially-digitalized intermediary renting DVDs, and later as a fully-digitalized intermediary streaming video provider. Now, *Netflix* is producing and delivering its own content, strengthening its ecosystem influence such that the company is universally recognized both as one of the industry's more powerful and innovative players. *Amazon,* on the other hand, has followed two very different paths in becoming a producer. Having *by necessity* developed (1) deep knowledge of the pipeline ecosystem that creates and delivers books to consumers and (2) strong digital capabilities as this ecosystem transitioned from hardcopy to digital books, *Amazon* has become a successful publisher of digital books through its *Kindle Direct Publishing* operation. Again, having *by necessity* developed superb digitalization capabilities in executing its massive B2C and B2B business models, *Amazon* has also become a successful provider of digitization services (e.g., computer processing power, data storage, content management, etc.) through its *Amazon Web Services* operation.

A Recap and Look Ahead

This chapter has both explained the economic foundations that have enabled pipeline ecosystems to dominate most industries over the past century and the manner by which digitization and digitalization have transformed pipeline organizations and pipeline ecosystems over the three eras of digital disruption. Given this understanding of pipeline ecosystems [...].

Post-Reading Questions

1. What are the effects of the digital revolution on the economy?
2. What is the information economy, and why is it important today?
3. Do network ecosystems benefit the economy? Explain why or why not.

UNIT II

Specific Issues Within the Information Economy

THIS UNIT FOCUSES ON THE IMPORTANT role of product versioning and the kinds of business models most often found in the information marketplace. *Product versioning* is simply the way information producers differentiate their information product for various markets. In other words, an information producer will offer its initial product in different versions and leave the customers to select the version best suited to their needs. This strategy appeals to customers as well, because the customer can still have access to an information product even if he or she cannot afford the premium version. It is also a way for an information producer to capture a large share of the market. In order to execute this strategy, information firms simply create a high-end version of their product and create slightly lower-quality versions derived from it. Information producers like this strategy for two primary reasons. First, the low-end version can be used to advertise the qualitatively superior product. Many users of stripped-down encyclopedias, databases, or music-editing programs can readily see the value of buying an upgraded version of the software. For example, users of Adobe's free Reader will quickly come to realize the usefulness of being able to create PDF files or transfer PDF files into other file formats, which requires the priced version of Adobe Acrobat. Second, by offering lower-priced versions of the information product, a firm can build a reliable customer base.

Various business models have been tried in the information marketplace. We are also seeing new experimentation in the information marketplace with the advent of the Creative Commons and other open licenses. These open licenses have paved the way for Open Educational Resources

(OERs) in the education industry. These information goods are often produced and distributed by institutions, foundations, and governments to offset the price of education. Other industries have begun experimenting with open licensing and business structures as well, but, at least for now, education has mostly put this education model to work.

Currently, the most popular business models are some kind of subscription or paid service or generating revenues through advertising. Digital advertising, of course, depends on the targeted market segment an information provider is trying to appeal to. The most popular form of online marketing is known as personalized online marketing. This form of marketing is used by social media sites and other information providers such as Amazon, YouTube, and Google. Basic personal information is gleaned from the user's accounts and collected from the user's digital traces by storing and accessing the URLs of all the websites the user has visited. In the social media industry, companies like Facebook will track all the communication of a user, including very personal data, and post advertisements believed to be very appealing to the user. If the user is provided the option of clicking away an advertisement the social media site will simply use that data as an opportunity to place more personalized advertisements on the user's account. Personalized advertising has become the main source of monetization for social media platforms. However, the legitimate need for privacy protection is quickly at odds with this form of marketing. This unit explores these themes and the issues involved in our digital economy.

Reading 4

Digitalized Business Models for Network Ecosystems

Vallabh Sambamurthy and Robert W. Zmud

TODAY, WHEN YOU USE YOUR SMARTPHONE or tablet to post content on *Facebook* statuses, to tweet, exchange photos, or search for information on the Internet, you expect these types of Internet-based services to be provided mostly free-of-charge. In economic terms, this amounts to a vast consumer surplus being provided by organizations offering such services. Why do organizations (e.g., *Facebook*, *Twitter*, *WhatsApp*, *Google*, etc.) offer these free services? The not-so-subtle answer is quite straightforward—to generate revenue streams (via advertising or access fees) by enabling other organizations to *touch* an expanding network of consumers or to gain access to information about these consumers.

But, how does this occur? Most often, it occurs through the creation of a *network (market-focused) ecosystem*, with the *core transaction* of the market being the free service: a *Facebook* post, a *Twitter* tweet, a *WhatsApp* photo-share, or a *Google* Internet search. The ***core transaction*** of a network ecosystem is the primary market exchange activity driving both producers and consumers to an ecosystem's *market platform*. The ***market platform*** of a network ecosystem is the organized collection of digital and business platforms that hosts the content and functionalities that establish, operate and govern the ecosystem's market. In order to better grasp the nature of a network ecosystem, let's take a closer look at *Google* and *Facebook*. Also, for the ease of understanding, we will refer to the *networks* being brought together within a network ecosystem as *communities*.

The core transaction enabled by *Google* is a consumer's search for specific content (some unit of information) believed to exist on one or more producer websites (see Figure 4.1). Note especially the third community involved with *Google*'s ecosystem: advertisers. Having developed state-of-the-art search algorithms and an innovative auction scheme for selling advertising associated with specified search outcomes, *Google* has built a business model that profitably monetizes Internet search by attracting large customer and advertiser communities. Interestingly, considerable overlap does exist across the three communities interacting through *Google*'s search

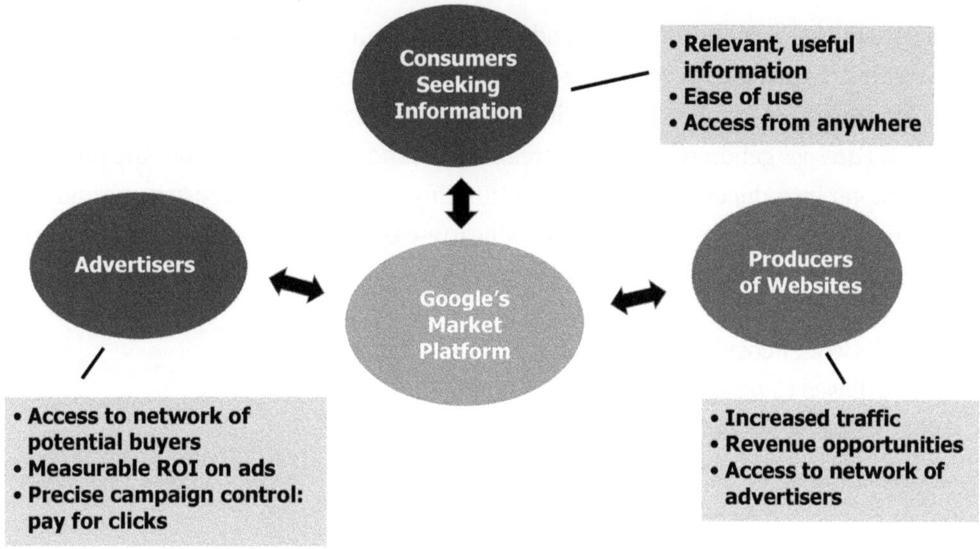

FIGURE 4.1 Google's Network Ecosystem.

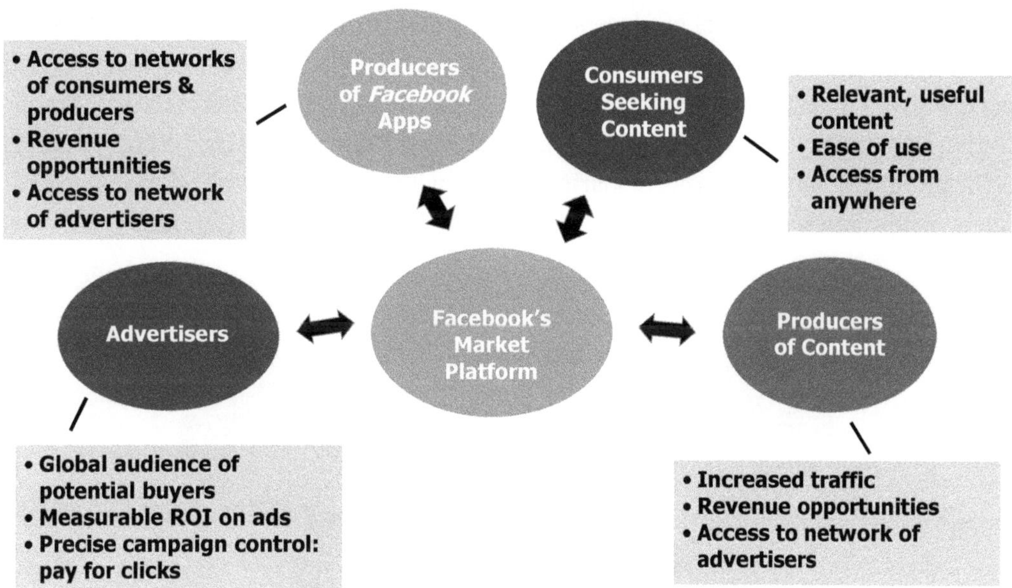

FIGURE 4.2 Facebook's Network Ecosystem.

platform: website producers and advertisers do Internet searches (that is, act as consumers), website producers do advertise, and advertisers do place content on websites.

The core transaction enabled by *Facebook* is a person's posting of content (accompanied by *Facebook* immediately notifying the consumer's *friends* of the posting). As depicted in Figure 4.2, the person posting content is a member of a producer community and the friends wishing to see the posted content are members of a consumer community. Somewhat unique to social media sites, these consumer and producer communities essentially overlap their memberships (aside from pure *lurkers* within the consumer community). Note also that *Facebook*'s ecosystem involves two additional communities: advertisers and *Facebook* App producers. *Facebook* generates revenue streams from these advertisers and App producers.

This chapter introduces intuitive ways of thinking about network ecosystems and about the digital and business platforms used to orchestrate the market spaces established by network ecosystems. The following topics are covered:

- Why Network Ecosystems Exist
- Crowd-Based Capitalism
- Digitalizing Network Ecosystems
- Blended Organizations

Why Network Ecosystems Exist

In explaining the economic concepts that underlie network ecosystems, we use the example of a simplified hypothetical social media ecosystem (see Figure 4.3). Here, community members take on the roles of producers and consumers in order to share content. By sharing content—and, hence, gaining exposure to each other's likes, dislikes, experiences and perspectives—members enrich their relationships with each other. What is the value proposition that drives a person to join, participate, and remain in a social media ecosystem? It is the promise of more-intensively sharing content with individuals with whom a personal relationship already exists or of sharing content with individuals with whom no (or, at best,

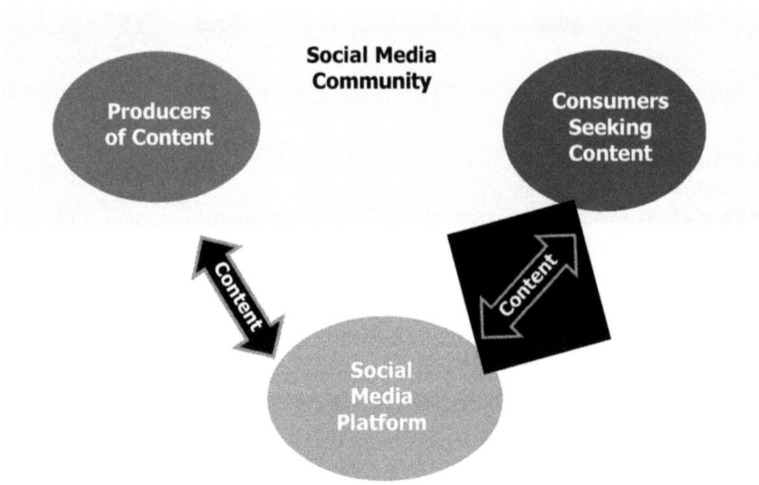

FIGURE 4.3 Simplified Social Media Ecosystem.

a casual) personal relationship currently exists, but with whom a richer personal relationship is desired.

This social media ecosystem value proposition is driven by what economists refer to as *network effects*. Stated simply, as the social community grows *linearly*, the number of possible relationships amongst the community's members grows *exponentially*: 1 member—0 possible relationships, 2 members –1 relationship, 4 members –6 possible relationships, 12 members –66 possible relationships, 100 members –4,950 possible relationships, and so on. Bigger networks, as a general rule, are more valuable to participants; thus, network effects give network ecosystems with the largest participant communities an advantage that is hard for competitors to overcome. We explore network effects further, starting with *two-sided markets*, moving on to *multi-sided markets*, and concluding with a discussion of *winner-take-all markets*—the competitive endgame of a market-focused network ecosystem.

Network Effects

Network effects, or what economists term a ***network externality***, refer to situations where the worth of or demand for a value-unit grows as an exponential function of the number of current consumers of a value-unit and/or the number of *complements* available to these consumers. A ***complement*** increases the perceived worth of a value-unit. A good example of a complement would be the apps available for a particular social media ecosystem, e.g., apps that make it easier to manipulate and share content across the ecosystem. Would you be more inclined to join a social media ecosystem that had more or fewer of your current friends as participants? And, is this more likely for larger or smaller social media ecosystems? Now, given two social media ecosystems comparable regarding the likelihood of you being able to share content with your friends, would you prefer the ecosystem with more or fewer valued complements (e.g., an image manipulation app)? And, would app producers be more inclined to create apps for larger or smaller social media ecosystems? This is the power of network effects!

How can firms capture the opportunities available through positive network effects? Positive network externalities occur only when a customer network is satisfied with—better yet, enthused about—the value-unit being offered. Much of *Apple*'s surge in product success (*iPod, iPhone, iPad, iTunes, iMusic, etc.*) is a direct result of positive word-of-mouth chatter. In contrast, negative customer experiences and perceptions can be devastating.

The competition between *HD DVD* and *Blu-ray* as the standard for DVD players provides an example of network externalities in action. Consider this quote from Matthew Smith, a former SVP of merchandising for *Blockbuster*:[1] *"The consumers are sending us a message.*

---

1 R. Harris, "Blu-ray vs. HD DVD: Game Over," http://blogs.zdnet.com/storage/?p=149.

I can't ignore what I'm seeing. Blockbuster has been renting both Blu-ray and HD DVD titles in 250 stores since late last year and found that consumers were choosing Blu-ray titles more than 70 percent of the time." Relatively quickly, word-of-mouth and consumer purchase decisions led to a positive network effect for *Blu-ray* titles, subsequent growth in the number of *Blu-ray* titles offered for sale or rent relative to the number of *HD* titles, and *Blu-ray* ultimately winning the DVD standards war.

Because of the power of network effects, it is critical for network ecosystems to exploit the influence of word-of-mouth and enlist their communities in growing both community membership and member participation within a community. Another tactic for capturing network effects with network ecosystems is to carefully define the architectural standards enabling connectivity and interoperability and promote these standards such that the standards become dominant in the network ecosystem market space. Winning *standards wars* is critical as this increases the number and variety of complements available to participants. A primary factor behind *Microsoft*'s dominance in PC operating systems was the wide variety of software applications compatible with the *Windows* operating system. This reinforces the dominance of *Windows* in the market for PC operating systems. Firms become successful in standards wars either by leveraging their brand and existing market presence (e.g., a *Microsoft*, an *IBM*, an *Apple*, a *Google*, etc.) or by forming alliances with other firms and collectively engaging in persuasive tactics to influence an industry-wide movement toward a favored standard (e.g., *Bluetooth*, *GSM* for mobility services, *Android* for smart phones, etc.).

Two-Sided Markets

A key notion for understanding the nature of network ecosystems involves the economics of *two-sided markets.*[2] With a ***two-sided market***, the ecosystem owner/builder—the *network orchestrator*—brings together two distinct communities to engage in value-unit exchanges. Most typically, this is accomplished by growing one side of the market as a means of attracting participants to the other side of the market. The two sides of the network ecosystem are perhaps best thought of as a ***subsidy-side*** and a ***money-side***, with the ecosystem's *market platform* providing the rules, functionalities and resources to attract participants and to facilitate value-unit exchanges. As a general rule, the subsidy-side is provided incentives to participate in a network ecosystem as the primary role of the subsidy-side is to attract the money-side, from which revenues are generated. The basic idea, thus, is to grow the subsidized community to the point that its size becomes sufficient to attractive money-side participants willing to pay a fee to gain access to the subsidy-side participants.

---

2 Eisenmann, G. Parker and M. Van Alstyne, "Strategies for Two-Sided Markets," *Harvard Business Review*, October 2006, pp. 92–101.

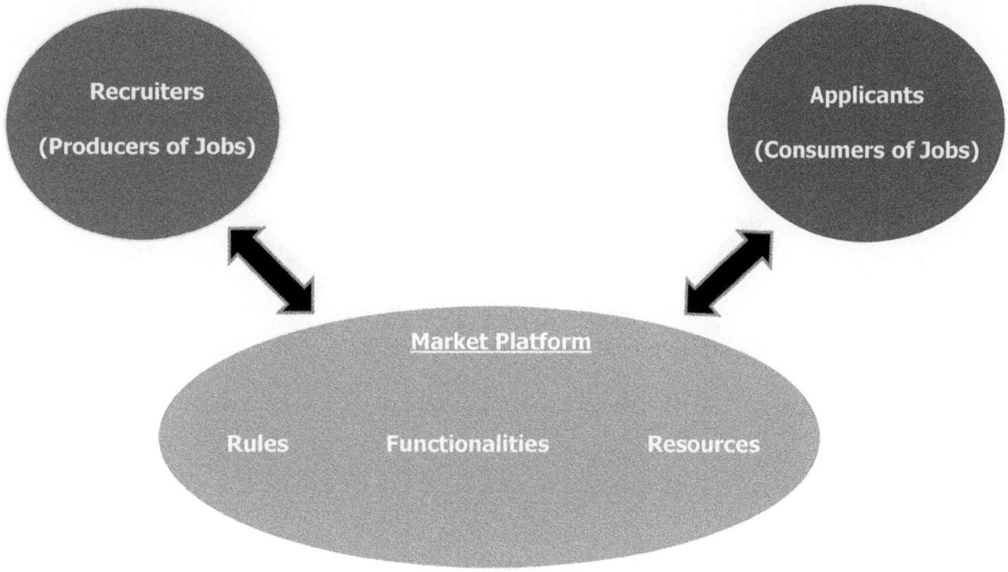

FIGURE 4.4 **Generic Job Recruiting Network Ecosystem.**

As an example of a two-sided market, consider Figure 4.4, which depicts a generic job-recruiting network ecosystem, e.g., *CareerBuilder*, *Monster*, *Job.com*, etc. The subsidy-side is the community of individuals looking for a job. By heavily subsidizing (free?) participation and by offering useful rules (e.g., privacy), functionalities (e.g., resume-builder) and resources (e.g., career advice content), a large pool of job candidates is built. If this pool of job applicants is large and of high quality (e.g., broad ranges of skills and experiences), a high likelihood exists that a sizable pool of recruiters will be attracted despite the participation fees being charged to these recruiters (typically, a recruiter might be charged a modest fee to post a job opportunity, a slightly larger fee for each match that occurs, and a much larger fee if and when an applicant is offered a position).

Another, quite different, example of a two-sided market involves *Adobe* and its *Adobe Reader* and *Adobe Acrobat* software (see Figure 4.5). Before *Adobe Reader* and *Acrobat* were released, the established standard for sharing and printing documents was a tool called *PostScript*. In order to make inroads into the lucrative document creation software market, *Adobe* made its document reader software freely available (subsidizing the consumers of digital documents) and encouraged adopters to share information about *Adobe Reader* and how to obtain it. With positive word-of-mouth by a large number of *Adobe Reader* adopters, *Adobe Reader* became the *de facto* standard for document reading and sharing. Once *Adobe Reader* became the dominant document reader for viewing any type of document, *Adobe* was able to sell its document-creation software, *Acrobat*, to all types of document creators: publishers, law firms, authors, etc. While *Adobe* continues to give *Adobe Reader* away for free,

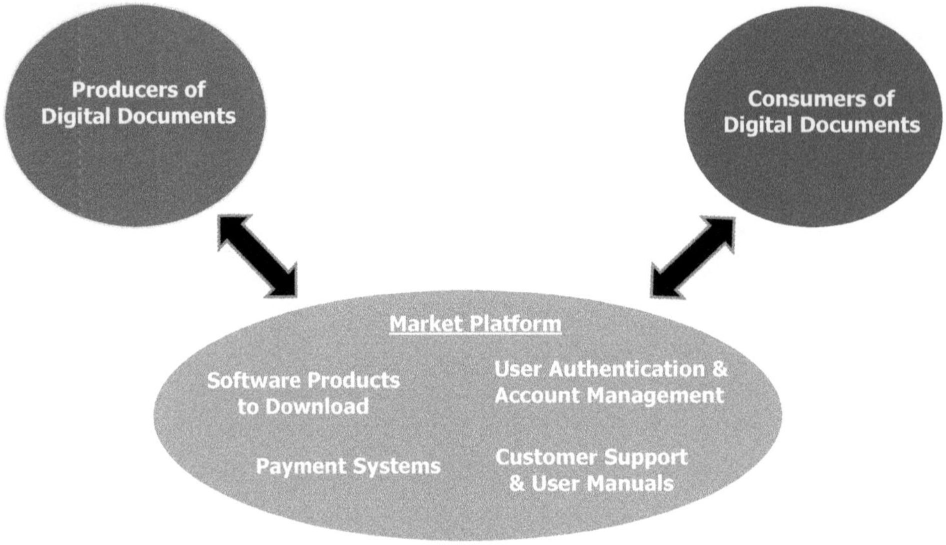

FIGURE 4.5 Adobe's Two-Sided Market Business Strategy.

it generates sizeable revenues through its Acrobat software (now available only by lease, a more-profitable pricing tactic).

What is important about *Adobe*'s strategy? *Adobe* could have enjoyed the benefits of network effects by only offering *Adobe Reader*—by standardizing their use around it, consumers of digital documents would be able to easily exchange documents and read them on any type of device. However, would this positive network effect benefit Adobe to the same extent it benefited *Adobe*'s customers? In other words, would *Adobe* have been able to eventually sell *Adobe Reader* at a price sufficient to generate a lucrative profit? What price could it charge without hurting its ability to build a critical mass of document reader users? *Adobe* recognized that rather severe limits existed regarding what people would be willing to pay for a document reader. But, *Adobe* also recognized that it could generate substantial revenue from document-creation software given that it could achieve a large, installed base of *Adobe Reader* users.

Figure 4.6 provides a more nuanced depiction of the logic underlying a two-sided market. Note that two types of positive network effects are in play. The first is called the ***same-side effect*** and refers to the possibility of network effects with each side of the market. In the case of *Adobe*, as more people adopt *Adobe Reader* for viewing documents, each is presented with more opportunities to easily share documents. This represents a *positive, same-side* network effect for the adopters of *Acrobat Reader*. Potential same-side network effects exist, as well, for document producers. As more producers adopt *Adobe Acrobat* for document creation, more opportunities arise for these producers to exchange content in order to create bundled offerings.

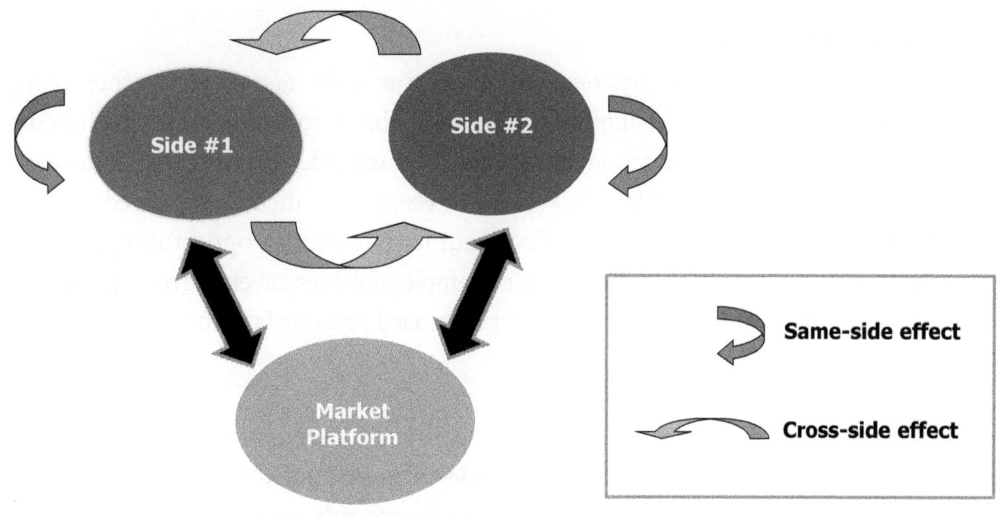

FIGURE 4.6 Same-Side and Cross-Side Network Effects.

The second type of positive network effect is called a ***cross-side effect***. This refers to the potential value that one side derives when there are more participants on the other side. Again, using the *Adobe* example, adopters of *Adobe Reader* benefit as more producers adopt the *Adobe Acrobat* document creation software (because of the increase in the number of compatible digital documents), and document producers benefit with an increase in the number of consumers reading digital documents through the use of *Acrobat Reader* (a larger consumer market for produced digital documents).

So far, our discussion has been based on the assumption that same-side and cross-side network effects are always positive. This is not the case, as these network effects could be negative. Refer back to the job recruiting network ecosystem portrayed earlier as Figure 4.4. Are the same-side network effects *positive* or *negative*? Does a growing pool of job applicants benefit each applicant participating in the ecosystem? Does a growing list of recruiters benefit each recruiter participating in the ecosystem? Possibly not, as this may translate into greater competition among applicants for the best jobs, as well as greater competition among recruiters for the best candidates. Even though each side benefits from positive, cross-side network effects, the potential for negative, same-side network effects could limit the number of job seekers or job providers willing to participate in the ecosystem.[3]

3 The way job recruiting network systems typically deal with negative, cross-side network effects is to segment the pools of available jobs and applicants into 'sub-markets' that become more-level playing fields for both recruiters and applicants.

Multi-Sided Markets

Increasingly, today's network ecosystems are designed as *multi-sided markets* rather than as two-sided markets. A ***multi-sided market*** involves more than two actively participating communities. In this chapter's introduction, we described a three-sided market (the *Google* search network ecosystem) and a four-sided market (the *Facebook* social media network ecosystem).

With multi-sided markets, each added community presents an opportunity to generate additional revenue streams. *Facebook*, for example, receives revenue from advertisers and from app producers. But, this potential for increased revenue is accompanied by three management challenges:

- Creating and then evolving attractive value propositions for each participating community.
- Identifying and optimizing positive same-side/cross-side network effects.
- Identifying and minimizing negative same-side/cross-side network effects.

As the number of communities participating in a multi-side network increases, the complexity of these management challenges tends to increase in a nonlinear fashion.

Winner-Take-All Markets

Increasingly, the payoff gap between being the best competitor in a market and the second-best is widening into a canyon. This applies to labor markets (e.g., professional athletes), to technology markets (e.g., technology producers), and especially to network ecosystems. In explaining the nature of winner-take-all markets, we begin with the most straightforward context—that of a digital product/service.

As positive network effects drive more consumers to adopt a product or service, the product/service can gain a ***critical mass*** of adopters and become dominant in its market space. This same phenomenon occurs with network ecosystems. A *critical mass* of network ecosystem participants is achieved when the momentum produced by an ecosystem's positive network effects is unlikely to be reversed by the entry into the market space of an appealing new network ecosystem, regardless of how appealing this new ecosystem's value-units might be. Think of the market dominance held by *Microsoft Windows* and *Office*, by *Google's Android* and *Gmail*, and by *Blu-ray* DVD players and movies. In each of these cases, the respective markets are said to have *tipped over* with the winner crowding out rival products or services. A ***winner-take-all market***, thus, refers to a market where the potential exists that a critical mass of consumers will adopt *one* producer's products/services.

Nintendo's entry into the home video gaming market nicely demonstrates how competition unfolds in winner-take-all markets. In 1985, *Atari* was the dominant firm in the video game market. By Christmas 1986, the *Nintendo Entertainment System* (*NES*) had emerged as a very popular product, creating positive network effects with both customers and, importantly, game developers, in turn attracting even more customers. At some point, the market tipped over to *Nintendo* as the dominant competitor. Once this occurred, game developers were willing to produce their software exclusively for *Nintendo* for a two-year period—indicating the significant rewards winners can obtain in winner-take-all markets. *Microsoft's* business strategies with its operating systems and its *Office* software suite reflect similar competitive dynamics.

Network ecosystems are particularly susceptible to winner-take-all markets. Three factors tend to characterize winner-take-all network ecosystems:

- Strong producer economies of scale.
- Strong positive cross-side network effects.
- High consumer switching costs.

The latter factor is especially important. When participating in a competitor network ecosystem is perceived as being costly (i.e., a non-trivial investment is required to participate in a network ecosystem and this investment is then lost in moving to a different ecosystem), consumers will be reluctant to either participate in multiple network ecosystems or to switch ecosystems.

Importantly, not all market spaces are susceptible to winner-take-all market dynamics. Consider the market space for *daily deals*, e.g., *Groupon* and *LivingSocial*.[4] Many early investors believed that strong cross-side network effects would produce high stock valuations for *Groupon* and for *LivingSocial*. However, as consumers participating in *Groupon* and in *LivingSocial* experienced very low switching costs, little allegiance was shown to any one market platform with consumers instead skipping through multiple platforms looking for the most attractive deals. As one might expect, the high valuations have yet to materialize.

Generally, a market space susceptible to winner-take-all dynamics is most likely to be seen as a winner-take-all network ecosystem when:

- Participants experience significant, positive network effects.
- Participants are reluctant to move to a competing ecosystem.
- One of the network ecosystems begins to attract a majority of the new participants entering the market space.
- This same ecosystem attracts an accelerating flow of participants from competing ecosystems.

---

4 A. Haigu, "Strategic Decisions for Multi-Sided Platforms," *Sloan Management Review*, Winter 2014, pp. 71–80.

Competition in early-stage winner-take-all network ecosystem market spaces can be fierce. More profitable competitors, *because they are more profitable*, are able to invest more in R&D and to provide greater incentives to participants—enabling their participating communities to grow even faster. This intense competition often results in winner-take-all market spaces being dominated by just a few firms (two or three, at most).

Crowd-Based Capitalism

The past decade has witnessed a reemergence of bartering, the earliest type of market-focused ecosystem, in the form of ***crowd-based capitalism***—that is, a two-sided market that brings together two crowds, or communities, of *individuals*: one community possessing an under-used asset or skill (the *value-unit*) and the other possessing a short-term need for such an asset or skill. This new bartering ecosystem differs from the original in two important ways:

- The medium for the short-term sharing of the value-unit is money. In other words, the person that owns the shared value-unit gets paid by the person being granted short-term use of the value-unit.
- The market is enabled through a digitalized market platform built, managed and owned by a third-party, the network orchestrator.

This form of market-focused ecosystem is the basis for what is popularly referred to as to as ***the sharing economy***.[5] Essentially, digital technologies (e.g., the Internet, interconnected smart devices, social media, payment systems, trust systems, etc.) are extending peoples' options for obtaining goods and services beyond family, friends, neighborhood stores and national/global retailers toward crowds of entrepreneurs.

Table 4.1 lists some of the crowd-based network ecosystems that have emerged over the last decade. As you look over this listing, notice the attributes of value-units likely to be shared via crowd-based capitalism: low-use and high-value. Low-use implies unused capacity (of an asset) or idle time (of a skill-provider); high-value infers that the value-created—the consumer payment subsequently appropriated and shared by a producer (an asset-owner or skill-provider) *and* a network orchestrator—will exceed the costs associated with an exchange.

---

5 A. Sundararajan, *The Sharing Economy: The End of Employment and the Rise of Crowd-Based Capitalism*, MIT Press, Cambridge, MA, 2016.

TABLE 4.1 Examples of Crowd-Based Network Ecosystems.

Crowd-Based Network Ecosystem	Value-Unit	Examples
Educational Services	Idle Skill Capacity	*SkillShare, TradeSchool, Udemy*
Freelance Work	Idle Expertise Capacity	*Amazon Mechanical Turk, InnoCentive, TopCoder, Upwork*
Fundraising	Idle Capital	*AngelList, FundiingCircle, Kickstarter*
Handyman Chores	Idle Labor Capacity	*Handy, TaskRabbit, TimesFree*
High-End Fashion	Unused Clothes	*Designer24, Rendevoux, Rent My Wardrobe, Rent the Runway, StyleLand*
Lodging	Unused Housing Capacity	*Airbnb, CouchSurfing*
Personal Services	Idle Labor Capacity	*Lux, Postmate, Shyp, Washio, Wag*
Philanthropy	Idle Capital	*DonorsChoose, Kiva*
Transportation	Unused Automobile Capacity	*BlaBlaCar, Getaround, Lyft, Turo, Uber, Zipcar*

Digitalizing Network Ecosystems

Network ecosystems existed prior to the eras of digital disruption. For example, three pervasive pre-digital network ecosystems were those involving (as network orchestrators) real estate brokerages, independent insurance agencies and travel agencies. In these network ecosystems, the network orchestrator (via the work processes shown in Figure 4.7):

- Built up a portfolio of offerings from a producer community.
- Attracted a consumer community.
- Enriched producers' offering creation capabilities.
- Enriched consumer demand.
- Matched the needs of individual consumers with the producer's offerings.
- Facilitated both exchange transactions and exchange fulfillment.
- Worked to retain the members of the producer and consumer communities.

With digitalized network ecosystems, the vast majority of work processes are carried out through a market platform (i.e., a collection of digital platforms and business platforms). The digitization and digitalization reflective of the three eras of digital disruption (see Table 4.2) have produced two types of effects on network ecosystems. First, the pre-digital network ecosystems have either radically transformed themselves through both digitalization and specialization or have exited their markets. Second, scores of new network ecosystems have emerged and continue to emerge (see Table 4.3).

FIGURE 4.7 A Network Orchestrator's Managerial and Operational Processes.

TABLE 4.2 Evolution of Network Ecosystems.

Era	Value-Units	Digitization & Digitalization	Exchange Currency	Trust Systems
1	Digital complements	• Data/document standards • Point-to-point connectivity • Intra- and inter-organizational (managerial and operational) process efficiencies	• Banking system • Credit/debit card systems	• Government & 3rd-party institutions • Contracts • Brand • Social capital
2	Digital value-units	• Internet • One-to-many connectivity • Data, process, analytic and collaboration platforms • Social media • Omni-channel producer-consumer interaction	• Digitalized payment systems	• 3rd-party digital trust seals • Consumer monitoring (product & producer reviews)
3	Social complements	• Many-to-many connectivity • Smart devices • Big Data platforms • Big Data analytic platforms • Social messaging platforms	• Reputation • Social capital • Bitcoins	• Community monitoring • Peer-regulation • Self-regulation

TABLE 4.3 Examples of Network Ecosystems.

Era	Variation	Examples	Community 1	Community 2	Community 3
1	Services Platform	*Visa, MasterCard*	Producing Organizations	Banks	Consumers
	Digital Architecture	*Microsoft's PC Operating System*	Application Producers	PC Producers	Consumers
2	B2B Horizontal Marketplace	*Alibaba.com, Thomasnet.com*	Producing Organizations	Advertisers	Consuming Organizations
	B2B Vertical Marketplace	*e-Steel, Farms.com*	Producing Organizations	Advertisers	Consuming Organizations
	B2C e-Commerce	*Amazon Marketplace*	Producing Organizations	Advertisers	Consumers
	C2C e-Commerce	*eBay, Craigslist*	Producers	Advertisers	Consumers
3	Search Platform	*Google*	Content Producers	Advertisers	Content Consumers
	Social Media Platform	*Twitter*	Content Producers	Advertisers	Content Consumers
	Crowd-Based Capitalism	*Airbnb, Uber*	Asset/Skill Owner	Advertisers	Asset/Skill User

Era 1

Two types of network ecosystems emerged during Era 1. The first of these applied proprietary, point-to-point connectivity to create new markets based on digitalized services. Perhaps the most familiar example is that of credit card providers, such as *Visa* and *MasterCard*. By establishing a digitalized (in part) services platform, merchants were able to offer a convenient, safe payment channel to consumers and banks gained a new revenue stream.

The second type of network ecosystem that emerged involved proprietary architectures for digital products and these product's complements. By promoting and licensing a product architecture that tips over a market, the architecture's creator is able to sustain high-margin sales for a lengthy period of time. Perhaps the most familiar example of this is that of personal computer (PC) operating systems, such as *Microsoft OS* (and then *Windows*). The *Intel* PC operating system market tipped over to *Microsoft OS* because the PC application software community gave priority to developing products to run on *OS* (and then on *Windows*)—increasing the likelihoods that software producers would gain large revenue streams and that consumers purchasing PCs would be able to run needed software.

Era 2

The availability of one-to-many connectivity enabled by the Internet triggered a rapid growth in network ecosystems. Four distinct types of e-commerce ecosystems emerged: B2B horizontal (producers offering a broad range of value-units to any type of consumer-business) marketplaces, B2B vertical (producers offering value-units to consumer-businesses in a single industry) marketplaces, B2C marketplaces, and C2C marketplaces.

B2B marketplaces generally operate in the upstream portions of industry value streams. Connecting (raw material and component) suppliers to producers, these intermediaries aim to disintermediate established supplier-producer relationships with the promise of a more efficient market. The value-propositions of these B2B marketplaces vary considerably, as reflected in the four levels of functionality that can be established between producers and consumers: information exchange, value-unit exchange/fulfillment transaction execution, logistical flow coordination, and collaboration enablement.

B2C and C2C marketplaces generally operate in the downstream portions of industry value chains. Connecting finished goods producers to consumers, these intermediaries aim to disintermediate established retailer-consumer relationships, again with the promise of a more efficient market. Notice in Table 4.3 (shown earlier) that the example given for an Era 2 B2C network ecosystem is *Amazon Marketplace* rather than *Amazon*, given *Amazon Marketplace*'s objective of bringing together a broad community of small producers to interact with *Amazon*'s consumer community. Two examples of C2C marketplaces, *eBay* and *Craigslist*, are used to illustrate the variety that exists. For example, *eBay* utilizes an auction pricing mechanism and offers the parties of value-unit exchanges a range of transactional and fulfillment services, while *Craigslist* utilizes fixed prices and offers little in the way of transactional and fulfillment services.

Era 3

The digital technologies associated with the third era of digital disruption—most notably many-to-many connectivity, smart devices, social messaging and peer regulation—triggered a fresh, explosive wave of network ecosystems focused on enabling and exploiting individuals' desires to maintain anytime, anywhere connections with the people, institutions and opportunities that are most important to them. As listed earlier in Table 4.3, the dominant types of Era 3 network ecosystems involve digital services (e.g., search, photo sharing, music sharing, etc.), social media, and crowd-based capitalism. As many of these network ecosystems involve participants and activities outside of the purview of established markets and institutions, new forms of community-based and peer-based trust systems have emerged. For example, there are limited regulations at present to assure consumers of the accuracy of host-provided *Airbnb* lodging descriptions. In response, *Airbnb* has implemented two trust mechanisms: the capturing and reporting of consumers' lodging reviews, and host identity verification systems that combine the digitized social capital of social media with governmental ID infrastructures. In addition, *Airbnb* proactively involves hosts and consumers in developing and evolving *standards and expectations* guidelines that must be agreed-to by hosts and consumers.

Blended Organizations

Today's most successful organizations are increasingly exhibiting the qualities of both pipeline ecosystems and network ecosystems, and in the process becoming a ***blended organization.*** This primarily occurs via one of two approaches:

- An organization operates multiple, largely independent business models, some of which are executed as a pipeline organization and others as a network organization.
- A pipeline organization incorporates a *private* or *semi-private* network-ecosystem as a means of enhancing efficiency, effectiveness or both.

Each of these approaches is briefly described.

The organization that best illustrates the first approach of operating both pipeline ecosystem and network ecosystem business models is *Amazon*. *Amazon's* initial business model was that of a pipeline ecosystem retailer: interacting physically with suppliers to stock product inventories, then interacting digitally with customers to sell these products, and then interacting physically and digitally with third-party package delivery providers in fulfilling customers' purchases from *Amazon's* brick-and-mortar distribution centers. Over time, *Amazon* has expanded its portfolio of business models to include operating as:

- A pipeline ecosystem retailer that stocks, sells and delivers digital products and smart devices.
- A pipeline ecosystem producer of digital technology services for businesses and for individuals.
- A network ecosystem orchestrator of media streaming services.
- A network ecosystem orchestrator of B2B and B2C marketplaces.

While *Amazon*'s various business models are targeted at distinct markets, they all make extensive use of *Amazon*'s world-class capabilities to design, build, operate and evolve digital platforms and business platforms.

The second approach to becoming a blended organization involves a focus on upstream, internal and/or downstream processes.

With regard to *upstream* processes, for many producers (e.g., automobiles, durable appliances, electronic products, etc.) a few of the raw materials used in procured components

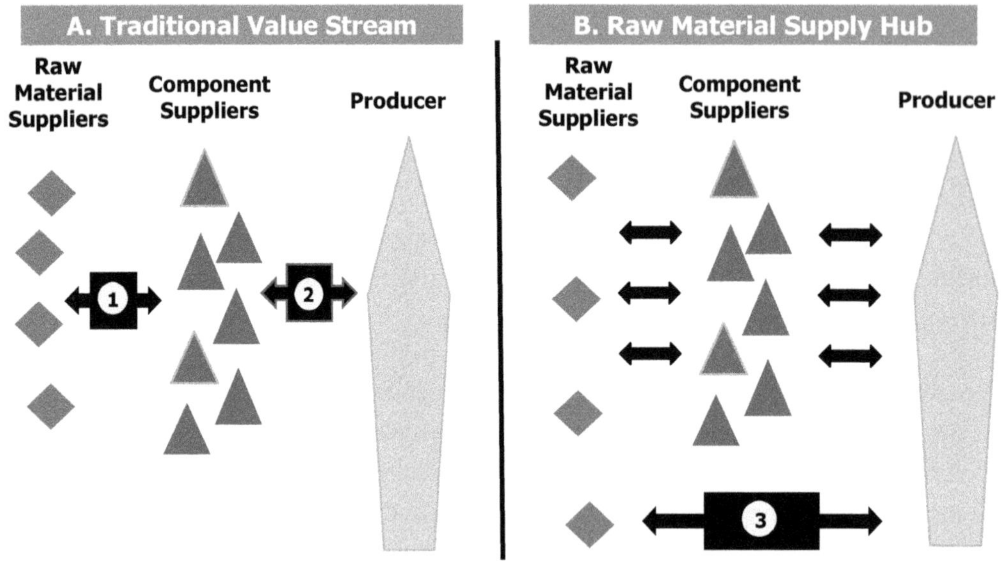

FIGURE 4.8 Introducing a Supply Hub into a Pipeline Ecosystem Value Stream.

represent a significant percentage of production costs. Part A of Figure 4.8 portrays a traditional *upstream value stream* for a pipeline manufacturing organization. Note that value stream participants engage with two largely-independent markets: *Market 1* involves raw material suppliers and component suppliers, and *Market 2* involves these component suppliers and the producers. Because of the potential for supply/demand imbalances and information asymmetries, component suppliers tend to be disadvantaged in *Market 1*, passing on market inefficiencies to the manufacturer in the form of higher prices and logistical delays in *Market 2*. Part B of Figure 4.8 introduces the notion of a *supply hub* as a means of overcoming these potential market inefficiencies in this upstream portion of the traditional pipeline value stream.[6] Here, the manufacturer creates a pseudo-market (*Market 3*) within the established market for raw materials. After aggregating raw material requirements and production plans across all component suppliers, a producer is able to apply a comprehensive understanding of component supplier demand (volumes and timings) in negotiating prices with raw material suppliers on behalf of the component suppliers.

With regard to *internal* processes, organizations can obtain a variety of benefits (e.g., productivity, employee goodwill, reputation enhancement, etc.) by employing a private network ecosystem solely inside their boundaries. The platforms used with such internal marketplaces can be developed in-house or licensed from a third-party platform-provider. A nice

6 A. Agrawal, A. De Meyer and L.N. Van Wassenhove, "Managing Value in Supply Chains: Case Studies on the Sourcing Hub Concept," *California Management Review*, Winter 2014, pp. 23–54.

TABLE 4.4 Introducing a C2C Marketplace into a Pipeline Ecosystem Value Stream.

Pipeline Organization	Network Ecosystem	Strategic Value
Ikea Group	*Ikea Family* loyalty program community: members post & sell used *Ikea* items.	• Supports *Ikea's* eco-friendly ethos. • Opens up room in members' homes for new Ikea items.
Patagonia	Partnership with eBay: consumers easily sell used *Patagonia* clothing items.	• Supports *Patagonia's* eco- friendly ethos. • Increases the visibility of the *Patagonia* brand both online and on the street.
DM (German Drugstore Chain)	Sponsors & arranges clothing swap events, at which makeup/styling products & techniques are demonstrated.	• Generates new consumers in the targeted demographic. • Enriches brand by leveraging the green spirit of sharing rather than buying. • Gains brand visibility as these events are featured on social media and by fashion bloggers.

example of using a private market ecosystem is that of *Zimride*, the ride-sharing platform that *Lyft*'s founders licensed to universities and businesses as a private ride-sharing service used solely by a subscribing university's/business's employees.[7] Zimride provides a useful benefit for employees in the form of a convenient and safe mechanism for solving employees' commuting-to-work problems and positions the organization as being socially-responsible, a quality likely valued by many of the organization's stakeholders.

With regard to *downstream* processes, Table 4.4 provides examples of three organizations that have appended C2C marketplaces as complements to their traditional sales channels. When carefully conceived and executed, the network effects engendered can be exploited to enrich a brand and grow the consumer base without cannibalizing pre-existing sales channels.

A Recap and Look Ahead

Network ecosystems, as introduced and fleshed out in this chapter, represent a rapidly increasing segment of most countries' GNPs. In the process, existing markets and industries are being transformed and new markets and industries are being formed. [...]

---

7 R. Lawler, "Lyft-Off: Zimride's Long Ride to Overnight Success," *TechCrunch*, August 29, 2014: https://techcrunch.com/2014/08/29/6000-words-about-a-pink-mustache/

Reading 5

Preannouncing Information Goods

Jay Pil Choi, Eirik Gaard Kristiansen, and Jae Nahm

5.1 Introduction

With the advent of digital technology, information goods are increasingly composed of bits, not atoms. This has profound implications for the industry of information goods as discussed in various chapters of this book. Software companies, for instance, face a number of challenges in their business strategy. They need to protect their innovations through patents [...] and copyright protection [...]. Versioning is another strategic instrument that plays an important role [...]. Software companies are also often part of a "sub-economy," that is, they are a component of a software platform [...]. As such, software solutions have impacted several related markets including digital music distribution [...] and electronic commerce [...].

In this chapter, we focus on a widely practiced business strategy of *preannouncing new products* in the industry of information goods. In particular, information goods in digital form are much more durable than tangible goods that are subject to wear and tear over time. This implies that one of the most important decisions for a consumer is choosing when to buy information goods, especially when the market is characterized by switching costs (Klemperer 1995) and ongoing technological progress.

Developing a new product is a lengthy process, and the expected arrival of a new product affects consumers and rival firms. As a result, firms usually make new product announcements well in advance of actual market availability. By making preannouncements, firms can deliver information on a product while it is being developed. The announcement may influence the decisions of rival firms and consumers. In particular, a firm in the process of developing a new product could make preannouncements aimed at persuading consumers to delay their purchase until its own product is available. The announcements could also be directed at potential rival firms. For instance, if there is a high duplicated R&D cost, a firm, by announcing that it is already very close to finishing its R&D project, could discourage potential competitors from investing in a similar project. This is especially true for information goods that are characterized by large sunk costs of development, but negligible marginal costs. Thus a firm has strategic reasons to convey its private information on a new product in order to change other parties' behavior in a way that is beneficial to the firm.

However, there is an issue of credibility associated with such announcements—that is, whether the firm would have incentives to be truthful in its announcements. In fact this practice has been called *vaporware* by industry commentators since, in many instances, these promised products were significantly delayed or the promised features did not meet expectations.[1] *Wired News*, for instance, puts out an annual list of the top ten vaporware products of the past year that includes various hardware, software, and game titles. In the most recent annual list (released on January 7, 2005), Alienware's Video Array topped the list, and 3D Realms's Duke Nukem Forever received a Lifetime Achievement Award for its endless delay. Whether these delays were an honest mistake due to unforeseen difficulties in the development process or whether the firm intentionally made a false announcement is debatable.

If a firm uses preannouncement as a strategic tool to stifle market competition, it could have perverse effects on market competition. For instance, when a rival firm introduces a new product, an entrenched dominant firm, by announcing that it would introduce a better product, may induce consumers to withhold purchasing the rival's product and prevent the loss of market shares. In this way, the incumbent can maintain its dominant position by using product preannouncement as a strategic tool. Thus product preannouncement has been a contentious issue in major antitrust cases. For instance, Microsoft was recently accused of this practice concerning its MS-DOS operating system.[2] IBM's announcement of its System/360 line of computers in the 1960s is another example.[3]

In this chapter, we conduct a selective review of the literature on the effects of product preannouncement on market competition; we provide a very simple model of vaporware in the context of reputation and discuss its implications for social welfare and antitrust policy. We also discuss several open issues in need of further research.

The remainder of the chapter is organized as follows. Sections 5.2 and 5.3 constitute a selective review of the related literature that analyzes announcements as a firm strategy. The literature can be classified broadly into two categories depending on the main purpose or audience of the announcement. In section 5.2, we review models of product preannouncement directed toward rival firms to deter entry. Section 5.3 focuses on models of product preannouncement directed toward consumers to delay their purchase decisions until a new product is available.[4] In reviewing the literature in sections 5.2 and 5.3, we highlight the main differences between the existing models and our own model. In section 5.4, we present a very simple cheap-talk model of vaporware with reputational concerns. We identify conditions under which product preannouncement can be informative and explore welfare implications of such a practice. Section 5.5 concludes with the discussion of potential extensions.

5.2 Announcements Aimed toward Rival Firms

By using preannouncement as a strategic tool, firms intend to influence other economic agents' choices in the relevant market. The announcements, for instance, can be directed toward rival firms, potential consumers, or both. In this section, we review a line of research that analyzes the effects of announcements directed mainly toward rival firms to dissuade entry.

5.2.1 Cheap Talk Models of Coordination

When there is a high sunk cost of entry or of developing a new product, a market can accommodate only a few firms. Suppose there are two potential entrants and that a market can accommodate only one firm. Then one firm's optimal entry decision depends on the other firm's entry decision, and the two firms need to communicate with each other to coordinate their entry decisions. There are two approaches for modeling the communication between firms. One is a signaling model, and the other is a cheap-talk model. In a signaling model, it is assumed that making a false announcement is costly. A firm that makes a false announcement could, for example, be penalized by an antitrust investigation. On the contrary, in a cheap-talk model, communication between firms does not entail any direct costs.

The main insight of the cheap-talk literature is that cheap talk can function as preplay communication among players to achieve coordination, even though it does not involve any direct cost or benefits of communication. Farrell (1987) and Park (2002), for instance, analyze how costless and nonbinding communication can achieve coordination among potential entrants.

To illustrate the main intuition, consider the following entry game analyzed in Farrell (1987). There are two potential entrants who must decide whether or not to enter simultaneously. The market can accommodate only one firm. If both firms enter, each firm loses L; if only one firm enters, the firm earns M, and the other firm earns B, where M is larger than B. If neither firm enters, each firm earns zero. One critical assumption is that $B > 0$. That is, even if it does not enter, each firm prefers that the other firm enter. The assumption reflects the case in which the new product is complementary to the firms' existing products. The game can be described by the following matrix (table 5.1).

The Pareto optimal allocation in this game is that only one firm chooses "In." There are multiple equilibria in this game, with two asymmetric pure-strategy equilibria and one symmetric mixed-strategy equilibrium. In the two asymmetric pure-strategy equilibria, one firm chooses "In" while the other chooses "Out," and the resulting equilibrium is Pareto optimal. However, the most natural equilibrium may be the

TABLE 5.1 Payoff Matrix of the Simultaneous Entry Game.

	In	Out
In	−L, −L	B, M
Out	M, B	0, 0

symmetric mixed-strategy equilibrium since both firms are symmetric in this game. Without communication, the unique, symmetric equilibrium is that each firm enters with probability $p = \frac{M}{B+L+M}$. With the symmetric mixed-strategy equilibrium, however, we have a coordination failure. With the probability of p^2, both firms choose "In," and with the probability of $(1-p)^2$, both firms choose "Out" and no entry occurs. Thus, the overall probability of coordination failure is given by $[p^2 + (1-p)^2]$.

Suppose the two firms can have a preplay "talk." More specifically, consider a game of preplay communication in which the two firms simultaneously announce "In" or "Out" before making their real entry decisions. If only one firm says "In," then the firm will choose "In," while the other firm stays out. If both firms say "In" or "Out," then they play the symmetric equilibrium we derived above—that is, each firm enters with the probability $p = \frac{M}{B+L+M}$. Then, in the unique symmetric equilibrium of the game with preplay communication, each firm says "In" with probability $q = \frac{M-pB}{B-2pB+B}$. Thus the probability of a failure of coordination (both enter or neither enters) is reduced from $[p^2 + (1-p)^2]$ to $[p^2 + (1-p)^2][q^2 + (1-q)^2]$. Thus the communication can help the coordination problem among potential entrants.[5]

Farrell and Saloner (1985) analyze coordination under incomplete information in the context of technology adoption with network externalities. They discuss the effects of preplay communication and show that "symmetric" or Pareto inertia due to incomplete information can be eliminated with simple communication through cheap talk.[6] However, they also point out the possibility that preplay communication exacerbates inertia where the preferences differ.[7]

5.2.2 Signaling Models of Entry Deterrence

Bayus et al. (2001) develop a signaling model that analyzes how firms' announcements of new products affects other firms' entry decisions. They consider a situation in which two firms simultaneously decide whether and when to introduce a new product. Each firm, by spending more on R&D, can introduce its product earlier. In contrast to Farrell (1987), Bayus et al. consider an asymmetric setting in which one firm is dominant in the sense that the other firm cannot operate profitably if it enters later than the dominant firm. There are two types of firms: the R&D cost of the low-type firm is lower than that of the high-type firm. Thus the low type can develop its product earlier than the high type for the same R&D spending. By announcing an earlier release time of the new product, the firm can signal that it is of the low type. Since the entry by the follower is unprofitable when the dominant firm is of the low cost type, intentional vaporware is associated with entry deterrence. In such a setting, Bayus et al. analyze the dominant firm's incentives for intentional vaporware, that is, the firm making an announcement on the release time knowing that it could miss the date. They show that there is a separating equilibrium in which the low-type firm engages in intentional vaporware, whereas the high-type firm announces its release time truthfully.

Penalty costs associated with false announcements are what enable separation of types in the model of Bayus et al. (2001). They assume a penalty cost function that is increasing and convex in the discrepancy between the announced time and the actual time of product introduction. They justify this assumption with potential antitrust investigation or loss in reputation associated with false announcements. Even though the assumption is reasonable, it is at best ad hoc in that there is no microfoundation for such penalty costs in their model. In particular, no one is deceived by intentional vaporware since all receivers can infer the actual timing of product introduction in equilibrium, even if it is different from the announced date. In section 5.4, we develop a model of vaporware in which the reputation cost is endogenously derived.

Haan (2003) also develops a model of premature announcements that are used strategically to deter other firms from developing a similar product. In his model, an incumbent sells a durable good in period one, but can introduce a new product in the second period. The new product makes an existing product obsolete. There is also a firm that considers entering the market. However, if the incumbent is about to introduce the new product, it is not optimal for this entrant to enter. Whether or not the incumbent has an innovation is private information. After observing the incumbent's output level, consumers in period one decide how much to pay for the incumbent product and the entrant decides whether or not to enter. The model is, technically, a two-audience signaling model in the spirit of Gertner, Gibbons, and Scharfstein (1988). The reason is that the price consumers are willing to pay in the first period depends on their beliefs about the market price in the second, which, in turn, depends on whether or not the incumbent firm introduces the drastic innovation in the future. In this setup, Haan (2003) shows that there is no separating equilibrium and that no information can be revealed in equilibrium. This is due to the incumbent's incentives to send different messages to different audiences. More specifically, the incumbent would like to have consumers believe that, in the next period, there will not be a new product that would make their purchases in the first period obsolete. In this way, the incumbent firm can sell the old technology at a higher price and have consumers make another purchase when the new product is introduced. For the potential entrant, in contrast, the incumbent would like to convince consumers that there will be a new product, which will make entry unprofitable. As a result, neither type has incentives to separate from the other type, and the resulting outcome is a pooling equilibrium in which neither type is revealed in equilibrium. We should mention that strictly speaking, since the means of signaling in Haan's model is the production level in the first period, he focuses on whether there is separation of types through the firm's production decision, and not on whether the firm has any incentives to make false announcements.

5.3 Announcements Aimed toward Consumers

This section describes the models that analyze the effects of announcements targeting consumers for the purpose of delaying their purchase decisions. Developing a new product usually takes time. If there is a high switching cost, consumers who buy a currently available product are locked into that product and find it difficult to switch to a new product when it is introduced. Thus consumers need to decide whether to buy currently available products or to wait for a new product. The consumers' optimal decisions depend on the expected quality of the new product. Conversely, the firm's R&D incentive to develop a new product depends on how many consumers are waiting for its product. Therefore, there are common interests between the firm and consumers, and they have incentives to "talk" to each other.

Suppose that in a two-period model, consumers can buy a currently available durable good. The currently available product provides consumers a flow consumption benefit of w per period. One firm is developing a new product and is able to introduce it in period two. The new product can provide consumers a flow benefit of $(w + s)$ per period, where s can be interpreted as the improvement of the new product over the currently available one and is assumed to be private information of the firm. For simplicity, there is no time discount between periods one and two. If consumers buy the currently available product in period one, they can enjoy $2w$ benefit for the two periods, while they can get $(w + s)$ by delaying their purchase until period two when the new product is available. Since consumers need to pay the opportunity cost of waiting w, consumers will delay their purchasing only if the additional consumer benefit from the new product is larger than w. If the firm can verify the size of s to consumers in period one, the firm's announcement can help consumers make better decisions.

By assuming that the firm can make a verifiable claim on its product quality, Farrell and Saloner (1986) provide an early analysis of how product preannouncements affect consumers' technology adoption decisions. They point out that, even though a product preannouncement helps consumers make better decisions, it could be anticompetitive in the presence of *network effects*. In particular, they construct a dynamic model of technology adoption in which consumers arrive sequentially in the market, and each decides which technology to choose given what others have done. In the model, the announcement of a new *incompatible* product can have an impact on the pattern of technology adoption, that is, whether or not the new product succeeds in replacing the existing technology. Upon hearing the announcement, some consumers decide to wait. Even if the potential users who decide to wait are well informed and their welfare is increased as a result of product preannouncement, due to the presence of network effects their adoption of the new technology may adversely affect both consumers with the old product and later adopters, who might have preferred the old technology to the new one.

Gerlach (2004) also analyzes the effects of advance announcements directed at consumers to increase their expected value of waiting and prevent the loss of potential future demand in a durable goods market with switching costs. He calls this positive effect of announcements for the firm the *demand pull effect*. Gerlach's model is noteworthy in that he allows the possibility that the advance information directed toward consumers spills over to the incumbent rival firm, which can respond preemptively to the revelation of new information on impending entry, strategically setting its price to deter the entry of the announcing firm.[8] This negative effect of announcement is called the *strategic reaction effect*.[9] Gerlach analyzes the entrant's incentive to make a pre-announcement on its product and shows that entrants do not always announce in equilibrium due to the tradeoff between the positive demand pull and the negative strategic reaction effect. Gerlach further demonstrates that such an equilibrium behavior maximizes ex ante social welfare, even though consumers might be better off with a ban on announcements.

However, both Farrell and Saloner (1986) and Gerlach (2004) consider the case in which firms can make verifiable statements about their products. The studies do not allow the possibility of false announcements, and nor do they analyze consumers' inference problems from announcements.[10] In most cases, firms cannot make a verifiable statement about their product, and consumers do not know the veracity of the announcement. Consumers need to rely on the information the firm provides, but the firm has an incentive to cheat consumers with regard to quality level. Suppose that the additional consumer surplus from the new product over the old product is between zero and w. Then it is optimal for consumers to buy the current product in period one without waiting for the new product. However, if consumers are induced to wait until period two, they will choose the new product over the old product since the new one provides a higher consumer surplus than the old product does. Thus as long as the firm can induce consumers to wait until period two, the firm can sell its product to consumers in period two. The firm has an incentive to inflate (or make a false claim about) its product's quality level. Also, since a new product is still in development, it is very difficult for the firm and consumers to make a contract based on the product's quality. For instance, when a software company promises in advance features of a new software program, it could be difficult to describe them in precise terms, without any ambiguity, so that the contract could be enforceable in court.

The question, then, is: what makes a firm's preannouncements credible since every firm has incentives to make consumers wait for its product? If a firm and consumers have only a one-time interaction, then it would be difficult for a product preannouncement to be informative. However, if a firm has repeated interactions with consumers, the firm will have a reputation concern, and the firm's reputation will depend on its past behavior. Fisher et al. (1983) argue:

> [T]here is no reason to inhibit the time when a firm announces or brings products to the marketplace. Customers will be the final arbiters of the product's quality and the firm's reputation. Broken promises and unattractive products can be expected to lead quickly to a loss of credibility and sales.

Levy (1997) explores antitrust implications of vaporware and echoes the argument in Fisher et al. (1983). More specifically, he considers a situation in which consumers do not know the veracity of the firm's announcements when they are made. He concludes that vaporware should not be of concern to antitrust authorities since reputation concerns prevent firms from intentionally making false announcements. However, he does not model reputation explicitly in his paper.

Dranove and Gandal (2003), in a rare paper, provide an empirical analysis of preannouncement effects in the DVD market. Regarding the standard war between the DVD and DIVX formats, they show that the preannouncement of DIVX slowed the adoption of DVD technology, which is consistent with the theory of product preannouncements in theoretical literature.

Choi, Kristiansen, and Nahm (2004) (hereafter referred to as CKN) analyze the role of preannouncement when a firm has a reputation concern. They model explicitly the formation of reputation in a repeated product preannouncement game and characterize the equilibrium in which private information held by the firm is partially revealed. The following section describes the CKN model in more detail.

5.4 Vaporware and Reputation

In this section, we construct a simple model to answer the question of whether preannouncements of a new product can help consumers make better purchasing decisions when a firm's announcement is nonbinding and nonverifiable. Indeed, if the game is played only once, there would be no room for the product preannouncements to be informative. However, if there are repeated interactions between the firm and consumers, the firm tries to build its reputation. Thus CKN (2004) consider a scenario in which the firm and consumers interact repeatedly and develop a reputation model of vaporware. CKN derive conditions under which product preannouncements can be informative and they analyze the welfare effect of product preannouncement. Let us present a simpler version of the CKN model with only two types.

Consider a game that is played by consumers and a firm that develops a *sequence* of new products. This would be the case if the industry were characterized by a constant stream of new products.[11] For instance, consumers expect computer and video game producers to introduce new titles over time. Computer hardware and software producers are also expected to continuously develop new gadgets and software programs. For simplicity, we assume there are two sequential product cycles and a firm can introduce a new product in each cycle. Let δ denote the time discount between the first and second product cycles. In each product cycle, there are two periods. More specifically, in the first period, an existing product is competitively supplied. The firm that develops a new product introduces the new product in the second period. For simplicity, there is no time discount between periods within the same product cycle. Consumers who have unit demand for the product in each product cycle have two options in the first period: they can either purchase the existing product at the competitive price or wait until the second period for the new product. For the first period purchase decision to have dynamic implications, we assume that the good is durable. In addition, once the consumers purchase in the first period, they are locked in and cannot switch to the new product in the second period due to switching costs (see Klemperer 1995).

The quality of the new product can be either high (H) or low (L). The ex ante probability that the firm can develop a high-quality product is denoted by θ, which can be considered the firm's type. There are two types of firm, θ_1 and θ_2, $\theta_1 < \theta_2$. The firm knows its own type, but consumers know only the distribution of the firm types. The prior belief that the firm is of type θ_2 is q. The firm's type is assumed to be invariant across product cycles and represents the firm's innovativeness or research capability. The realization of quality, however, is independent across product cycles. The firm that is in the process of developing a new product knows the quality of the product in the first period of each product cycle. The firm can announce the quality of the product to consumers in period one to persuade consumers to delay their purchase. We assume that product preannouncements are cheap talk and do not entail any costs to make.

If a consumer buys the currently available product in period one, the consumer's surplus per period is w. When consumers wait, they forego the current consumption benefit that can be considered their waiting costs.[12] The new product developed by the firm is superior to the existing product, regardless of its quality realizations. Let s_H and s_L be the expected value of the indirect utility difference between the new and old products when the quality of the new product is high and low, respectively. This implies that the consumer surplus from waiting until period two is $w + s_i$, where $i = H$ or L, depending on the quality realization of the new product, while that of buying the current product in period one is $2w$.

We assume that $s_H > s_L > 0$, which implies that consumers get a higher surplus from the high-quality product than from the low-quality product and that consumers will buy even the low-quality product in period two if they wait until period two. Consumers are more willing to wait if the new product is of high quality.[13] To have a meaningful analysis of consumers' waiting decision, we assume that $s_L < w < s_H$. That is, consumers are willing to delay their purchase if and only if the new product is of high quality. We also assume that $\theta_2 s_H + (1-\theta_2)s_L > w$ and that $\theta_1 s_H (1-\theta_1)s_L < w$. That is, if the firm's type is known to be θ_2, the expected quality of the new product is high enough that consumers will wait until period two. However, if the firm's type is known to be θ_1, consumers will not wait.

Let $\pi^H (\pi^L)$ denote the profit for the firm that introduces a high-quality product and a low-quality product, respectively, when consumers wait. We assume that $\pi^H > \pi^L > 0$. Since $\pi^H > 0$ and $s_H > w$, if the new product is of high quality, it is mutually beneficial for consumers and the firm that consumers wait for the new product. We assume that if consumers do not wait, the firm profit is zero. This assumption can be justified because significant switching costs prevent consumers from buying the new product once they have purchased in the first period. This implies that if announcing a high-quality product induces consumers to wait until period two, the firm with the low-quality product has an incentive to mislead consumers and announce a high-quality product. Therefore, product preannouncements cannot impart any information to consumers if the game is played only once. Next we analyze whether or not we can have an informative equilibrium in such a situation if the announcement game is played repeatedly.

As usual, we derive an equilibrium with backward induction and analyze the second product cycle first. In the second product cycle, the firm's announcement does not convey any credible information since it is the last interaction between the firm and consumers. Consumers, thus, make their decision based only on their updated belief about the firm's type derived from its history.

Let μ denote consumers' belief that the firm has a high-quality product. Then we can define a critical level of belief $\bar{\mu}$ at which consumers are indifferent between purchasing the currently available product in the first period and waiting for the new product until the second period.

$$\bar{\mu} s_H + (1-\bar{\mu}) s_L = w$$

That is,

$$\bar{\mu} = \frac{w - s_L}{s_H - s_L} \tag{5.1}$$

Since $\theta_2 s_H + (1-\theta_2)s_L > w$ and $\theta_1 s_H + (1-\theta_1)s_L < w$, $\bar{\mu}$ is between θ_1 and θ_2.

Let μ_2 denote the consumers' updated belief of the firm's probability to deliver a high-quality product in the second product cycle. We interpret μ_2 as the reputation level of the firm. If μ_2 is higher than $\bar{\mu} = \frac{w-s_L}{s_H-s_L}$, consumers will wait until period two in the second product cycle.

If consumers do not wait until the second product cycle, the firm's profit is zero. However, if consumers wait, the firm's ex ante expected profit (that is, before knowing whether it has a high- or low-quality product) is $\theta\pi^H + (1-\theta)\pi^L$, which increases in θ. That is, even though all types benefit from consumers' waiting, type θ_2 has a higher return from it than type θ_1 does. That is, type θ_2 has more reputation concerns than type θ_1 does if a higher reputation leads consumers to wait, which implies that the Spence-Mirrlees single crossing property holds.[14] Due to the single crossing property, we can get a separating equilibrium in which higher types make an honest announcement, while lower types could make an intentionally false announcement. We are interested in conditions under which the firm's reputation concerns leads the firm to make an honest announcement on the quality of its product in the first product cycle.

In particular, we are looking for an informative equilibrium with the following properties:

1. If the firm has a high-quality product in the first cycle, both types (truthfully) announce a high-quality product. Consumers take the announcements as partially true and wait until the second period in the first product cycle. Since their beliefs are confirmed, consumers update their beliefs upward and also wait for a new product in the second product cycle.
2. If the firm has a low-quality product in the first cycle,
   (i) the θ_1-type firm makes a false announcement that its product is of high quality, and consumers are misled into waiting for the new product in the first cycle. They will revise their beliefs downward and not wait in the second cycle.
   (ii) the θ_2-type firm makes a truthful announcement (or does not make an announcement), and consumers do not wait in the first cycle. However, they revise their beliefs upward and reward the firm by waiting in the second product cycle.

Knowing that a firm might make an intentionally false announcement, consumers update their beliefs about the new product's quality based on the firm's announcement strategy. Given the equilibrium strategies of the firm above, if the firm announces a high-quality product in the first cycle, the updated belief that the product is of high quality in the first cycle is given by:

$$\mu_1^H = \frac{q}{q\theta_2 + (1-q)}\theta_2 + \left(\frac{1-q}{q\theta_2 + (1-q)}\right)\theta_1 \tag{5.2}$$

For the product preannouncements to have impacts on consumers' waiting decision, we assume the following:

$$\mu_1^H > \bar{\mu} \tag{5.3}$$

That is, when the firm announces a high-quality product, consumers will wait for the new product in the first cycle. If the announcement turns out to be true, then consumers will update their beliefs about the firm's type according to the Bayes rule. The posterior probability that the firm is of high type can be derived as:

$$
\begin{aligned}
&\Pr(\theta = \theta_2 \mid Quality = H) \\
&= \frac{\Pr(\theta = \theta_2)\Pr(Quality = H \mid \theta = \theta_2)}{\Pr(\theta = \theta_2)\Pr(Quality = H \mid \theta = \theta_2) + \Pr(\theta = \theta_1)\Pr(Quality = H \mid \theta = \theta_2)} \\
&= \frac{q\theta_2}{q\theta_2 + (1-q)\theta_1}
\end{aligned}
$$

Thus μ_2 becomes $\frac{q\theta_2}{q\theta_2+(1-q)\theta_1}\theta_2 + \left(\frac{(1-q)\theta_1}{q\theta_2+(1-q)\theta_1}\right)\theta_1$. If the announcement turns out to be false, then μ_2 becomes θ_1. Since $\frac{q\theta_2}{q\theta_2+(1-q)\theta_1} > \frac{q\theta_2}{q\theta_2+(1-q)}$, equation (5.3) implies that $\frac{q\theta_2}{q\theta_2+(1-q)\theta_1}\theta_2 + \left(\frac{(1-q)\theta_1}{q\theta_2+(1-q)\theta_1}\right)\theta_1 > \bar{\mu}$. That is, if the firm introduces a high-quality product in the first cycle, consumers will wait in the second cycle as stipulated in the description of the equilibrium.

Finally, if the firm does not make an announcement in the first cycle, then consumers do not wait in the first cycle, but μ_2 becomes θ_2. Since we assume that $\theta_2 s_H + (1-\theta_2)s_L > w$, that is, $\theta_2 > \bar{\mu}$, consumers will wait in the second cycle.

Let us check whether the firm's strategies described satisfy incentive compatibility constraints in the first product cycle. If the firm has a high-quality product in the first cycle, it is obvious that it is an optimal strategy for the firm to make an honest announcement. Now consider the case in which the firm has a low-quality product in the first cycle. If the firm makes a false announcement, consumers will wait, and the firm's profit in the first product cycle is π^L. However, the firm loses its reputation and consumers will not wait in the second product cycle. In contrast, if the firm does not make any announcement, it gets zero profit in the first product cycle whereas its expected profit in the second product cycle is $\delta[\theta\pi^H + (1-\theta)\pi^L]$. Consumers wait in the second product cycle and the firm's expected profit in such a scenario depends on its ex ante probability that the firm can develop a high quality product, that is, the firm's type θ.

The incentive compatibility conditions for type θ_2 with a low-quality product to make a true announcement in the first cycle, while for type θ_1 with a low-quality product to make a false announcement, are satisfied if the following condition holds:

$$\theta_1 < \frac{1-\delta}{\delta} \frac{\pi_L}{\pi_H - \pi_L} < \theta_2 \tag{5.4}$$

Thus we can conclude that if conditions (5.3) and (5.4) are satisfied, we can have the informative equilibrium described.[15] We summarize our main result in the following proposition.

Proposition 5.1 Suppose that conditions (5.3) and (5.4) hold. Then there exists an informative equilibrium with the following properties:

5.4.1 Firm Behavior

If the firm has a high-quality product in the first cycle, both types (truthfully) announce a high-quality product. If the firm has a low-quality product in the first cycle, the low-type firm (θ_1) makes a false announcement that its product is of high quality whereas the high-type firm (θ_2) makes a truthful announcement (or does not make an announcement).

5.4.2 Consumer Behavior

When the firm makes an announcement of high quality in the first cycle, consumers take the announcements as partially true and wait until the second period in the first product cycle. If the product is of high quality and their beliefs are confirmed, consumers update their beliefs upward and also wait for a new product in the second product cycle. If the product is of low quality and consumers are misled into waiting for the new product in the first cycle, they will revise their beliefs downward and not wait in the second product cycle. If there is an announcement of low quality (or no announcement) consumers do not wait in the first cycle. However, they revise their beliefs upward and reward the firm by waiting in the second product cycle.

In this simple, twice-repeated cheap-talk game, we can also show that in any informative equilibrium, a firm's announcement always ex ante improves consumer welfare, even though a firm might make a false announcement. This implies that, as long as consumers understand the low-type firm's incentives to mislead with its announcements and take them into account in making their purchase decisions, consumers cannot be worse off with product preannouncements. Our model thus formalizes the argument in Fisher et al. (1983)

and Levy (1997) that firms will refrain from making false announcements due to concerns about reputation.

Proposition 5.2 The welfare effect of product preannouncements on consumers is positive.

Proof See the appendix.

5.5 Concluding Remarks

We have conducted a selective review of the related literature and highlighted the differences between the existing models and our own. In a simplified version of the CKN model, we also show that reputational concerns can be used as an incentive device to make cheap talk *partially informative*. As a result, consumers are able to make a better intertemporal purchase decision; they are better off with the possibility of product preannouncements as long as consumers are rational and understand the incentives of low-type firms to mislead consumers. We conclude by discussing potential extensions of our chapter and several open issues in need of further research.

5.5.1 Strategic Price-Setting by the Incumbents

As in Farrell and Saloner (1986), we do not consider strategic pricing by the incumbent firms, but instead assume that the old product is competitively supplied. It would be an interesting extension of our model to allow the possibility that the incumbent firms can respond to product preannouncements by innovators of a new product, as in Gerlach (2004).

5.5.2 Network Effects

The welfare result in our model depends crucially on the assumption that there are no externalities associated with consumers' purchase decisions. However, product preannouncements have been prominent in industries characterized by network effects, such as the computer software industry. In such a case, we cannot rule out the possibility that product preannouncements might influence which product prevails in the marketplace and lead to socially inefficient technology adoption. This may be true even if those who make purchase-or-wait decisions are better informed, with the potential source of inefficiency being incompatibility between the old and new products. Farrell and Saloner (1986) demonstrate the possibility that preannouncement can lower social welfare in a dynamic model of technology adoption. We can surely derive a similar result in our model if we introduce network effects. This possibility certainly provides a caution against blanket approval of product preannouncements.

5.5.3 Intentional versus Unintentional Vaporware

To analyze the possibility of the informativeness of product pre-announcements, we focus exclusively on *intentional* vaporware, assuming that the innovating firm can predict the quality of the product or the timing of the product introduction without any error. In reality, however, such a prediction inevitably entails some error due to unforeseen events in the development process. With such a possibility, consumers' inference problem can be more complex. When there is a discrepancy between the announced timing and quality of the new product and the actual delivery, consumers have to assess the cause of the discrepancy: was the firm dishonest, or was the delay due to an honest mistake? If the consumers are lenient and give the firm the benefit of the doubt when the actual delivery does not meet expectations, the incentives to tell the truth would be destroyed. However, if the consumers are too harsh and treat any discrepancy as a proof of dishonesty, the innovating firms would refrain from providing any information for fear of a mistake. This could block a useful channel of information between producers and consumers. The optimal punishment scheme should balance these two conflicting effects, as in the design of the optimal collusive scheme under uncertainty (see Green and Porter 1984).

The possibility of unintentional vaporware also poses a problem for antitrust policymakers. If all product preannouncements can be made and ex post fact verified without any error, the best public policy would be to prohibit any false announcements. Such a policy would lead to perfect information revelation, as in Grossman (1981). In reality, however, it would be difficult to implement such a policy because of the difficulty and ambiguity associated with ascertaining whether the firm actually delivered the promised quality, especially when the features promised are something nonexistent at the time of announcement—a fact that makes direct contracting between the firm and consumers infeasible in the first place. Also, another hurdle in implementing such a policy is the difficulty of determining whether or not the firm made its product announcements in good faith.

5.5.4 The Finite Horizon versus Infinite Horizon

We develop a reputational model of a cheap-talk game with a finite number of product cycles. If we considered an infinite horizon of product cycles, we would have a similar result, with the high types always telling the truth and the low types lying when they have a low-quality product. The mechanism in the infinite horizon model through which the high types tell the truth would be similar to the one in Choi's (1998) model of brand extension. In Choi (1998), as long as all previous products with the same brand name were of high quality, consumers believe that a new product under that brand name will be of high quality, as well. Once the brand name is extended to a low-quality product, consumers ignore any signaling value of brand extension. In response, the monopolists extend brand name only to a high-quality product, and consumers' beliefs are confirmed. In our model, consumers would believe product preannouncements as long as all the previous announcements were true. Once the firm makes a false announcement, consumers will ignore any future announcement made by the firm. One major difference in Choi's brand extension model is that his model is of moral hazard, and there is no uncertainty about the firm type. In contrast, in our model there is also an adverse selection problem about the firm type, with the separation of types taking place over time.

Appendix: Proof of Proposition 5.2 The Effect of Product Announcements on Consumer Welfare

In this section, we analyze how the firm's product announcements affect consumer welfare in the simple two-type model. We refer the reader to CKN (2004) for a more detailed welfare analysis for a general setting.

When the firm is allowed to make product preannouncements, the expected total consumer welfare in the informative equilibrium is as follows,

$$\begin{aligned} W^A &= W_1^A + \delta W_2^A \\ &= (1-q)(\theta_1(s_H + w) + (1-\theta_1)(s_L + w)) + q(\theta_2(s_H + w) \\ &\quad + (1-\theta_2)2w) + \delta[(1-q)(\theta_1(w + \theta_1 s_H + (1-\theta_1)s_L) \\ &\quad + (1-\theta_1)2w) + q(w + \theta_2 s_H + (1-\theta_2)s_L)]. \end{aligned}$$

(where W_i^A denotes consumer welfare in period i; $i = 1$; 2 when preannouncements are allowed)

Let us analyze how prohibiting preannouncements affects consumers' welfare. First, suppose that $q\theta_2 + (1-q)\theta_1 < \bar{\mu}$. Then if the social planner prohibits preannouncements, consumers will buy the currently available product and get $2w$ in the first cycle. In the second cycle, consumers will update their beliefs about the product's quality based on whether the product in period one is of high quality. If the firm produced a high-quality product in the first cycle, then the updated belief that the product is of high quality in the second cycle is given by $\frac{q\theta_2}{(1-q)\theta_1+q\theta_2}\theta_2 + \left(1-\frac{q\theta_2}{(1-q)\theta_1+q\theta_2}\right)\theta_1$. In contrast, if the firm produced a low-quality product in the first cycle, the updated belief is given by $\frac{q(1-\theta_2)}{(1-q)(1-\theta_1)+q(1-\theta_2)}\theta_2 + \frac{(1-q)(1-\theta_1)}{(1-q)(1-\theta_1)+q(1-\theta_2)}\theta_1$. By condition (5.3) and the fact that $\frac{q(1-\theta_2)}{(1-q)(1-\theta_1)+q(1-\theta_2)} < q$, consumers will wait for a new product in the second cycle only if the product in the first cycle is of high quality. The total expected consumer welfare is as follows:

$$\begin{aligned} W^{NA} &= W_1^{NA} + \delta W_2^{NA} \\ &= 2w + \delta[(1-q)((1-\theta_1)2w + \theta_1(w + \theta_1 s_H + (1-\theta_1)s_L)) \\ &\quad + q((1-\theta_2)2w + \theta_2(w + \theta_2 s_H + (1-\theta_2)s_L))]. \end{aligned}$$

Let us compare W^A and W^{NA}. First, $W_1^A - W_1^{NA} = ((1-q)\theta_1 + q\theta_2)s_H + (1-q)(1-\theta_1)s_L - (1-q+q\theta_2)w$. If we divide both sides by $(1-q+q\theta_2)$, we get $\mu_1^H s_H + (1-\mu_1^H)s_L - w$, where $\mu_1^H = \frac{q\theta_2}{q\theta_2+(1-q)} + \left(\frac{1-q}{q\theta_2+(1-q)}\right)\theta_1$. Since $\mu_1^H > \bar{\mu}$, we have that $W_1^A - W_1^{NA} > 0$. Second, $W_2^A - W_2^{NA} = q(1-\theta_2)(\theta_2 s_H + (1-\theta_2)s_L - w)$. Since $\theta_2 > \bar{\mu}$, $W_2^A - W_2^{NA} > 0$. Thus, we have $W^A > W^{NA}$.

Second, suppose that $q > \bar{\mu}$. Then, if the firm is not allowed to make product preannouncements, consumers will wait for a new product in the first cycle. Consumers will wait in the second cycle only if the product in the first cycle is of high quality, as in the previous case. In the second case, the expected consumer welfare can be written as follows:

$$\begin{aligned} \mathring{W}^{NA} &= \mathring{W}_1^{NA} + \delta \mathring{W}_2^{NA} \\ &= (w + (1-q)(\theta_1 s_H + (1-\theta_1)s_L) + q(\theta_2 s_H + (1-\theta_2)s_L)) \\ &\quad + \delta(1-q)((1-\theta_1)2w + \theta_1(w + \theta_1 s_H + (1-\theta_1)s_L)) \\ &\quad + \delta q((1-\theta_2)2w + \theta_2(w + \theta_2 s_H + (1-\theta_2)s_L)) \end{aligned}$$

Let us compare W^A and $\mathring{W}^{NA}$. First, $W_1^A - \mathring{W}_1^{NA} = q(1-\theta_2)(w - s_L) > 0$. Second, since $\mathring{W}_2^{NA} = W_2^{NA}$, we have $W_2^A - \mathring{W}_2^{NA} > 0$. Thus, we have $W^A > \mathring{W}^{NA}$.

Combining these two cases together, we can conclude that allowing preannouncements always helps consumers make a better decision, and its effect on consumer welfare is positive.

End Notes

This paper was prepared for the CESifo Economic Studies Conference on "Understanding the Digital Economy" held in Munich on July 2–3, 2004. We thank Christian Wey, editor Martin Peitz, two anonymous referees, and participants in the conference for helpful and constructive comments on the previous version of the paper.

1. See Bayus et al. (2001) for the origin of the term *vaporware*.
2. Although Microsoft announced that its DOS 5.0 would be released in the first quarter of 1991, it was not released until June 1991. It was also alleged that some of the announcements about its features were spurious.
3. See Fisher et al. (1983) for details.
4. There also are papers that allow the spillover of announcement information.
5. Another efficiency argument for product preannouncements directed to business firms can be made in systems markets with complementarities. In such a market, a product's value depends on the availability of complements. An announcement by industry leaders, such as IBM or Microsoft, about the features or characteristics of the new platform product coordinates the research and development efforts of suppliers of complements. We thank our discussant Christian Wey for pointing this out.
6. Symmetric excess inertia refers to a situation in which the new technology is not adopted when adoption is favored by both firms.
7. It is a general result in the cheap talk literature that preplay communication is more effective when the players' interests are more aligned. See Farrell and Rabin (1996) for a survey of the cheap talk literature.
8. Technically speaking, Gerlach (2004) is a model of cheap talk with two audiences in which the sender's (the entrant's) preferences are aligned with one type of audience (consumers), but are opposed to the other (the incumbent). In a model of cheap talk with one audience, Crawford and Sobel (1982) show that the sender's message can be more informative the more aligned the preferences of the sender and the audience.
9. In Farrell and Saloner (1986) and our model in section 5.4, this information spillover would not matter since the current product market is assumed to be perfectly competitive, and the prices of the products are exogenously set. Thus, the announcement of the new product does not affect pricing of the old product, and the strategic reaction effect does not exist.
10. Even though Gerlach's (2004) main analysis is of the case of verifiable announcement, he also considers the possibility of false announcements. He shows that when the entrant's claims are not verifiable, the announcements cannot be informative in equilibrium. In contrast, in our model in section 5.4, we construct a reputational model of cheap talk, and the central question is whether or not nonverifiable announcements can be informative in a sequence of announcements.
11. Our model also would apply if the firm is expected to introduce a sequence of upgrades that would render the previous generations of the product obsolete.
12. For simplicity, we assume that consumers are homogeneous in their waiting costs (w) and, therefore, make the same decision as to purchase or wait in the first period. We can relax this assumption and allow different consumption patterns according to their waiting costs without affecting the main qualitative results. See Choi et al. (2004) for more details.
13. See Choi et al. (2004) for a microfoundation of the assumptions we make.
14. See Mas-Colell, Whinston, and Green (1995) for more details.
15. It can be easily verified that the set of parameters satisfying conditions (5.3) and (5.4) is nonempty.

References

Bayus, B. L., S. Jain, and A. G. Rao (2001), "Truth or Consequences: An Analysis of Vaporware and New Product Announcements," *Journal of Marketing Research* 38, 3–13.

Choi, J. P. (1998), "Brand Extension as Informational Leverage," *Review of Economic Studies*, 655–670.

Choi, J. P., E. G. Kristiansen, and J. Nahm (2004), "Vaporware," unpublished manuscript.

Crawford, V. P., and J. Sobel (1982), "Stratgic Information Transmission," *Econometrica* vol. 50, 1431–1451.

Dranove, D., and N. Gandal (2003), "The DVD vs. DIVX Standard War: Empirical Evidence of Vaporware," *Journal of Economics and Management Strategy* 12, 363–386.

Farrell, J. (1987), "Cheap Talk, Coordination, and Entry," *Rand Journal of Economics* vol. 18, no. 1, 34–39.

Farrell, J., and M. Rabin (1996), "Cheap Talk," *Journal of Economic Perspectives* 10(3), 103–118.

Farrell, J., and G. Saloner (1985), "Standardization, Compatibility, and Coordination," *Rand Journal of Economics*, 70–83.

Farrell, J., and G. Saloner (1986), "Installed Base and Compatibility: Innovation, Product Pre-announcements, and Predation," *American Economic Review* 76, 940–955.

Fisher, F. M., J. J. McGowan, and J. E. Greenwood (1983), "Folded, Spindled, and Mutilated: Economic Analysis and U.S. vs. IBM," The MIT Press, Cambridge.

Gerlach, H. A. (2004), "Announcement, Entry, and Preemption When Consumers Have Switching Costs," *Rand Journal of Economics* 35, 184–202.

Gertner, R., R. Gibbons, and D. Scharfstein (1988), "Simultaneous Signaling to the Capital and Product Market," *Rand Journal of Economics* 19, 173–190.

Green, E., and R. Porter (1984), "Noncooperative Collusion under Imperfect Price Information," *Econometrica* vol. 52, 87–100.

Grossman, S. J. (1981), "The Informational Role of Warranties and Private Disclosure about Product Quality," *Journal of Law and Economics* 24, 461–483.

Haan, A. M. (2003), "Vaporware as a Means of Entry Deterrence," *Journal of Industrial Economics*, Volume LI, 345–358.

Klemperer, P. (1995), "Competition When Consumers Have Switching Costs," *Review of Economic Studies* (62), 515–539.

Levy, S. M. (1997), "Should 'Vaporware' be an Antitrust Concern?," *The Antitrust Bulletin*, 33–49.

Mas-Colell, A., M. D. Whinston, and J. R. Green (1995), "Microeconomic Theory," Oxford University Press.

Park, I. (2002), "Cheap-Talk Coordination of Entry by Privately Informed Firms," *Rand Journal of Economics* vol. 33, no. 3, 377–393.

Reading 6

Versioning Information Goods

Paul Belleflamme

6.1 Introduction

Information can be defined very broadly as anything that can be digitized (that is, encoded as a stream of bits): text, images, voice, data, audio, and video (see Varian 1998). Basic information is transacted under a wide range of formats or packages (which are not necessarily digital). These formats are generically called *information goods*. Books, movies, music, magazines, software, games, databases, telephone conversations, stock quotes, Web pages, news, ringtones, etc. all fall into this category. Information goods have the distinguishing characteristic of involving high fixed costs but low (often zero) marginal costs. In this case, cost-based pricing is not a sensible approach for firms and must give way to *value-based pricing*: an information good must be priced according to the value consumers attach to it, not according to its production cost. Moreover, as different consumers attach very different values to the same information good, the producer should set not a single *but several* value-based prices for its information good. This practice is known as *price discrimination*. More precisely, price discrimination implies that two varieties of a good are sold (by the same seller) to two buyers at different net prices, the net price being the price (paid by the buyer) corrected for the cost associated with the product differentiation.[1]

We begin by addressing the *feasibility of price discrimination*. In a perfectly competitive market, there cannot be two different prices for the same product, for it would otherwise be possible to earn a profit by engaging in *arbitrage*, that is, by buying at the low price and selling at the high price. Implicit behind this "law of one price" are the assumptions that arbitrage is perfect (costless) and that agents are perfectly informed about the different prices. However, in the real world (and especially for information goods), examples abound in which different prices are observed for what is apparently the same product. First, it must be the case that firms enjoy some market power, so that they are in a position to set prices. Second, leaving aside the possibility of imperfect consumer information, it must be that arbitrage costs are so high that consumers do not find it profitable to transfer the good between them.[2]

Let us now distinguish between different *types of price discrimination*. Following Pigou (1920), it is customary to distinguish three types, according to the information that firms have about buyers. The most favorable case for the firm is when it has complete information about individual preferences. The firm is then able to charge an individualized price for each buyer and for each unit purchased by each buyer, thereby extracting all of the consumer surplus. In Pigou's taxonomy, this practice is known as *first-degree price discrimination* (or *perfect discrimination*). Shapiro and Varian (1999) propose the more descriptive term of *personalized pricing*. It is often argued that personalized pricing cannot be applied in practice because of the enormous amount of information it requires. However, firms are now able to use information technologies to improve their knowledge of consumers' preferences and, thereby, to personalize price offers.[3]

When the firm does not know exactly each consumer's willingness to pay, it may still manage to extract a fraction of the consumer surplus by relying on some indicators (such as age, occupation, and location) that are related to the consumers' preferences. If the firm can observe a buyer's characteristics, then it can charge different prices as a function of these characteristics. This type of price discrimination is referred to as *third-degree price discrimination* in Pigou's taxonomy, or as *group pricing* in Shapiro and Varian's. This practice is common in the software industry: for example, office software often are sold at different prices to home users and to professionals, and students enjoy special discounts on Mathematica.[4] As group pricing can be seen as a special case of a multiproduct firm's pricing problem (see Tirole 1988), we shall not discuss it further in this chapter.

When buyers' characteristics are not directly observable, the firm still has the option to use self-selecting devices to extract some consumer surplus. The idea is to discriminate between heterogeneous buyers by targeting a specific package (that is, a selling contract that includes various clauses in addition to price) for each class of buyers. The firm faces then the problem of designing the menu of packages in such a way that consumers indeed choose the packages targeted for them. Pigou describes this practice as *second-degree price discrimination*, whereas Shapiro and Varian refer to it, more descriptively, as *versioning*. Examples of such practice abound for information goods (see section 6.2). As Peitz and Waelbroeck indicate in their analysis of digital music [...], digital rights management (DRM) solutions facilitate the practice of versioning: using DRM, the producer of a digital music file has the possibility to create different versions by attaching different liberalities of use to the file (in terms of, for example, number of access, number of copies on different devices, number of people one can share the file with, rights to modify or excerpt, or even time of possession).[5]

Versioning is our main focus in this chapter. In section 6.2, we present an integrated model that allows us to study how to implement versioning and when it is optimal to do so. Then in section 6.3, we consider a number of specific strategies for discriminating between consumers in the information economy: bundling or tying different goods together, "functional degradation" (that is, creating a new version by disabling some functions of an existing version), and conditioning prices on purchase history. Section 6.4 gives some concluding remarks.

[...]

6.2 Versioning: How and When?

In the nineteenth century, Jules Dupuit (a French engineer and economist, quoted by Ekelund, 1970) analyzes the practice of the three-class rail system as follows:

It is not because of the few thousand francs which would have to be spent to put a roof over the third-class carriages or to upholster the third-class seats that some company or other has open carriages with wooden benches. ... What the company is trying to do is prevent the passengers who can pay the second-class fare from traveling third-class; it hits the poor, not because it wants to hurt them, but to frighten the rich. ... And it is again for the same reason that the companies, having proved almost cruel to third-class passengers and mean to second-class ones, become lavish in dealing with first-class passengers. Having refused the poor what is necessary, they give the rich what is superfluous.

What Dupuit describes is a classical example of versioning: by offering the same product under a number of "packages" (that is, some combinations of price and product characteristics), the seller is able to sort consumers according to their willingness to pay. The key is to identify some dimensions of the product that are valued differently across consumers, and to design the product line so as to emphasize differences along those dimensions. The next step consists in pricing the different versions in such a way that consumers will sort themselves out by selecting the version that most appeals to them.

Examples of such practice abound in the information economy. The dimension along which information goods are versioned is usually their *quality*, which is to be understood in a broad sense (for instance, the quality of a software might be measured by its convenience, its flexibility of use, the performance of the user interface). Shapiro and Varian (1998) give a series of specific examples. For instance, referring to "nagware" (that is, a form of shareware that is distributed freely but displays a screen encouraging users to pay a registration fee, or displaying ads), they illustrate how annoyance can be used as a discriminating device: some users will be willing to pay to turn off the annoying screen. Versioning of information goods can also be based on *time*, following the tactic of delay. For example, new books often appear first in hardcover and later as less expensive paperbacks. Similarly, movies can be viewed first in theaters; a few months later, they are released on DVD and are shown on premium cable television; eventually, they are broadcast on terrestrial television. The price of these choices usually declines with the viewing date. Finally, versioning can be based on *quantity*. Meurer (2001) gives some examples: software site licenses often provide discounted royalties as the number of networked machines or users grow; online databases offer discounts based on number of users or on usage by a particular user (measured by the number of searches performed, the quantity downloaded or printed, etc.); music performance licenses use factors like the number of square meters in a bar or store, or the size of the audience for a radio or television station to set quantity-based royalties; magazine and newspaper subscriptions feature quantity discounts.

We now develop a simple model to understand how monopolists should choose prices to induce self-selection of the consumers between different versions of the product. We also identify conditions under which versioning allows the monopolists to increase profits.

6.2.1 A Simple Model of Versioning

We consider the problem of monopolists choosing packages of quality and price level for an information good when consumers have unit demands.[6] The monopolists have identified one particular dimension of the good for which consumers have different value. In particular, we suppose that there is a continuum of potential consumers who are characterized by their valuation, θ, for this dimension of the information good. We assume that the "taste parameter" θ is uniformly distributed on the interval $[0, 1]$. The monopolists can produce this dimension of the good at two levels of quality, which are given exogenously. We note the two levels s_1 and s_2, with $s_2 > s_1$. As for the other dimensions of the information good, consumers are assumed to share the same valuation. Consumers' preferences are then described as follows: when consuming a unit of the good of quality s_i sold at price p_i, a consumer of type θ enjoys a (net) utility of

$$u(\theta, s_i) = k + \theta s_i - p_i, \tag{6.1}$$

where $k \geq 0$ represents the common valuation for the other dimensions of the information good. We assume that $k < s_1$, meaning that the consumer with the highest taste parameter ($\theta = 1$) values the particular dimension (at its lowest quality level) more than all the other dimensions of the good. Finally, we pose that consumers' utility is zero if they refrain from buying.

Monopolists face the following problem. They know the aggregate distribution of the taste parameters but are unable to identify a particular consumer's type. Two options are available: they can either sell a unique quality at a single price, or price discriminate by offering the two qualities at different prices. Let us examine the two options in turn, assuming that there is a constant marginal cost $c_i \geq 0$ to produce one unit of the good of quality s_i (with $c_i \leq k$ for $i = 1, 2$, meaning that the less eager consumer would buy either version if priced at marginal cost). Assumption 1 summarizes the relationship between the parameters of the model. For reasons that will become clear immediately, we also assume that the cost of producing the high quality (c_2) is not too large with respect to the cost of producing the low quality (c_1). Assumption 2 makes this condition precise.

Assumption 6.1 $0 \leq c_1, c_2 \leq k < s_1 < s_2$.

Assumption 6.2 $c_2 < c_1 + x$, with $x \equiv k + s_2 - c_1 - \sqrt{s_2/s_1}(k + s_1 - c_1) > 0$.

6.2.1.1 Selling a Single Quality

Under Assumption 2, the monopolists will choose to produce quality s_2 if they decide to sell a single quality. For a given price p_2 of quality s_2, the marginal consumer who is indifferent between buying and not buying is identified by $\theta_{20}(p_2)$, which solves $k + \theta_{20}(p_2)s_2 - p_2 = 0 \Leftrightarrow \theta_{20}(p_2) = \frac{p_2 - k}{s_2}$. Since all consumers with a higher valuation than $\theta_{20}(p_2)$ will buy the good, the monopolists' profit-maximization problem writes as

$$\max_{p_2} \pi_{1q} = (p_2 - c_2)[1 - \theta_{20}(p_2)] = (p_2 - c_2)\left(1 - \frac{p_2 - k}{s_2}\right).$$

The optimal price and profit are easily computed as

$$\hat{p}_2 = \frac{k + s_2 + c_2}{2} \quad \text{and} \quad \hat{\pi}_{1q} = \frac{(k + s_2 - c_2)^2}{4s_2}.$$

6.2.1.2 Selling the Two Qualities

We need now to find the profit-maximizing price pair (p_1, p_2) that induces some consumers to select quality s_1 and other consumers to select quality s_2. Given (p_1, p_2), we denote by θ_{12} the marginal consumer who is indifferent between consuming either of the two qualities, and by θ_{10}, the marginal consumer who is indifferent between consuming quality s_1 and not consuming at all. By definition, we have

$$k+\theta_{12}s_1-p_1=k+\theta_{12}s_2-p_2 \Leftrightarrow \theta_{12}(p_1,p_2)=\frac{p_2-p_1}{s_2-s_1},$$

$$k+\theta_{10}s_1-p_1=0 \Leftrightarrow \theta_{10}(p_1)=\frac{p_1-k}{s_1}.$$

To achieve price discrimination, prices must be such that $0 \le \theta_{10} < \theta_{12} < 1$. In that case, the population of consumers is divided into two (possibly three) groups: consumers with $\theta \ge \theta_{12}$ buy quality s_2, while consumers with $\theta_{10} \le \theta < \theta_{12}$ buy quality s_1 (and if $\theta_{10} > 0$, consumers with $0 \le \theta < \theta_{10}$ do not buy any quality). Prices must thus satisfy the following two constraints.

$$\theta_{12}(p_1,p_2)<1 \Leftrightarrow p_2<p_1+(s_2-s_1), \quad \text{(A)}$$

$$\theta_{10}(p_1)<\theta_{12}(p_1,p_2) \Leftrightarrow s_1/(p_1-k)>s_2/(p_2-k). \quad \text{(B)}$$

These are the so-called *self-selection constraints* (also known as "incentive-compatibility constraints"). If the menu $(s_i, p_i)_{i=1,2}$ is to be feasible in the sense that it will be chosen voluntarily by the consumers, then consumers of each group must prefer consuming the package intended for them as compared to consuming the other group's package or not consuming any package. Constraint (A) states that the price of the high-quality version must be lower than the price of the low-quality version, augmented by the quality gap (as valued by the most eager consumer, that is, $\theta = 1$). This is a necessary condition for positive sales of the high-quality version. Constraint (B) states that the low-quality version must offer a better "quality-price ratio" (computed here as $\frac{s_i}{p_i-k}$ for version i) than the high-quality one. This is a necessary condition for positive sales of the low-quality version.

Expressing p_2 as $p_1+\Delta$, we can write the monopolists' profit-maximization problem as follows

$$\max_{p_1,\Delta} \pi_{2q}=(p_1-c_1)[\theta_{12}(\Delta)-\theta_{10}(p_1)]+(p_1+\Delta-c_2)[1-\theta_{12}(\Delta)]$$
$$\text{s.t. (A) and (B) are met.}$$

That is, the monopolists set the price of the low-quality version (p_1) and the premium over that price associated with the high-quality version (Δ). The two first-order conditions are given by

$$\frac{\partial \pi_{2q}}{\partial p_1}=[1-\theta_{10}(p_1)]-(p_1-c_1)\frac{\partial \theta_{10}(p_1)}{\partial p_1}=0;$$

$$\frac{\partial \pi_{2q}}{\partial \Delta} = [1 - \theta_{12}(\Delta)] - (\Delta - c_2 + c_1)\frac{\partial \theta_{12}(\Delta)}{\partial \Delta} = 0.$$

The former condition shows that an increase in p_1 has a twofold effect on profits: on one hand, revenues are gained from the consumers of the two versions, but on the other hand, margins are lost from consumers of the low-quality version who leave the market because of the price increase. The latter condition indicates two similar effects: a higher premium Δ gives rise to increased revenue from the consumers of the high-quality version but makes some consumers switch to the low-quality version (which is sold at a margin $p_1 - c_1$ instead of $p_2 - c_2$).

Replacing θ_{12} and θ_{10} by their respective value and solving for each first-order condition, we compute the profit-maximizing prices as

$$p_1^* = \frac{k + s_1 + c_1}{2}, \quad \Delta^* = \frac{c_2 - c_1 + s_2 - s_1}{2} \Rightarrow p_2^* = \frac{k + s_2 + c_2}{2}.$$

Do these prices meet the constraints? We first check that the market is not fully covered at these prices: our assumption that $s_1 > k$ implies that $\theta_{10}(p_1^*) > 0$, so that consumers with very low values of θ do not purchase any version. Next, a few lines of computations establish for which regions of parameters the self-selection constraints are met:

$$p_2^* < p_1^* + (s_2 - s_1) \Leftrightarrow c_2 < c_1 + (s_2 - s_1), \tag{A'}$$

$$s_1 / (p_1^* - k) > s_2 / (p_2^* - k) \Leftrightarrow s_1 / (c_1 - k) > s_2 / (c_2 - k). \tag{B'}$$

Conditions (A′) and (B′) are nothing but the self-selection constraints (A) and (B) expressed in the case of marginal-cost pricing (that is, $p_1 = c_1$ and $p_2 = c_2$). We now discuss the optimality of versioning under different scenarios for the values of the parameters k, c_1, and c_2.

6.2.2 When Is Versioning Optimal?

We have just shown that conditions (A′) and (B′) are necessary for versioning to be feasible. Using a simple "revealed preference" argument, we can also say that versioning is more profitable than selling a single version when conditions (A′) and (B′) are met. Indeed if the monopolies decide to set a pair of prices that induces some consumers to purchase the low-quality version, it is because this strategy increases profits (otherwise, they would choose prices such that only the high-quality version is purchased).

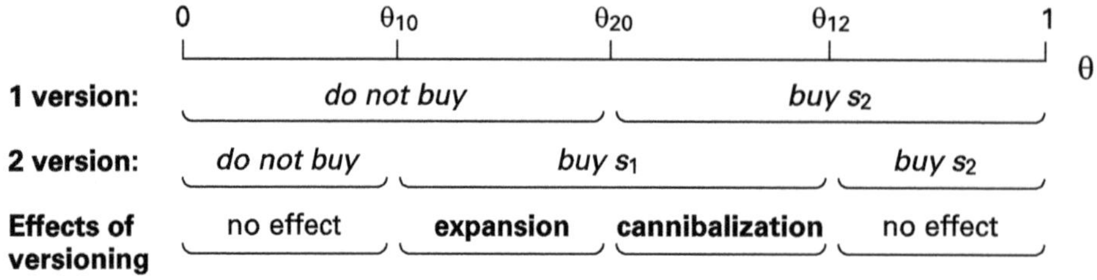

FIGURE 6.1 Effects of Versioning on Firm's Profits.

6.2.2.1 Cannibalization vs. Market Expansion

To understand the importance of the two conditions, let us detail the two conflicting effects versioning induces on the monopolist's profits (see figure 6.1). Under conditions (A′) and (B′), the marginal consumers in the two options are ranked as follows:

$$0 < \theta_{10}(p_1^*) < \theta_{20}(\hat{p}_2) < \theta_{12}(p_1^*, p_2^*) < 1.$$

That is, the effect of versioning on consumers' choices is twofold: first, because $\theta_{20}(\hat{p}_2) < \theta_{12}(p_1^*, p_2^*)$, fewer consumers buy the high-quality good; second, because $\theta_{10}(p_1^*) < \theta_{20}(\hat{p}_2)$, some previous nonconsumers now buy the low-quality good. How does this affect profits? The first thing to note is that nothing changes for the consumers with very high taste parameters $(\theta > \theta_{12}(p_1^*, p_2^*))$: in the two options, they buy quality s_2 at the same price $(p_2^* = \hat{p}_2)$. Going down the distribution of θ, we encounter consumers who would buy quality s_2 if it were the only quality available, but who would buy quality s_1 otherwise. This *cannibalization effect* has the following *negative* impact on the monopolist's profit:

$$\begin{aligned} d\pi_{ca} &= [\theta_{12}(p_1^*, p_2^*) - \theta_{20}(\hat{p}_2)][(p_1^* - c_1) - (\hat{p}_2 - c_2)] \\ &= -\frac{[s_2 - s_1 - (c_2 - c_1)][s_2(k - c_1) - s_1(k - c_2)]}{4s_2(s_2 - s_1)} < 0. \end{aligned}$$

Finally, versioning has a *market expansion effect*: there are consumers who would buy quality s_1 when it is offered but who would not buy quality s_2 were it the only quality available. The *positive* impact on profit is equal to

$$\begin{aligned} d\pi_{me} &= [\theta_{20}(\hat{p}_2) - \theta_{10}(p_1^*)](p_1^* - c_1) \\ &= \frac{[s_2(k - c_1) - s_1(k - c_2)](k + s_1 - c_1)}{4s_1 s_2} > 0. \end{aligned}$$

Adding the two effects, we find that under conditions (A′) and (B′), price discrimination is indeed the most profitable option:

$$\pi_{2q}(p_1^*, p_2^*) - \pi_{1q}(\hat{p}_2) = d\pi_{ca} + d\pi_{me} = \frac{[s_2(k - c_1) - s_1(k - c_2)]^2}{4s_1 s_2(s_2 - s_1)} > 0.$$

6.2.2.2 Is Versioning Optimal for Information Goods?

Information goods have the distinguishing characteristic of involving high fixed costs but low (often zero) marginal costs. More generally, the marginal cost of production is invariant with product quality. In our setting, this would mean that $c_1 = c_2 \equiv c$. With c being near zero, we observe that assuming $0 < k < s_1$ suffices to guarantee that conditions (A′) and (B′) are met and that versioning is optimal.[7] Note that for $c_1 = c_2 = 0$, we have that

$$\Delta_{ca} + \Delta_{me} = -\frac{s_2 - s_1}{4s_2}k + \frac{(s_2 - s_1)(k + s_1)}{4s_1 s_2}k = \frac{s_2 - s_1}{4s_1 s_2}k^2 > 0 \Leftrightarrow k > 0.$$

We record our main result below.

Result 6.1 Suppose the consumers' utility for the information good can be separated along two dimensions: a "key dimension" for which consumers have different valuations, and a "secondary dimension" for which all consumers have the same, positive, valuation. Suppose also that some consumers value the key dimension more than the secondary dimension, and that the marginal cost of producing any level of quality for the key dimension is near zero. Then versioning the information good along the key dimension is the most profitable option for the monopolists.

6.2.2.3 Damaged Goods

One extreme form of versioning occurs when firms intentionally damage a portion of their goods in order to price discriminate. Such *"damaged goods strategy"* is widely used in software markets: initially, the producer develops a complete full-featured version and then introduces additional low-quality versions by degrading quality of the original version.[8] Denekere and McAfee (1996) report other instances where firms actually incur an extra cost to produce the low-quality version (for instance, Sony recordable Mini-Discs (MDs) come in two formats—60′ and 74′ disks—which are sold at different prices. Yet the two formats are physically identical: a code in the table of contents identifies a 60′ disc and prevents recording beyond this length, even though there is room on the media). They model this extra cost by assuming that the marginal cost of production is higher for the low-quality version. In the above setting, this would mean that $c_1 > c_2 \geq 0$. Continuing to assume that $0 < k < s_1$, let us examine whether versioning could be optimal under this alternative scenario. Condition

(A′) is clearly satisfied as $c_2 - c_1 < 0$. As for condition (B′), it can be satisfied if the "damaging cost" $(c_1 - c_2)$ is not too large.

Looking at the examples provided in Denekere and McAfee (1996), one could argue that the damaged good strategy is more likely to require some additional fixed cost rather than an increase in marginal cost. In this case, supposing $c_1 = c_2 = 0$ and letting $F > 0$ denote the fixed cost of creating quality s_1 by damaging quality s_2, we have that the damaged good strategy is optimal if and only if

$$\pi_{2q}(p_1^*, p_2^*) - F > \pi_{1q}(\hat{p}_2) \Leftrightarrow F < \frac{s_2 - s_1}{4s_1s_2}k^2.$$

To sum up, the introduction of a different version of the product aims at inducing consumers to reveal their preference for quality, so that the producer is able to extract a larger surplus from them. It is optimal to do so as long as the increase in surplus covers the cost of creating a new version of the product. We record thus the following result:

Result 6.2 Versioning can be feasible, and thus optimal, even if it is more costly to produce the low-quality version of the product.

6.3 Versioning: Applications

We discuss now three specific ways, observed in the information economy, of inducing consumers' self-selection in order to capture a larger share of the consumer surplus: bundling, functional degradation, and conditioning prices on purchase history.

6.3.1 Bundling

Just as inducing self-selection by offering a menu of versions enhances the monopolists' ability to extract surplus, so can selling different products as a combination package. Two such techniques are bundling and tying. The practice of *bundling* consists of selling two or more products in a single package (bundling is said to be "pure" when only the package is available, or "mixed" when the products are also available separately). The distinguishing feature of bundling is that the bundled goods are always combined in fixed proportions. In contrast, the related practice of *tying* (or *tie-in sales*) is less restrictive in that proportions might vary in the mix of goods. It takes only a little reflection to recognize how common practices bundling and tying are in the information economy. Examples abound both on the content side and on the infrastructure side, as illustrated on the following page.

Examples of Bundling in the Information Economy

Content Side (1) A subscription to cable television is typically a package of channels together, rather than a subscription to each channel separately; similarly for subscriptions to magazines, for CDs (which can be seen as bundles of different songs), or for newspapers (which can be seen as a bundle of news, arts, lifestyle, and sports content). (2) Software companies sell individual products but also offer packages (or "suites") consisting of several applications (for example, Microsoft Office suite). (3) As for software platforms, as indicated by Evans, Hagiu, and Schmalensee [...], many tasks that were performed by stand-alone applications have become integrated into other applications (for example, spell checkers, which were originally sold separately from word processors) or into the software platform itself. (4) Movie distributors frequently force theaters to acquire "bad" movies if they want to show "good" movies from the same distributor.

Infrastructure Side (1) Evans, Hagiu, and Schmalensee point out that computer systems comprise many components. Typically, the microprocessor, memory, and other components are combined to create a hardware platform such as a PalmOne Zire PDA, a Nokia mobile phone handset, or an Xbox game console. (2) Audio equipment usually can be bought as separate components or as a complete system. (3) Photocopier manufacturers offer bundles that include the copier itself as well as maintenance; they also offer the alternative of buying the copier and servicing separately. (4) A classic example of tying is the practice adopted by IBM in the era of punch-card computers: IBM sold its machines with the condition that the buyer use only IBM-produced tabulating cards. Current examples involve computer printers (ink cartridges are generally specific to a particular model of a particular manufacturer) or some photographic films (only Polaroid films fit a Polaroid Instamatic).

Economists have given different explanations for bundling and tying. First, some explanations are too transparent to merit formal treatment. In the case of perfectly complementary products, such as matching right and left shoes, no one questions the rationale of bundling: there is virtually no demand for separate products and bundling them together presumably conserves on packaging and inventory costs. In other cases where products are not necessarily complements, various cost efficiencies might provide a basis for profitable bundling. More interestingly, even in the absence of cost efficiencies, there are demand-side incentives that make bundling and tying profitable strategies. On one hand, both practices can serve as an effective tool for sorting consumers and price discriminate between them; it is this rationale we concentrate on in this section.[9] On the other hand, bundling and tying are also particularly effective entry-deterrent strategies; the recent case brought against Microsoft by the European Commission follows this line of argument.[10]

We now present a simple example to illustrate the use of bundling as an alternative strategy for (second-degree) price discrimination.[11] Consider two monopolized products, which are independent both in terms of demand (that is, the value a consumer places on one product does not depend on the consumption of the other product) and in terms of costs (that is, there are no cost advantages of multiproduct production; in particular, we assume zero marginal cost for both goods). We still have a continuum of potential consumers who are characterized by a taste parameter θ, which is assumed to be uniformly distributed over the interval [0; 1]. Consumers have a unit demand for each of two information goods (indexed by $i = 1; 2$). A typical consumer θ has the following (gross) utility function:

$$u(\theta) = \begin{cases} u_1(\theta) = \theta & \text{if consuming good 1,} \\ u_2(\theta) = \alpha\theta + (1-\alpha)(1-\theta) & \text{if consuming good 2,} \\ u_b(\theta) = u_1(\theta) + u_2(\theta) & \text{if consuming the bundle.} \end{cases}$$

where $\alpha \in [0, 1]$ measures the correlation between the two distributions of utilities across consumers: for α in $\left[0, \frac{1}{2}\right)$ there is perfectly *negative* correlation, for $\alpha = \frac{1}{2}$ there is no correlation, and for α in $\left(\frac{1}{2}, 1\right]$ there is perfectly *positive* correlation. Note that for $\alpha = \frac{1}{2}$ the valuation for product 2 is constant across consumers.

We now compare two options for the monopolists: either selling the two goods separately (*separate sales*), or selling them together as a bundle (*pure bundling*).

6.3.1.1 Separate Sales

Let p_i denote the price of good i ($i = 1, 2$). We identify two pivotal consumers:

- Consumer $\theta_1(p_1)$ is such that $u_1(\theta) - p_1 = 0$: this consumer is indifferent between buying good 1 only and not buying any good (or between buying the two goods and buying good 2 only); as $u_1(\theta)$ is an increasing function of θ, consumers with a value of θ larger than $\theta_1(p_1)$ strictly prefer the first option.
- Consumer $\theta_2(p_2)$ is such that $u_2(\theta) - p_2 = 0$: this consumer is indifferent between buying good 2 only and not buying any good (or between buying the two goods and buying good 1 only); if $\alpha \geq \frac{1}{2}$ (positive correlation), $u_2(\theta)$ is an increasing function of θ and consumers with a value of θ larger than $\theta_2(p_2)$ strictly prefer the first option; otherwise (negative correlation), $u_2(\theta)$ is a *decreasing* function of θ and the consumers who strictly prefer the first option are those with a value of θ *smaller* than $\theta_2(p_2)$.

Consider first the case of *negative correlation* $(0 \leq \alpha < \frac{1}{2})$. Using the definition of the pivotal consumers, we see that consumers would prefer to buy nothing if their value of θ was comprised between $\theta_2(p_2)$ and $\theta_1(p_1)$: as $\theta > \theta_2(p_2)$, they are better off buying nothing than buying good 2 only; moreover, as $\theta < \theta_1(p_1)$, they are also better off buying nothing than buying good 1 only. Inverting the argument, we conclude that the monopolists will cover the whole market (that is, sell at least one good to each and every consumer) if they set prices so that

$$\theta_1(p_1) = p_1 \leq \theta_2(p_2) = \frac{1-\alpha-p_2}{1-2\alpha}.$$

Under this condition, consumers are split into three groups: those with $0 \leq \theta < \theta_1(p_1)$ buy good 2 only, those with $\theta_1(p_1) \leq \theta < \theta_2(p_2)$ buy the two goods, and those with $\theta_2(p_2) \leq \theta < 1$ buy good 1 only. The monopolists' maximization program writes thus as

$$\begin{aligned} \max_{p_1, p_2} \pi_s &= p_1(1-p_1) + p_2\frac{1-\alpha-p_2}{1-2\alpha} \\ \text{s.t. } 0 &\leq p_1 \leq \frac{1-\alpha-p_2}{1-2\alpha} \leq 1. \end{aligned} \tag{6.2}$$

The unconstrained prices are easily found as $p_1^* = \frac{1}{2} > 0$ and $p_2^* = \frac{1-\alpha}{2}$. One checks that $(1-2\alpha)p_1^* < 1-\alpha-p_2^*$. However, the last constraint is satisfied if and only if $\alpha \leq \frac{1}{3}$. For $\frac{1}{3} < \alpha < \frac{1}{2}$, we have a corner solution: $\bar{p}_2 = \alpha$ and no consumer buys good 1 only. A quick analysis reveals that the latter solution also holds in the special case where $\alpha = \frac{1}{2}$ and all consumers have the same utility for good 2.

Consider next the case of *positive correlation* $(\frac{1}{2} < \alpha < 1)$. Now, by the definition of the pivotal consumers, we find that consumers with a value of θ larger than $\max\{\theta_1(p_1), \theta_2(p_2)\}$ buy both goods, while those with a value of θ comprised between $\min\{\theta_1(p_1), \theta_2(p_2)\}$ and $\max\{\theta_1(p_1), \theta_2(p_2)\}$ buy only a single good. Whatever the ranking of $\theta_1(p_1)$ and $\theta_2(p_2)$, the monopolists' profit writes now as

$$\pi_s = p_1(1-p_1) + p_2\left(1 - \frac{p_2-(1-\alpha)}{2\alpha-1}\right).$$

The profit-maximizing prices are: $p_1^* = \frac{1}{2}$ and $p_2^* = \frac{\alpha}{2}$. At these prices, one checks that $\theta_2(p_2^*) < \theta_1(p_1^*) < 1$. For the solution to be interior, we still need that $\theta_2(p_2^*) > 0 \Leftrightarrow \alpha > \frac{2}{3}$. If the latter condition is not satisfied, we have a corner solution: $\bar{p}_2 = 1-\alpha$, and the market is fully covered.

Collecting our previous results, we can compute the optimal profit under separate sales for all values of α:

$$\pi_s^* = \begin{cases} \frac{\alpha^2-4\alpha+2}{4(1-2\alpha)} & \text{for } 0 \le \alpha \le \frac{1}{3}, \\ \alpha + \frac{1}{4} & \text{for } \frac{1}{3} < \alpha \le \frac{1}{2}, \\ 1-\alpha+\frac{1}{4} & \text{for } \frac{1}{2} < \alpha \le \frac{2}{3}, \\ \frac{\alpha^2+2\alpha-1}{4(2\alpha-1)} & \text{for } \frac{2}{3} < \alpha \le 1. \end{cases} \tag{6.3}$$

6.3.1.2 Pure Bundling

Let p_b denote the price of the bundle (which is the only available good in the present case). Consumer θ's net utility is given by $u_b(\theta) - p_b = (1-\alpha) + 2\alpha\theta - p_b$. Consider first the special case of *perfect negative correlation* ($\alpha = 0$). In that case, all consumers have the same utility for the bundle: $u_b(\theta) = 1-\alpha = 1$. The monopolists will thus set $p_b = 1$ and sell the bundle to the whole population of consumers, achieving a profit of $\pi_b = 1$. For $\alpha > 0$, we can identify the consumer who is indifferent between buying the bundle or not as $\theta_b(p_b) = \frac{p_b-1+\alpha}{2\alpha}$. The monopolists' profit-maximization program is given by

$$\max_{p_b} \pi_b = p_b\left(1-\frac{p_b-1+\alpha}{2\alpha}\right) \text{ s.t. } 1-\alpha \le p_b \le 1+\alpha. \tag{6.4}$$

Solving for the first-order condition, we find $p_b^* = \frac{1+\alpha}{2}$. This solution meets the constraints if and only if $\alpha \ge \frac{1}{3}$. Otherwise, we have a corner solution: $\bar{p}_b = 1-\alpha$ and the market is fully covered. In sum, the optimal profit under pure bundling is equal to

$$\pi_b^* = \begin{cases} 1-\alpha & \text{for } 0 \le \alpha < \frac{1}{3}, \\ \frac{(1+\alpha)^2}{8\alpha} & \text{for } \frac{1}{3} \le \alpha < 1. \end{cases} \tag{6.5}$$

Note that the optimal profit under pure bundling is a decreasing function of α.

TABLE 6.1 Change in Profit: Bundling vs. Separate Sales.

$\alpha = 0.2$	Purchasing decision	Change in profit
$0 \le \theta \le 1/2$	(S) buy 2 at $p_2 = 0.4$ (B) buy bundle at $p_b = 0.8$	+0.2
$1/2 \le \theta \le 2/3$	(S) buy 1 and 2 at $p_1 + p_2 = 0.9$ (B) buy bundle at $p_b = 0.8$	−0.0167
$2/3 \le \theta \le 1$	(S) buy 1 at $p_1 = 0.5$ (B) buy bundle at $p_b = 0.8$	+0.1
TOTAL		**+0.2833**
$\alpha = 0.4$	**Purchasing decision**	**Change in profit**
$0 \le \theta \le 1/8$	(S) buy 2 at $p_2 = 0.4$ (B) buy nothing	−0.05
$1/8 \le \theta \le 1/2$	(S) buy 2 at $p_2 = 0.4$ (B) buy bundle at $p_b = 0.7$	+0.1125
$1/2 \le \theta \le 1$	(S) buy 1 and 2 at $p_1 + p_2 = 0.9$ (B) buy bundle at $p_b = 0.7$	−0.1
TOTAL		**−0.0375**

6.3.1.3 When Is Pure Bundling More Profitable than Separate Sales?

From the previous analysis, we observe that, as α increases, bundling becomes less profitable for two reasons. First, we have just shown that because the demand for the bundle rotates, lower profits are obtained when selling the bundle. Second, for larger values of α, there is a smaller proportion of consumers who buy a single good when sold separately but who buy the bundle when it is offered. These two effects are illustrated in table 6.1 where we compute the change in profit that bundling (B) yields compared to separate sales (S) for $\alpha = 0.2$ and $\alpha = 0.4$.

More precisely, comparing expressions (6.3) and (6.5) for all values of α, we find the following (see figure 6.2):

$$\text{for } 0 \le \alpha \le \frac{1}{3},\quad \pi_b^* = 1 - \alpha > \pi_s^* = \frac{\alpha^2 - 4\alpha + 2}{4(1 - 2\alpha)};$$

$$\text{for } \frac{1}{3} < \alpha < \sqrt{\frac{1}{7}},\quad \pi_b^* = \frac{(1+\alpha)^2}{8\alpha} > \pi_s^* = \alpha + \frac{1}{4};$$

$$\text{for } \sqrt{\frac{1}{7}} \le \alpha < \frac{1}{2},\quad \pi_b^* = \frac{(1+\alpha)^2}{8\alpha} < \pi_s^* = \alpha + \frac{1}{4};$$

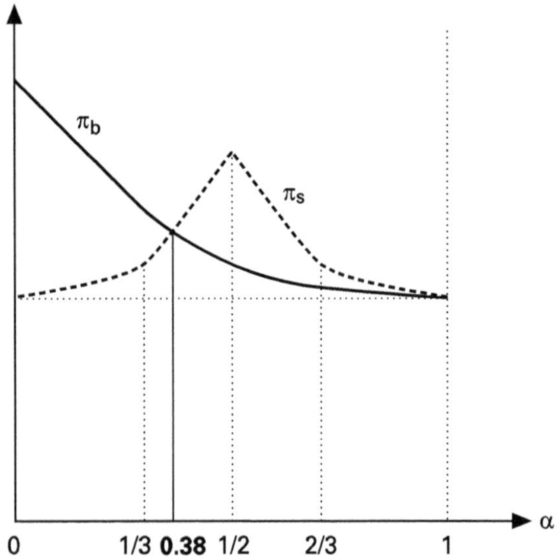

FIGURE 6.2 Comparison of Profits Under Separate Sales and Pure Bundling.

for

$$\frac{1}{2} < \alpha \leq \frac{2}{3}, \quad \pi_b^* = \frac{(1+\alpha)^2}{8\alpha} < \pi_s^* = 1 - \alpha + \frac{1}{4};$$

for

$$\frac{2}{3} < \alpha \leq 1, \quad \pi_b^* = \frac{(1+\alpha)^2}{8\alpha} < \pi_s^* = \frac{\alpha^2 + 2\alpha - 1}{4(2\alpha - 1)}.$$

We therefore conclude

Result 6.3 Profits are higher under bundling than under separate sales if and only if the correlation between the distributions of consumer utilities for the two goods is sufficiently negative, that is, if and only if $\alpha \leq \sqrt{\frac{1}{7}} \simeq 0.38$).

The intuition for this result has been explained. By selling a bundle at a lower price, the monopolists attempt to attract consumers who place a relatively low value on either of the two goods but who are willing to pay a reasonable sum for the bundle. When the two goods are sold separately, these consumers would buy a single good, but if the goods are sold as a bundle, they would buy the bundle and, therefore, acquire a good they would not have purchased otherwise. This strategy works, however, provided that willingnesses to pay for the individual products are sufficiently different. In their discussion of bundling, Evans, Hagiu, and Schmalensee [...] propose a similar intuition by pointing out that bundling reduces variation in reservation prices and, thereby, enables the seller to capture more of the product's value.

6.3.2 Functional Degradation

We now examine the logic behind a practice that becomes increasingly common nowadays: *functional degradation* of computer software. Well-known examples of this practice are software such as *Acrobat Reader, RealPlayer, Mathematica Reader*, and various *Microsoft Office* (*Word, Excel, PowerPoint*) *Viewers*. These software are designed to view and print (or play) contents written in a specific format, but are not capable of producing the contents in the specific format. The software manufacturers typically provide two different versions of a product, the read-only (or play-only) version and the full version. They offer the viewer or player almost free of charge by allowing consumers to download it on the Internet. However, the viewer (or player) is viewing and printing (or playing) only. To be able to create and edit contents (as well as view or play them), users need to purchase the corresponding full version, which is of course sold at a positive price. In the following simple model, based on Csorba and Hahn (2003), we show that this practice is based on a mixture of economic motivations: versioning, damaged good strategy, network building through free versions, and unbundling.

Suppose a firm is the sole supplier of a software that combines a read and a write function: the write function is required to produce documents that can be read using the read function. Since not all consumers are interested in writing documents, it is natural to offer the software under two versions: a *full* (write and read) version and a *read-only* version.[12] As before, we assume that there is a continuum of potential consumers who buy at most one unit of the good. Consumers are identified by a parameter θ (drawn from a uniform distribution on the unit interval), which indicates their valuation for the two functions of the good. More precisely, the valuations for the two functions are assumed to be proportional: θ is the valuation for the *write* function, while $\beta\theta$ (with $\beta > 0$) is the valuation for the *read* function. That is, we restrict the attention to cases where users who value highly one function also value highly the other function (and *vice versa*).[13]

The software exhibits *two-sided network effects*, insofar as the users' utility from reading (respectively writing) increases with the number of writers (respectively readers).[14] Letting p_f and p_r denote the prices of the full and the read-only versions, and n_f and n_r denote the numbers of consumers who buy the full and the read-only versions, we can express the (net) utility of consumer θ as follows:

$$u(\theta) = \begin{cases} \theta(n_f + n_r) + \beta\theta n_f - p_f & \text{if buying the full version,} \\ \beta\theta n_f - p_r & \text{if buying the read-only version,} \\ 0 & \text{if not buying.} \end{cases}$$

Let us detail this utility function. The full version can be seen as a bundle combining the two functions. Utility is assumed to be additively separable in the two functions. The first term is the utility from the write function: users owning the full version enjoy a network effect exerted by the users able to read the documents they produce (that is, those users who own either version of the good). The second term is the utility from the read function: the network effect, here, is exerted by the users able to write documents and is valued at $\beta\theta$ (instead of θ for the write function). Naturally, utility from owning the read-only version is limited to the latter term.

Because the firm cannot observe the consumers' types, it cannot resort to personalized or group pricing. Two options are available: either sell the full version only (which can be seen as pure bundling), or sell the two versions (which is a form of versioning or of mixed bundling). We consider the two options in turn.

6.3.2.1 Sell the Full Version Only

When selling only the full version, the firm is in the position of monopolists pricing a good that exhibits network effects. If the read-only version is not available, n_r is necessarily equal to zero and the consumer θ's options are restricted to buying the full version (which yields a net utility of $[1+\beta]\theta n_f^e - p_f)$ not buying the product. Note that n_f^e denotes the *expected* number of consumers buying the good: as choices are simultaneous, consumers base their purchasing decision on the expectations they form about future network sizes. The consumer who is indifferent between the two options is thus identified by θ_f, with

$$(1+\beta)\theta_f n_f^e - p_f = 0 \Leftrightarrow \theta_f = \frac{p_f}{(1+\beta)n_f^e}.$$

We suppose that consumers form rational expectations. Therefore, we have in equilibrium that $n_f^e = 1-\theta_f$ (because all consumers with a higher valuation than θ_f decide to buy the full version), which means that

$$p_f = n_f^e(1+\beta)(1-n_f^e). \tag{6.6}$$

Because of the presence of network effects, there may exist more than one n_f (that is, more than one quantity) that satisfies the equilibrium condition (6.6) for a given price. For instance, $p_f = 0$ for $n_f^e = 0$ and $n_f^e = 1$. We thus need a rule to choose between multiple solutions. We apply the *Pareto criterion*: if, at a certain price, there exist more than one number of consumers ("quantity") that satisfies the equilibrium condition and one of these "quantities" Pareto-dominates (that is, makes everyone better off than) the other quantities, consumers expect this allocation to prevail in equilibrium. In the present case, the larger n_f (which corresponds to the lower θ_f) that satisfies (6.6) gives a larger value to the network good, so everyone would be better off by coordinating on this solution. This is thus the value we pick when following the Pareto criterion.

We can now express the firm's problem as

$$\max_{n_f} \; p_f n_f = n_f^2(1+\beta)(1-n_f).$$

The first-order condition for profit maximization is $n_f(2-3n_f) = 0$, which admits two roots: $n_f = 0$ and $n_f = \frac{2}{3}$. Checking for the second-order condition, we find that the former corresponds to a minimum while the latter corresponds to a maximum. It follows that, when selling the full version, the firm's optimal network size, price, and profit are given by (with the superscript *F* meaning "full version only"):

$$n_f^F = \frac{2}{3}, \quad p_f^F = \frac{2(1+\beta)}{9}, \quad \pi^F = \frac{4(1+\beta)}{27}. \tag{6.7}$$

6.3.2.2 Introducing the Read-Only Version

The introduction of the read-only version aims to achieve versioning. The idea is to segment the market into two groups: the full version is targeted toward consumers with a high valuation, and the read-only version toward consumers with a low valuation. We can therefore follow the same methology as in section 6.2.1. We identify two pivotal consumers. Let θ_{fr} denote the consumer who is indifferent between the two versions.

That is,

$$\theta_{fr}(n_f^e + n_r^e) + \beta\theta_{fr}n_f^e - p_f = \beta\theta_{fr}n_f^e - p_r \Leftrightarrow \theta_{fr} = \frac{p_f - p_r}{n_f^e + n_r^e}.$$

Similarly, let θ_{ro} denote the consumer who is indifferent between the read-only version and no purchase:

$$\beta\theta_{ro}n_f^e - p_r = 0 \Leftrightarrow \theta_{ro} = \frac{p_r}{\beta n_f^e}.$$

To achieve the desired segmentation, the firm must choose p_f and p_r so that $0 \le \theta_{ro} < \theta_{fr} < 1$. Suppose for now it is the case. Because consumers form rational expectations, the expectations about the respective network sizes must be fulfilled at equilibrium. It follows that $n_f = 1 - \theta_{fr}$ and $n_r = \theta_{fr} - \theta_{ro}$. Plugging the values of θ_{fr} and θ_{ro} into the latter two expressions, we can solve for the prices and derive the following two equilibrium conditions:

$$p_f = (n_f + n_r)(1 - n_f) + \beta n_f(1 - n_f - n_r), \tag{6.8}$$

$$p_r = \beta n_f(1 - n_f - n_r). \tag{6.9}$$

As before, there can be multiple pairs of (n_f, n_r) that meet the two conditions for a given pair (p_f, p_r). It can be shown, however, that different equilibrium pairs always can be ordered, in the sense that a larger value of n_f always corresponds to a larger value of n_r.[15] Since larger network sizes confer higher utility to all consumers, the Pareto criterion tells us that consumers expect the largest pair (n_f, n_r) satisfying (6.8) and (6.9) to be the equilibrium.

We can now write the firm's profit-maximization problem in the case where the read-only version is used as a versioning device:

$$\max\ p_f n_f + p_r n_r = n_f(n_f + n_r)((1+\beta)(1 - n_f) - \beta n_r)$$

$$\text{Subject to } 0 \leq \theta_{ro} < \theta_{fr} < 1.$$

To find the (unconstrained) profit-maximizing values of n_f and n_r, we proceed in three steps. First, solving for the FOC with respect to n_r, we find that

$$n_r = \left(\frac{1}{2}\beta\right)(1+\beta-(1+2\beta)n_f). \tag{6.10}$$

Second, we plug this value into the FOC with respect to n_f, which then rewrites as

$$\left(\frac{1}{4}\beta\right)(n_f - 1 - \beta)(3n_f - 1 - \beta) = 0.$$

Third, we consider the two possible roots of the latter equation. Either $n_f = 1+\beta$ or $n_f = \frac{1+\beta}{3}$. Using expression (6.10), we observe that for $n_f = 1+\beta$, $n_r = -(1+\beta)$, while for $n_f = \frac{1+\beta}{3}$, $n_r = \frac{1-\beta^2}{3\beta}$. Since we impose $\theta_{ro} < \theta_{fr}$ (that is, $n_r > 0$), we can reject the former solution. As for the latter solution, it satisfies the constraints providing (1) $n_r > 0 \Leftrightarrow \beta < 1$, and (2) $n_f + n_r = \frac{1+\beta}{3\beta} \leq 1 \Leftrightarrow \beta \geq \frac{1}{2}$. Therefore, there are three cases to consider according to the value of β (that is, the ratio between the valuations of the reading and writing functions).

1. *If the reading function is valued relatively higher than the writing function ($\beta \geq 1$), there is no interior solution to the above problem.* The firm does not find it profitable to introduce the read-only version (which amounts to set $n_r = 0$) and there is no versioning.
2. *If the reading function is valued relatively lower than the writing function ($\beta < 1$), versioning is profitable.* Two cases of interest appear.
   (a) For $\frac{1}{2} < \beta < 1$, $n_f = \frac{1+\beta}{3}$ and $n_r = \frac{1-\beta^2}{3\beta}$ meet the constraints. The corresponding optimal prices are both strictly positive and are given by (with the superscript V for "versioning")

$$p_r^V = \frac{(1+\beta)(2\beta-1)}{9}, \quad p_f^V = p_r^V + \frac{(1+\beta)(2-\beta)}{9\beta}.$$

We compute the resulting profit as

$$\pi^V = \frac{(1+\beta)^3}{27\beta},$$

and we check that $\pi^V > \pi^F \forall \left(\frac{1}{2}\right) < \beta < 1$.

   (b) For $0 < \beta \leq \frac{1}{2}$, the valuation for the reading function becomes relatively very small and the firm finds it optimal to cover the whole market (that is, the constraint $n_f + n_r \leq 1$ is binding). Since $n_f + n_r = 1$, it follows from (6.9) that $p_r = 0$: *the read-only version is introduced for free.* It also follows from (6.8) that $p_f = 1 - n_f$, meaning that

the firm maximizes $\pi = n_f(1 - n_f)$ by choosing $n_f = \frac{1}{2}$ (which implies that $n_r = \frac{1}{2}$ too). In sum, the optimum when $0 < \beta \leq \frac{1}{2}$ is (with the superscript o for "versioning with a free read-only version")

$$p_r^0 = 0, \quad p_f^0 = \frac{1}{2}, \quad \pi^0 = \frac{1}{4}.$$

Again, it is easily checked that $\pi^0 > \pi^F \forall 0 < \beta \leq \frac{1}{2}$.

The latter result shows that the seller might find it profitable to give away a degraded version of the software in order to build the network of the full version. In their analysis of digital piracy, Gayer and Shy [...] reach a similar conclusion. They show a case where, in the presence of network effects, a copyright-owner's losses from piracy diminish when moving from nondigital to digital copying technologies. Because the quality of copies is enhanced, more (illegitimate) users copy the product, which generates larger network effects and thereby raises the price paid by legitimate users.

To conclude, we summarize our findings.

Result 6.4 Consider a software that combines a read and a write function. Suppose that consumers' valuations for the two functions are proportional. As long as the reading function is valued relatively lower than the writing function, the seller finds it profitable to engage in versioning by selling a read-only version along with the full (read and write) version of the software. If the relative valuation of the reading function is sufficiently low, it is even profitable to give away the read-only version for free.

6.3.3 Conditioning Prices on Purchase History

In the ecommerce world, sellers are able to monitor consumer transactions, typically through the use of *cookies*. A cookie is a unique identifier that is sent by a website for storage by the consumer's Web browser software. The cookie contains information about the current transaction and persists after the session has ended. As a result, for the next visit to the website by that consumer, the server can retrieve identification and match it with details of past interactions, which allows the sellers to condition the price offers that they make today on past behavior.

In other words, cookies make price discrimination on an individual basis feasible. Note that other technologies can be used toward the same objective: static IP addresses, credit card numbers, user authentication, and a variety of other mechanisms can be used to identify user history. Of course, users can take defensive measures. No one is forced to join a loyalty program, and it is possible to set one's browser to reject cookies or to erase them after a session is over.[16]

In sum, online technologies allow e-commerce sellers to post prices, observe the purchasing behavior at these prices, and condition future prices on observed behavior. Yet consumers are free to hide their previous behavior (possibly at some cost) and can always pretend that they visit a website for the first time. Therefore, as usual in versioning, sellers are bound to offer buyers some extra benefits to prevent them from hiding their identity.

We now extend the model of section 6.2.1 to investigate this type of strategic interaction between buyers and sellers in an e-commerce environment.[17] A single profit-maximizing seller provides a good at constant marginal cost (which, for simplicity, is set to zero). The seller can set cookies for recording consumers' purchase history. However, consumers can delete cookies at some cost (and inconvenience) denoted by $\gamma > 0$. Consumers can visit the seller's online store in two consecutive periods. In period $i = 1, 2$, the utility from purchasing one unit of the good is described as in expression (6.1):

$$u(\theta, s_i) = k + \theta s_i - p_i$$

(where, as assumed before, $0 < k < s_i$). We assume that $s_2 > s_1$ to capture the idea that the second unit of consumption is more valuable than the first. This might occur because the second visit to the online store is more efficient than the first one (for example, it is easier to find one's way through the Web pages), or because the seller offers enhanced services to second-time visitors (such as one-click shopping, loyalty rewards, and targeted recommendations).

Let us first examine the benchmark case where the seller sets a *flat price each period*, denoted by p. In period i, the consumer who is indifferent between buying the good and not buying is identified by $\theta_i(p) = \frac{p-k}{s_i}$. The seller thus chooses p to maximize

$$\pi_F = p(1 - \theta_1(p)) + p(1 - \theta_2(p)) = \frac{p}{s_1 s_2}(2s_1 s_2 + k(s_1 + s_2) - p(s_1 + s_2)).$$

The optimal price and profit are found easily as

$$p_F = \frac{k}{2} + \frac{s_1 s_2}{s_1 + s_2} \quad \text{and} \quad \pi_F = \frac{[2s_1 s_2 + k(s_1 + s_2)]^2}{4 s_1 s_2 (s_1 + s_2)}.$$

Naturally, the seller will try to take advantage of cookies and *condition prices on purchase history*. To do so, the seller designs the following pricing scheme:

1. the price p_o is charged to consumers having no cookie indicating a prior visit;
2. the price p_b is charged to consumers with a cookie indicating that they made a purchase on a prior visit;
3. the price p_n is charged to consumers with a cookie indicating that they did not make a purchase on a prior visit.

We investigate how to implement a solution where consumers with a high θ consumes in both periods (and do not delete their cookies) and consumers with a lower θ consume only in the first period. We identify two pivotal consumers:

- consumer θ_0 is indifferent between buying in the first period only and not buying at all: $k + \theta_0 s_1 - p_0 = 0 \Leftrightarrow \theta_0(p_0) = \frac{p_0 - k}{s_1}$;
- consumer θ_b is indifferent between buying in both periods (and keeping the cookie) and buying in period 1 only: $2k + \theta_b(s_1 + s_2) - p_0 - p_b = k + \theta_b s_1 - p_0 \Leftrightarrow \theta_b(p_b) = \frac{p_b - k}{s_2}$.

If the proposed pricing scheme is correctly designed, the seller's profit writes as

$$\pi_C = p_0(\theta_b(p_b) - \theta_0(p_0)) + (p_0 + p_b)(1 - \theta_b(p_b))$$
$$= p_0\left(1 - \frac{p_0 - k}{s_1}\right) + p_b\left(1 - \frac{p_b - k}{s_2}\right).$$

Solving for the first-order conditions, one computes the optimal prices as

$$p_0^* = \frac{k + s_1}{2} \text{ and } p_b^* = \frac{k + s_2}{2}.$$

Our assumption of enhanced services at the second visit ($s_2 > s_1$) guarantees that $\theta_b(p_b^*) = \frac{s_2 - k}{2s_2} > \theta_0(p_0^*) = \frac{s_1 - k}{2s_1}$. We still need to check, however, that all consumers behave rationally.

- Consider first the consumers with $\theta \geq \theta_b(p_b^*)$ who are supposed to prefer buying in both periods and are not deleting their cookies. From the definition of θ_b and θ_0, we know already that these consumers are worse off if they buy in period 1 only, or if they do not buy at all. There remain two options. First, they could buy in both periods but delete their cookies, securing a net utility of $2k + \theta(s_1 + s_2) - 2p_0 - \gamma$ (that is, by hiding their prior purchase, they continue to pay the low price p_0 but have to incur the cost γ). This option is dominated if and only if

$$p_b^* \leq p_0^* + \gamma \Leftrightarrow \gamma \geq \frac{1}{2}(s_2 - s_1). \tag{6.11}$$

Second, consumers could buy in the second period only and obtain a net utility of $k + \theta s_2 - p_n$. This option is dominated if and only if $\theta s_1 \geq p_0^* + p_b^* - p_n - k$, or

$$\theta \geq \frac{s_1 + s_2}{2s_1} - \frac{p_n}{s_1}.$$

The latter condition always is satisfied for these consumers if

$$\theta_b(p_b^*) = \frac{s_2 - k}{2s_2} \geq \frac{s_1 + s_2}{2s_1} - \frac{p_n}{s_1} \Leftrightarrow$$
$$p_n \geq \frac{s_2^2 + s_1 k}{2s_2} = p_0^* + \frac{(s_2 - k)(s_2 - s_1)}{2s_2}. \tag{6.12}$$

- Consider next the consumers situated between $\theta_0(p_0^*)$ and $\theta_b(p_b^*)$ who are supposed to buy in period 1 only. Again, the definition of the two pivotal consumers guarantees that these consumers are worse off if they buy in both periods (and keep their cookies) or if they do not buy at all. We still need to check whether they are also worse off in the same two remaining options as above. First, consuming in both periods and deleting the cookies leaves them worse off if and only if $k + \theta s_1 - p_0^* \geq 2k + \theta(s_1 + s_2) - 2p_0^* - \gamma$, or

$$\theta \leq \frac{p_0^* - k + \gamma}{s_2} = \frac{s_1 - k + 2\gamma}{2s_2}.$$

This inequality always is satisfied for these consumers if

$$\theta_b(p_b^*) = \frac{s_2 - k}{2s_2} \leq \frac{s_1 - k + 2\gamma}{2s_2} \Leftrightarrow \gamma \geq \frac{1}{2}(s_2 - s_1),$$

which is equivalent to condition (6.11). Second, consuming in period 2 only is dominated if and only if $k + \theta s_1 - p_0^* \geq k + \theta s_2 - p_n$, or

$$\theta \leq \frac{p_n - p_0^*}{s_2 - s_1}.$$

Again, all consumers in the range satisfy this condition if

$$\theta_b(p_b^*) = \frac{s_2 - k}{2s_2} \leq \frac{p_n - p_0^*}{s_2 - s_1} \Leftrightarrow p_n \geq p_0^* + \frac{(s_2 - k)(s_2 - s_1)}{2s_2},$$

which is equivalent to condition (6.12).

So, as long as the cost of deleting cookies is large enough (that is, as long as condition [6.11] is met), conditioning prices on purchase history is feasible (and thus profitable). The seller sets a low price for (genuine or pretended) first visitors, $p_0^* = \frac{k+s_1}{2} < p_F$, and a higher price for identified second-time buyers, $p_b^* = \frac{k+s_2}{2} > p_F$. The difference between this price and the first-visitor price is, however, inferior to the cost of deleting cookies. Finally, the price for consumers who visit the website for a second time but who have not purchased earlier, p_n^*, is set high enough (that is, in accordance with condition [6.12]) to discourage such behavior. As the seller keeps the possibility of setting $p_0^* = p_b^*$, fixing different prices must be profit-enhancing. We check indeed that

$$\pi_C = \frac{(k^2 + s_1 s_2)(s_1 + s_2) + 4ks_1 s_2}{s_1 s_2} = \pi_F + \frac{1}{4}\frac{(s_2 - s_1)^2}{s_1 + s_2}.$$

Note that conditioning prices on past purchase behavior would not be feasible if the second unit of consumption (or the second visit to the website) did not provide consumers with a higher value than the first unit. Indeed if $s_2 = s_1$, then $\theta_b(p_b^*) = \theta_0(p_0^*)$ and the market cannot be segmented.[18]

We can summarize our findings as follows.

Result 6.5 If the second visit to an online store is more valuable than the first visit, and if the cost of deleting cookies is large enough, conditioning prices on purchase history is feasible (and thus profitable). The seller sets a low price for (genuine or pretended) first visitors, and a higher price for identified second-time buyers; the difference between this price and the first-visitor price is inferior to the cost of deleting cookies. The price for consumers who visit the website for a second time but who have not purchased earlier is set high enough to discourage such behavior.

6.4 Conclusion

Price discrimination consists of selling the same product (or different versions of it) to different buyers at different prices. When sellers cannot relate to some observable characteristics a buyer's willingness to pay, price discrimination can be achieved by targeting a specific package (that is, a selling contract that includes various clauses in addition to price) for each class of buyers. The seller faces then the problem of designing the menu of packages in such a way that consumers indeed choose the package targeted for them. This practice, known as versioning (or as second-degree price discrimination), is widespread in the information economy: it is not only particularly well-suited for information goods (for which consumers' valuations might differ widely), but it is also facilitated by the use of information technologies (which allow the creation of different versions of the same good at very low cost and along many possible dimensions).

In this chapter, we have used a simple unified framework to expose the general theory behind versioning, and to consider a number of specific applications. In the general exposition, we have studied how to implement versioning and when it is optimal to do so. Applying the general analysis to information goods, we have shown that when the consumers' utility for an information good can be separated along two dimensions (a "key dimension" for which consumers have different valuations, and a "secondary dimension" for which all consumers have the same valuation), versioning the information good along the key dimension is the most profitable option for the monopolists.

We then extended our theoretical framework to shed light on three specific versioning strategies used in the information economy: bundling, functional degradation, and conditioning prices on purchase history. *Bundling* consists in selling different products as a combination package (like a word processor and a spreadsheet sold in an "office suite"). It is more profitable than separating sales if the correlation between the distributions of consumer utilities for the various goods comprised in the bundle is sufficiently negative. Under this condition, bundling induces a sufficient number of consumers to acquire a good they would not have purchased otherwise. *Functional degradation* is a practice by which a software firm removes some functions of its original product and sells the degraded version at a lower or zero price. For instance, Adobe sells Acrobat Reader along with Adobe Acrobat. The former software, available free of charge, is designed to view and print contents written in PDF format, but is not capable of producing the contents in this format. To be able to create and edit contents, users need to purchase the latter software, which is sold at a positive price. In a model involving two-sided network effects, we have shown the following: As long as the reading function is valued (by all users) relatively lower than the writing function, the seller finds it profitable to engage in versioning by selling a read-only version along with the full (read and write) version of the software. If the relative valuation of the reading function is sufficiently low, it is even profitable to give away the read-only version for free. Finally, we have considered the practice of *conditioning prices on purchase history.* Indeed online technologies allow e-commerce sellers to post prices, observe the purchasing behavior at these prices, and condition future prices on observed behavior. Yet consumers are free to hide their previous behavior (possibly at some cost) and can always pretend that they visit a website for the first time. Not surprisingly, the analysis revealed that the profitable use of such practice is conditional on the cost of hiding previous purchasing behavior being sufficiently large.

Notes

Useful comments and suggestions by Martin Peitz and two anonymous referees are gratefully acknowledged.

1. This definition is adapted from Phlips (1983, p. 6). As Phlips argues, this definition seems more acceptable than the standard definition, which identifies price discrimination as the practice of

setting different prices for the same good. Indeed one often observes that it is not the same product, but differentiated products, that are sold at discriminatory prices.

2. As Tirole (1988) points out, arbitrage costs might be associated either with the *transferrability of the good itself* (for example, it is too time-consuming to unbundle a "3-for-the-price-of-2 package" in order to resell individual units), or with the *transferrability of demand* between different packages aimed at different consumers (see section 6.2).

3. See Ulph and Vulkan (2000) for a study of personalized pricing in a duopoly setting.

4. These two examples present, however, the following difference: the home and office products are generally the same, but the student version of Mathematica lacks some features with respect to the nonstudent version. We return to this practice of *functional degradation* in sections 6.2.2 and 6.3.2.

5. For an economic analysis of DRM, see Bomsel and Geffroy (2005).

6. This problem was initially examined by Mussa and Rosen (1978). We use here the results of the extended analysis of Bhargava and Choudhary (2001).

7. However, if $k = 0$ and $c_1 = c_2$, condition (B′) cannot be met and the monopolists will prefer to offer the high quality only. This is the result reached by Salant (1989) under the assumption that the marginal cost function for quality is linear.

8. See the discussion of functional degradation in section 6.3.2 for further examples.

9. For related literature, see Adams and Yellen (1976), Schmalensee (1984), or McAfee, McMillan, and Whinston (1989).

10. Three papers addressing this topic are Whinston (1990), Choi and Stefanidis (2003), and Nalebuff (2004).

11. Regarding tying, let us simply mention that it can be viewed as a price-discrimination device because it enables the monopolists to charge more to consumers who value the good the most. Here, the value consumers place on the primary product (for example, the printer) depends on the frequency with which they use it, which is itself measured by their consumption of the tied product (for example, the ink cartridges). Those who most need the primary product will consume more of the secondary product and, thereby, pay a higher effective price.

12. A "write-only" version does not make much sense, as it seems hard to write a document without being able to read it.

13. In other words, there is positive correlation between the distribution of utilities for the two functions. Applying the analysis of the previous section, we can anticipate that this positive correlation is likely to drive the monopolists to "unbundle" the two functions.

14. For more on two-sided or multi-sided markets, see the analyses by Evans, Hagiu, and Schmalensee (chapter 3) and by Jullien (chapter 10) in this book.

15. See Csorba and Hahn (2003).

16. According to the Jupiter Research 2004 survey, an increasing number of people are blocking cookies or deleting them to protect their privacy or security: nearly 58 percent of online users deleted the small files; as many as 39 percent may be deleting cookies from their primary computer every month. (Sharma, D.C., C|Net News.com, March 16, 2005).

17. This model is adapted from Acquisti and Varian (2004).
18. The same conclusion holds when $k = 0$, which is reminiscent of what we observed in the general model of section 6.2.2.

References

Acquisti, A., and H. R. Varian (2004). Conditioning prices on purchase history. Mimeo. University of California, Berkeley.

Adams, W. J., and J. L. Yellen (1976). Commodity bundling and the burden of monopoly. *Quarterly Journal of Economics* 90: 475–498.

Bhargava, H. K., and V. Choudhary (2001). Second-degree price discrimination for information goods under nonlinear utility functions. In *Proceedings of the 34th Hawaii International Conference on System Sciences*.

Bomsel, O., and A.-G. Geffroy (2005). Economic Analysis of Digital Rights Management systems (DRMs). Mimeo. Cerna, Centre d'économie industrielle. Ecole Nationale Supérieure des Mines de Paris.

Choi, J. P., and C. Stefanidis (2003). Bundling, entry deterrence, and specialist innovators. Mimeo. Michigan State University.

Csorba, G., and Y. Hahn (2003). Functional degradation and two-sided network effects: An application to software markets. Mimeo. Keele University.

Denekere, R. J., and R. P. McAfee (1996). Damaged goods. *Journal of Economics and Management Strategy* 5: 149–174.

Ekelund, R. B. (1970). Price discrimination and product differentiation in economic theory: An early analysis. *Quarterly Journal of Economics* 84: 268–278.

McAfee, R. P., J. McMillan, and M. Whinston (1989). Multiproduct monopoly, commodity bundling and correlation of values. *Quarterly Journal of Economics* 104: 371–384.

Meurer, M. J. (2001). Copyright law and price discrimination. 23 *Cardozo Law Review* 55.

Mussa, M., and S. Rosen (1978). Monopoly and product quality. *Journal of Economic Theory* 18: 301–317.

Nalebuff, B. (2004). Bundling as an entry deterrent. *Quarterly Journal of Economics* 119: 159–188.

Pigou, A. C. (1920). *The Economics of Welfare*. Macmillan, London.

Phlips, L. (1983). *Economics of Price Discrimination. Four Essays in Applied Price Theory*. Cambridge University Press, Cambridge.

Salant, S. W. (1989). When is inducing self-selection suboptimal for a monopolist? *Quarterly Journal of Economics* 104: 391–397.

Shapiro, C., and H. Varian (1998). Versioning: the smart way to sell information. *Harvard Business Review*, Nov–Dec.

Shapiro, C., and H. Varian (1999). *Information Rules: A Strategic Guide to the Network Economy*. Harvard Business School Press, Boston, Mass.

Schmalensee, R. (1984). Gaussian demand and commodity bundling. *Journal of Business* 57: 58–73.

Tirole, J. (1988). *The Theory of Industrial Organization*. The MIT Press, Cambridge, Mass.

Ulph, D., and N. Vulkan (2000). Electronic Commerce and Competitive First-Degree Price Discrimination. Mimeo. Department of Economics, University College London.

Varian, H. R. (1998). Markets for information goods. Mimeo. University of California, Berkeley.

Whinston, M. (1990). Tying, foreclosure, and exclusion. *American Economic Review* 80: 837–869.

Post-Reading Questions

1. Which digitized business model is the most appropriate for a software development firm? Which one would work best for an online retailer?
2. What kinds of information goods benefit the most by preannouncing them? When would this strategy be less likely to succeed?
3. What are the benefits of versioning information goods? Name some information producers who version their information products.

UNIT III

Digital Currency: Bitcoin and Blockchain

THIS UNIT FOCUSES ON THE RELATIVELY recent developments in digital economics called Bitcoin and blockchain. Sometimes, the terms *Bitcoin* and *blockchain* are used synonymously, but they are actually different tools (blockchain is now used for more than tracking digital cryptocurrencies). So first, we will examine what Bitcoin is. Bitcoin is a cryptocurrency that allows for the peer-to-peer transfer of money without the mediation of a bank or other financial institution. Cryptocurrency is simply a form of digital money that can be exchanged and transferred digitally on the Internet. For security reasons, the digital currency is encrypted. Bitcoin was invented by an anonymous individual or group of people called Satoshi Nakamoto. In 2008, Nakamoto published a paper titled "Bitcoin: A Peer-to-Peer Electronic Cash System," in which the foundational principles of Bitcoin are developed and explained. In 2009, Nakamoto released Bitcoin as an open source code, and it was distributed across the world. Proponents of Bitcoin do not consider the actual identity of Nakamoto an important element of the Bitcoin system. Instead, they focus on the attributes of the Bitcoin currency, such as the fact that it is completely open and transparent, yet very secure, and that there is no central server, storage space, or government that can claim central authority over it.

Bitcoin has several interesting features. It allows users to bypass traditional banking methods and the fiat currencies used by nations. This way, users can avoid the fees and penalties imposed by most banks. The efficiency, speed, and security of Bitcoin transactions make Bitcoin an enticing option in the market of currencies. Furthermore, transactions using Bitcoin are completely anonymous, making it appealing to those concerned about personal privacy because there is no bank recording personal information. Funds are not tied to real-world financial institutions but rather digitally corresponding Bitcoin addresses. Owners of Bitcoin addresses are not explicitly identified, but all transactions on the blockchain are public. These benefits are made possible because it is by nature a decentralized open source project.

The technology that underlies Bitcoin is the public ledger known as blockchain. Transactions are recorded in the form of payer to payee using readily available software applications. Network computers can validate transactions and then add them to their copy of the ledger, and then broadcast these ledger additions to others in the network. To achieve independent verification of the chain of ownership each network node stores its own copy of the blockchain. Once a transaction is entered into the blockchain it is immune from revision. This is an important security feature that keeps others from tampering with the transactions and prevents what is known as the double-spending problem (the possibility of spending a digital currency twice). Each record has its own identifier and cannot be changed. This also builds a coherent and internal system of trust for those who use Bitcoin.

These are the themes explored in this unit. These readings serve as an entry-level guide to Bitcoin and blockchain. It is important to remember that Bitcoin has already demonstrated all the benefits and problems inherent to an open source project. It is true that many open source programs are very versatile, agile, and efficient. However, Bitcoin has undergone several forks, a phenomenon that often occurs when a group or community of developers disagree about the mission of the software (or foundation that has authority over the software) and takes the project in different directions. This can be very confusing for Bitcoin users and shows instability to the public at large. In a larger economic perspective, investing in Bitcoin can be seen as a high-risk investment; that is, an investment in Bitcoin is not like an investment in a real firm or product that provides tangible value in the marketplace. Furthermore, while Bitcoin has succeeded to build trust coherently within its system, many distrust it as a currency in the broader economy. Currencies are rarely used if they are not publicly trusted. At this point in history Bitcoin has developed interesting characteristics using innovative technology and it has solved some problems. However, it is unclear given its volatility whether it will gain larger public acceptance and not simply remain as a niche player in the digital marketplace.

Reading 7

Global Virtual Currency—Brief Overview

Suhail Abboushi

Executive Summary

Virtual currencies are becoming increasingly common and used for financial transactions worldwide. Bitcoin is the most prominent virtual currency using digital currency units, and operates directly from user to user with no involvement by a bank or other financial institution. Price of Bitcoin started at under ten cents in 2010 and currently trades at above five hundred dollars per Bitcoin unit. Some virtual currencies are convertible to real money and others are not. Government responses to the technology varied from complete ban to application of current or new laws. Virtual currency is expected to continue growing especially with the emergence of newer technologies and applications, and the rise in potential benefits.

Keywords: Virtual Currency, Bitcoin, Blockchain, Digital Currency, Cryptocurrency

Introduction

Advances in encryption and network technologies are introducing transformational changes in the valuation, exchange and accounting of economic assets and commercial transactions, and the recent emergence of virtual currency (VC), which makes possible exchange of economic value between parties without the involvement of traditional clearing house or bank, is a notable example of transformation. VC does not fit the legal concept of real currency because real currency (RC) banknotes and coins are issued by sovereign government whereas VC is not issued nor protected by government. Nor does it measure up to the economic role of real money due to the sharp volatility of its value which undermines its role as a medium for money transactions and purposes such as starting a savings plan for future financial security. VC is issued and exchanged without the backing of sovereign government, and VC-related account ledgers maintain complete and secure records of all transactions without the need for a central registry. The development holds promise for some benefits but also poses serious risks. VC is new and growing rapidly and is constantly open to newer technologies and innovations from interested participants in its global open source system, all of which make the future of VC not easy to predict, long term or short. So, an appropriate question to start with is: What is virtual currency?

Virtual Currency and How It Works

Given the newness of the phenomenon and its rapid change, suggesting a universal but encompassing definition of VC is a challenge. That being said though, core features or dimensions can be defined: (1) VC is a form of *digital currency* (DC) which is digital representation and measurement of economic value for an object or transaction; (2) it is issued by non-government party and remitted for the exclusive use by another private party; (3) it is denominated in units of account of its own system that may or may not be exchangeable to real currency; and, (4) it is used as a *medium* of exchange similar to RC but does not have legal tender status in any jurisdiction in the world. It is not illegal, but it also is not *protected* by government. Now, as for the basic or generic concept of digital currency mentioned in (1) above, it covers a wide array of DCs ranging from simple "promises" or IOUs such as digital 5% coupon issued by a retailer and retrieved as digital code on mobile device, to digital currencies backed by tangible economic assets such as gold or national currency, to the more sophisticated and increasingly popular "cryptocurrency," the algorithms used to exchange economic value between parties using principle of cryptography that are secure and unbreakable. The most famous cryptocurrency at the present is Bitcoin, the current leader in VC industry as measured by its market value, volume, and growing acceptance worldwide, and the symbol for which is similar to the dollar sign $ with B in place of S as shown in the following table. Table 7.1 identifies types of digital currency ranging from the simple digital payment system such as Pay Pal, to the cryptographic cryptocurrency, their units of denomination, and key features or examples.

To further explain the nature and characteristics of VC in general and Bitcoin in particular, it is compared to US home currency and a foreign currency (as in the case of Euro used

TABLE 7.1 Digital Currencies.

Type of Currency	Denomination	Key Feature
Digital currency (not virtual currency)	Denominated in real currency, e.g. US Dollar	Digital payment mechanism, e.g. e-money, Pay Pal, digital bank wallet
Non-convertible VC	Own units. Non-convertible to RC or other VC	Use only nonconvertible "coins"
Convertible VC	Own units. Convertible to RC, goods, and more	Centralized or decentralized VC system
Cryptocurrency	Basic Bitcoin unit, BTC, value depends on prevailing exchange rate, MilliBitoin mBTC is 0.001 BTC, MicroBTC is 0.000001 BTC, *satoshi* (smallest unit) is 0.00000001 BTC.	Use only cryptography to validate value and transaction. Bitcoin sign

Sources: https://en.bitcoin.it and IMF 2016,

TABLE 7.2 Comparison of Currency Characteristics.

Characteristic	Bitcoin VC	US Dollar	Euro
Intrinsic value	None	None	None
Legal tender	No	Yes	Not in the US
Medium of exchange	Small, among participants	Yes	Limited in the US
Used to store value	Limited and risky	Yes	Yes, subject to exchange
Structure	Decentralized	Monopoly	Monopoly
Supply source	Private	Public	Public/foreign
Cost of production	Computer utility power	Low	Low
Risk of inflation	No	Yes	Yes
Issuer is lender of last resort	No	Yes	Yes

Source: Redish (1993), IMF (2016), Bordo (1981).

in the US) on the dimensions of intrinsic value, legal tender, medium of exchange, structure, supply source, cost of production, risk of inflation, and the possibility of the issuer being the lender of last resort. A summary of these issues is presented in Table 7.2.

VC can be non-convertible to RC and operates within a closed system with restrictions on transactions outside its virtual online domain, or convertible that allows exchange to RC, and can be used for purchases and commercial transactions in real economy especially that a growing number of businesses have started accepting VC especially Bitcoin. Not unexpectedly, convertible VC, Bitcoin in particular, does more business with real economy than non-convertible closed VC.

VC system must have organization structure to oversee issuance and redemption of payments, monitor circulation, and control transaction settlements, and this structure can either be decentralized or centralized A decentralized system, most notably Bitcoin, operates free of a centralized administration, where transactions are done electronically between participating Bitcoin account holders. The system operates on a myriad of software protocols, such as Bitcoin's SHA-256 which is cryptographic hash functions, to initiate and complete remittances and verify accuracy of transactions, and ultimately record them in a virtual public ledger that contains all accounts. In Bitcoin, the work of verifying transactions and recording them in the ledger is done by a global network of Bitcoin participant account holders referred to as "miners" because they are rewarded by "mining" for newly created bitcoins, and who are generally speaking equipped with special computers (such as ASIC machines) referred to as nodes, and the complicated work of transaction verification and recording they do is referred to as "mining" (Brito & Castillo, 2013). The decentralized cryptocurrency system has the interesting and important feature of pseudonymity whereby the participants in the system, senders and receivers, are identified only by their virtual "addresses" made up of bits and bytes, which they create when they sign up for Bitcoin and obtain a pair of identification codes known as keys, a private key generated by digital signature algorithm, that works like password and is known only to the account holder, and a public key that is referred to as "address" because it is the address (account) to which the bitcoin remittance is sent. Both keys are unidirectional in design and cannot be traced back to the participants' real identity. This level of pseudonymity is a famous feature of Bitcoin, perhaps the most famous and attractive feature.

An interesting and rather transformational feature of decentralized cryptocurrency, CC, is the accounting system alluded to earlier. While participants in cryptocurrency are anonymous, their transactions are not. CC transactions are recorded in a virtual ledger referred to as *Blockchain,* and is transparent to all participants worldwide without revealing participant identity. (If reader wishes to see a live blockchain board with virtual transactions posted almost every second, the following Website is useful: https://blockchain.info.) Miners, who in effect perform mathematically challenging transaction recording and auditing, do the important task of collecting new transactions, grouping them into newly created "blocks" of transactions, and using cryptographic hash to connect (chain) them to previous blocks. That is why the ledger is called blockchain—it is a chain of blocks of verified transactions. Miners add the new blocks to their copy of the chain, and broadcast the updated ledger to the global Bitcoin network for verification. With all nodes maintaining copies of the same ledger, they provide independent universal verification of the millions of transactions and an updated registry of ownership of all bitcoins. This is how Bitcoin system operates—decentralized, peer-to-peer, maintained and validated by its worldwide participants without a centralized monitoring and intervening authority. An interesting system that observers believe may hold promise beyond VC.

A centralized VC system on the other hand has a centralized repository and administrator who performs the myriad of originating, controlling and recording transactions described above except for the major difference that the work in here is done by a central administrator, quite often a commercial company such as the famous Liberty Reserve Company that at one time processed $8 billion worth of VC transactions on behalf of 5.5 million users/account holders around the globe.

With regard to the source of VC, participants purchase them with real currency through the services of a VC exchanger, a trade platform where buyers and sellers offer and bid for VCs, from other VC holders, or, more recently and in the case of Bitcoin, from ATM-like stations through which one may sign up for an account, create the virtual pair of identity keys, the private and the public *address,* and purchase BTCs. Holders of VCs usually store them in what is known as "VC wallet", and their account balances are recorded in the blockchain.

History

VC is not the first privately issued currency in a decentralized system that does not have legal tender status. Historically, central banks in major economies started as being private financial institutions issuing currencies that did not have legal tender nor did the institutions have monopoly power as the exclusive issuer of currency. Table 7.3 provides examples of major economies and the origins of their central bank powers. And in the United States, many private banks issued notes that did not have legal tender status during the US Greenback era of the Civil War and that lasted until the central bank was founded in 1913. Public centralized systems became necessary to limit the likelihood of over-supply of currency and related inflation.

Some researchers continue to advocate *laissez-faire* monetary system and propose theoretical arguments on the feasibility of privately issued currency under conditions of competition (Selgin & White, 1994). The famous Milton Friedman argued that regulated system may come under question in times of crises and floating rates of money may be considered (Friedman & Schwartz, 1986) and in 1999 he is reported to have made explicit prediction that *the one thing that is missing but that will soon be developed is a reliable e-cash, a method whereby on the Internet you can transfer funds from A to B, without A knowing B or B knowing A* (Brito & Castillo, 2013, vii). It has been argued that the creation and emergence of Bitcoin coincided with the collapse of the global commercial financial system in 2008 and 2009. It was in November 2008 that Bitcoin "white paper" was published on the Internet under the virtual or pseudo name Satoshi Nakamoto, whose identity has been claimed but never adequately verified (Gold & Vigna, 2016). In 2009, bitcoin network came into existence with the issuance of the first BTC, and the first purchase made was two pizzas from Papa John's on May 22, 2010 for the value of 10,000 BTC which at the time, and at the prevailing exchange rate were worth about $25. Those prices, though, are long gone. In the evolution of this young currency, its exchange rate rose and fluctuated dramatically. BTC value in dollars went from $0.08 in July 2010 to $14.31 in 2011, $6.79 in 2012, $74.56 in 2013, $629.91 in 2014, $269.64 in 2015, and traded around $754.68 per BTC in June 2016 (BPI, 2016), as illustrated in figure 7.1.

TABLE 7.3 Origins of Central Bank Powers.

Country	Date Founded	Monopoly over Note Issue	Notes Made Legal Tender	Government Ownership
France	1800	1848	1878	1945
Germany	1875	1875	1909	1948
England	1694	1844	1833	1946
United States	1913	1913	1933	N/A

Source: Redish (1993).

Benefits and Risk

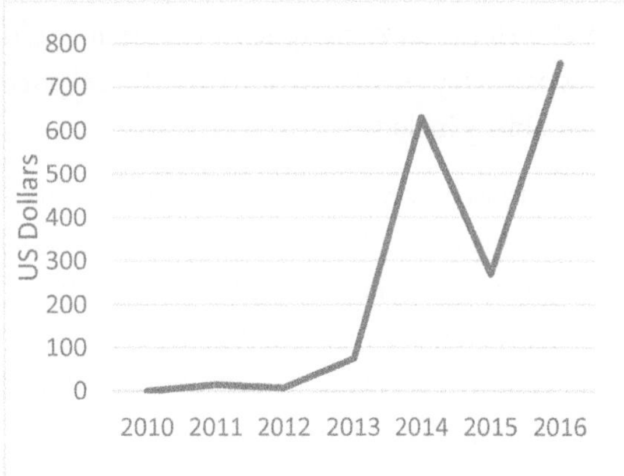

FIGURE 7.1 **Dollar Bitcoin Exchange Rate (Number of US $ to a Bitcoin).**

Source: BPI, 2016

VC is new but has already created unprecedented benefits such as (a) expedited transactions that take minutes instead of days; (b) record keeping system that is accurate, secure, and monitored by global networks of account-holders free of central authority; (c) reduced the cost of international financial transactions especially remittances that on average cost 7 percent through the bank but only 1 percent through Bitcoin; (d) offered small and medium size companies a low-cost alternative to expensive credit card transactions; and, (e) raised expectations that ledger technology may be extendable to non-VC transactions such as land and gold. Another big benefit of VC and especially Bitcoin is expanding the reach of virtual finance to people in third world countries who currently do not have access to traditional banking services. It is estimated that 64 percent of the population in developing countries lack access to the services of commercial financial institutions who shun poor rural areas due to high costs of extending banking services to those areas. People in many developing countries have turned to mobile banking for their financial needs, which contributed to the growth of electronic payment services such as M-Pesa used in Kenya, Tanzania, Afghanistan and others (Fong, 2013). Such mobile banking services can be augmented considerably by using Bitcoin VC system. The benefits and the potential for much more has encouraged a growing number of companies to accept Bitcoin payments. In February 2015, the number of businesses accepting BTC surpassed 100,000 (Cuthbertson, 2015). The list includes such famous household names like Dell, Amazon, Target, CVS, Subway, Victoria Secret, Pay Pal, Expedia, Zappos, Sears, Kmart, Home Depot, Gap, Whole Foods, and even a political party—The Libertarian Party! The list continues to grow among all companies, small and large, including Fortune 500 (Chokun, 2016). But the absence of regulation has left unaddressed risks that VC may pose, especially the risks posed by cryptocurrency with its solid pseudonymity. The risks range from concern about illegal money laundering, illicit use of VC to support global crime, tax evasion, and unsupervised capital traffic. To complicate matters, VC has been defined as currency, commodity, property, or payment system, and these different classifications produce diverse regulatory treatment. For example, the IRS has classified VC as "property" for tax purposes, whereas Treasure Department classified it as "value" for purposes of anti-crime anti-terrorism regulation.

VC systems have many attributes that could entice illicit users of the system for purposes of money laundering and other illegal purposes. The reasons why VC system has such vulnerability include:

1. Users may remain pseudonymous. This is a huge attraction to the system.
2. Being decentralized, the system does not have an administrator to keep information on users and report questionable activity to government. Not only are users pseudonymous, they are unreported!
3. The system is rather easy to use, and the fees are either voluntary or minimal.
4. It is global and can be accessed wherever there is an Internet connection.
5. The system has been substantially safe against hackers or intrusions.
6. Transactions are usually irrevocable.

These attributes may appeal to parties tempted to use the system for illicit purposes especially when coupled with the fact that *anti-money laundering* (AML) and *counter terrorist financing* (CFT) laws in different jurisdictions across the globe are weak and have varying degrees of rigor, consistency and enforcement. If financial institution that deal with VC globally do not have in place universally agreed to and consistent AML/CFT measures, the system may very well attract illicit users (Treasury, 2013). The possibility has actually happened few times. One of the more famous cases is the company known as Liberty Reserve, mentioned earlier, which used its centralized VC to facilitate $6 billion money laundering used by criminal organizations engaged in credit card fraud, identity theft, investment fraud and the like, and to allow cybercriminals to conceal and move their illegal proceeds anonymously. This company operated from 2005 until 2013 when the US government shut it down (Hong, 2016).

A key factor that has burdened the global effort to combat VC risk is the multitude of policies and regulations among countries of the world as shown in Table 7.4. Some countries went as far as banning VC, others addressed some of the immediate risks such as AML/CFT. A number of countries have yet to adopt any formal position on VC.

Outlook and Recommendations

Virtual currency is a relatively recent phenomenon in global finance, and as such, its identity, structure and function are continually evolving, but in the meanwhile, it is increasingly recognized as bona fide medium for global finance with immense potential. Bitcoin is the largest and most common VC, and while its initial introduction in 2009 was met with skepticism, hardly a week goes by these days that a large institution does not announce interest in Bitcoin whether it is UBS that says it could lead to massive simplification of banking, or

TABLE 7.4 Country Responses to VC Risk.

Country	AML/CFT	Tax Treatment	Consumer Warnings	Financial Sector	Ban on Issuance/use
Argentina	Warning on ML/TF risk		Consumer warning	Warning on reporting matters	
Bolivia					Yes
Canada	Amend existing regulations	Clarified tax treatment	Consumer advisory		
China				Ban	
France	Application of current laws	Clarified tax treatment	Warning		
Germany	Application of current laws				
Italy			Warning	Warning	
Japan	Plan new rules		Warning	Plan new rules	
Russia	Application of current laws		Warning		Yes—draft law
U.K.	Application of current laws	Clarified tax treatment			
U.S.	Application of current laws	Clarified tax treatment	Warning	State licensing requirements	

Source: Various public sources, and IMF (2016).

Bank of England who believes it will someday have far-reaching implications, or Nasdaq who is testing bitcoin technology for use on its stock exchange (Mims, 2015). Indeed, in 2009 total transactions were barely above 30,000 a year by die-hard dedicated fans of cryptography, but growth continued, as shown in figure 7.2, and will likely continue with the support by big name institutions such as Microsoft, endorsement by growing number of governments like Mexico and Britain, and the growing availability of Bitcoin now that special ATMs are becoming increasingly available ever since the first Bitcoin ATM was installed in Vancouver, Canada on October 29, 2013 (Liljas, 2013). The blockchain technology may one day provide digital alternative to a wide range of record

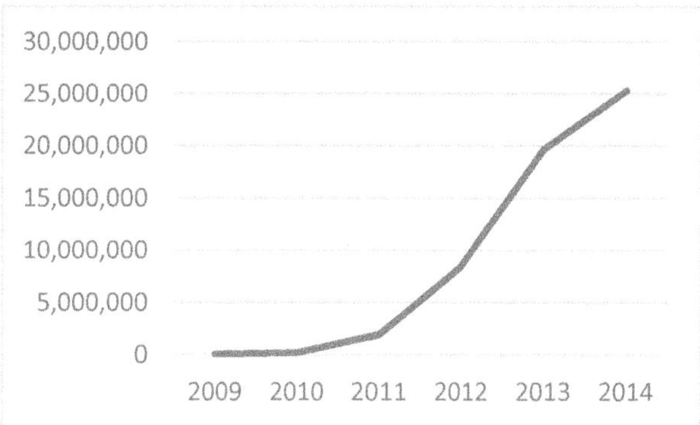

FIGURE 7.2 Growth in Annual Bitcoin Transactions.

Source: http://www.coincadence.com accessed June 13, 2016

keeping systems. In the opinion of senior VP at IBM, *the number of places that a distributed ledger can be used could become almost limitless* (McMillan, 2016).

How big will Bitcoin become? It had been proclaimed dead 89 times already, labeled a Ponzi scheme and a failed experiment. But beyond the rhetoric, observers have compared Bitcoin to another technology: The World Wide Web (Donnelly, 2016). Bitcoin is only seven years old and its base layer protocol is stable and performing to capacity, but like all new technologies, it is experiencing limitations such as the slow pace of operation manifested by the limited ability to handle only three transactions per second (TPS). Second layer infrastructure is needed and fortunately efforts are under way by dedicated companies like Bloq, BitGo, and Coinbase to build newer technology to open new frontiers and fulfill VC potential to become accessible to millions of people in the markets lacking global banking services. Experiments are also underway to introduce Bitcoin-like *digital gold,* which surprisingly, is already receiving acceptance and some trading activity in Argentina, India and Brazil (Donnelly, 2016). So what is Bitcoin's future? It is here to stay but where does it go from here that is difficult to predict.

The eminent growth of Bitcoin and the potential entry into new spheres of global economy, is putting pressure on governments to develop regulatory policies to allow and encourage useful purposes and protect against risk. There is not one path for VC public policy but key principles and guidelines may be worth considering. First, policy should protect against risk but not go beyond that to stifle the innovation with its remarkable potential. Outright ban is wrong but selective strategic targeting is more reasonable. It is suggested that regulating VC intermediaries such as exchangers or VC wallet providers, as the State of New York has recently done, is better than total intervention. Second, policy should address market conduct to protect against illicit users. A good example is AML/CFT discussed earlier which has proven effective to protect against illegal use without intervening in the core virtual technology. Third, government has to monitor growth of VC systems into new spheres of the economy and society as in cryptocurrency technology used to trade precious metals anonymously. And finally, international collaboration and coordination is essential to strengthen international understanding of VC and coordinate policies affecting the above mentioned priorities.

References

Bordo, M. D. (1981). The classical gold standard: Some lessons for today. *Federal Reserve Bank of St. Louis Review,* (May), 2–17.

Brito, J., & Castillo, A. (2013). Bitcoin: A primer for policymakers. Mercatus Center, George Mason University Retrieved April 18, 2016 from www.mercatus.org

BPI. (2016). BPI value data. Retrieved June 2, 2016 from www.coindesk.com

Chokun, J. (2016). Who accepts Bitcoins as payment? List of companies, stores, shops. Retrieved June 11, 2016 from *http://www.bitcoinvalues.net/who-accepts-bitcoins-payment-companies-stores-take-bitcoins.html*

Cuthbertson, A. (2015). Bitcoin now accepted by 100,000 merchants worldwide. *International Business Times,* Retrieved April 19, 2016 from www.ibtimes.com

Donnelly, J. (2016). Here is what the future of bitcoin looks like–and it's bright. Retrieved April 25, 2016 from www.venturebeat.com

Friedman, M., & Schwartz, A. J. (1986). Has government any role in money? *Journal of Monetary Economics,* 17(1), 37–62.

Fong, J. (2013). How Bitcoin could help the world's poorest people. *PolicyMic.* Retrieved July 6, 2016 from http://mic.com/articles/41561/bitcoin-price-2013-how-bitcoin-could-help-the-world-s-poorest-people

Gold, R., & Vigna, P. (2016). Craig Wright claims he is Bitcoin inventor "Satoshi Nakamoto." *Wall Street Journal.* Retrieved June 16, 2016 from *www.wsj.com*

Hong, N. (2016). Liberty reserve head sentenced to 20 years in prison. *Wall Street Journal.* Retrieved June 4, 2016 from www.wsj.com

IMF. (2016). Virtual currencies and beyond: Initial considerations. *IMF Staff Discussion Note,* January 2016.*

Liljas, P. (2013). World's first Bitcoin ATM launched in Canada. *Time.* Retrieved May 16, 2016 from www.business.time.com

McMillan, R. (2016). IBM bets on Bitcoin ledger. *Wall Street Journal,* February 16, B1–B2.

Mims, C. (2015). How future Bitcoin can prevent a future Greece. *Wall Street Journal,* July 13, B1.

Redish, A. (1993). Anchors aweigh: The transition from commodity money to fiat money in Western economies. *Canadian Journal of Economics,* 26(4), 777–795.

Selgin, G., & White, L. (1994). How would the invisible hand handle money? *Journal of Economic Literature,* 32(4), 1718–1749.

Treasury. (2013). *Statement of Jennifer Shasky Calvery, Director Financial Crimes Enforcement Network of the United States Department of Treasury.* United States Senate Committee on Banking, Housing and Urban Affairs, Subcommittee on National Security and International Trade and Finance, November 19. www.fincen.gov, retrieved June 1, 2016.

*IMF staff comprised: Dong He, Karl Habermeier, Ross Leckow, Vikram Haksar, Yasmin Almeida, Mikari Kashima, Nadim Kyriakos-Saad, Hiroko Oura, Tahsin Saadi Sedik, Natalia Stetsenko, and Concepcion Verdugo-Yepes.

Reading 8

The Bitcoin Revolution

Bennett T. McCallum

THE LIKELIHOOD OF THE BITCOIN SYSTEM replacing the Federal Reserve as the main provider of money in the United States and the desirability of such a transformation are the topics of this article.[1] With respect to the first of these topics, one needs to consider how far the so-called Bitcoin Revolution has progressed by estimating the average volume of transactions conducted per time period by means of Bitcoin payments, and then compare recent values of that magnitude with the total volume per period of dollar payments in the United States.[2]

Francois Velde of the Federal Reserve Bank of Chicago has estimated that, as of late 2013, the average volume of bitcoin transactions per minute totaled less than four-tenths of 1 percent of average dollar transactions per minute—actually, not *total* dollar transactions but only the *subset* conducted by means of Visa credit card payments (Velde 2013). In the months since the publication of Velde's article the volume of bitcoin payments has been growing rapidly, but their quantitative extent is still negligible from a macroeconomic perspective. In fact, this 0.004 magnitude is quite close to the ratio implied by magnitudes of Bitcoin and Visa daily transactions averaged over the most recent 12 months as reported on August 7, 2014, by the *coinometrics.com* web site. These magnitudes are $57.3 million and $16,518 million, so the implied ratio is 0.00345. Alternatively, in terms of *stocks*, rather than transactions, the M1 measure of the U.S. money supply (currency plus demand deposits) is currently about $2,835 billion (as of August 7, 2014) with bitcoins worth $7.7 billion, for a ratio of 0.00272—again, of the same order of magnitude.

Another way to express the point that Bitcoin is not at this time a quantitatively important money is to reflect on the economist's standard definition of money—namely, an entity that serves as a medium of exchange, store of value, and unit of account.[3] Doing so, one recognizes

1 I have not attempted to explain the workings of the Bitcoin system in this article because it would require space and because I could not do this better than Velde (2013).

2 In what follows, I will use "Bitcoin" as the name of the system, "bitcoin" as an adjective or a singular noun, and "bitcoins" to refer to specified quantities.

3 See, for example, Jevons (1875: 13–18), Wicksell (1935: 6–7), and Clower (1967: 4–5)

Bennett T. McCallum, "The Bitcoin Revolution," *Cato Journal*, vol. 35, no. 2, pp. 347-356.

that some clarification in this common description is necessary to make it analytically coherent. First, traditional money is typically a tangible object (e.g., metallic coins, government issued currency, or legal claims to such coins or currency) and thus is not itself a unit of account, which is intangible. Indeed, careful terminology would replace "unit of account" with "medium of account," a specified amount of which serves as the unit of account.[4]

Also, it is necessary to recognize that in developed economies tangible money does not rank highly as a store of value. For example, in the United States, during the first quarter of 2014, aggregate assets of households and nonprofit organizations together totaled $95,549 billion whereas checkable deposits and currency holdings by these units came to only $1,096 billion (roughly 1/100 of their assets).[5] Much larger components of household plus nonprofit-organization wealth include the reported monetary value of houses, furniture, automobiles, etc. Some major categories are real estate ($22,820 billion), corporate equities ($13,502 billion), corporate and foreign bonds ($2,626 billion), and pension entitlements ($19,766 billion).

Accordingly, it is the medium-of-exchange role that is the primary attribute that serves to define money.[6] But an important qualifier often made explicit is that money is a *generally acceptable* medium of exchange. By that standard bitcoins do not qualify as money. Indeed, for most members of the U.S. population there are very few, if any, of their basic payments that could be made using bitcoins.

None of the foregoing arguments rule out the possibility that Bitcoin will become a major—or even the main—medium of exchange in the future.[7] But as of today it seems likely that for law-abiding U.S. citizens the practical attractions of Bitcoin are primarily as a financial investment with very high volatility and as a means of participating in an intellectually fascinating, avant-garde, and potentially revolutionary, social experiment.[8] One would have to admit, however, that there are certain categories of transactions for which bitcoin payments are (or could be) quite important.

Anonymity

Before proceeding, it should be mentioned that, as a novice to the Bitcoin world, I have found it confusing that some experts tout anonymity as a great advantage of Bitcoin over other

4 This semantic point has been made by Niehans (1978: 118), McCallum (1989: 17), and White (1999: 7)

5 These figures came from: www.federalreserve.gov/releases/z1/current/z1r-5.pdf.

6 That the medium-of-exchange property is the essential one is mentioned by Wicksell (1935: 7), Clower (1967: 4), and (implicitly) Jevons (1875: 13–18).

7 For a reasonably optimistic outlook, and suggestions for improving it, see Luther and White (2014).

8 For an analytically impressive argument to the contrary, see Selgin (2013).

payment systems while other, also qualified, experts—e.g., Spear (2014)—state that anonymity is not a feature at all. Apparently, however, both are correct but have in mind anonymity in two quite different respects. One is whether it is possible to follow the transactions of an individual Bitcoin user. Since all transactions are recorded and retained in the system's "block chain," which is a public ledger, there is no anonymity at all of this nature. The public ledger does not, however, associate a particular Bitcoin transactor with any specific person (or group of persons). It might be possible, therefore, for an individual to keep secret his ownership of his bitcoin account. A useful brief statement on this topic by Grinberg (2011: 179) is: "All Bitcoin transactions are public, but are considered anonymous because nothing ties individuals or organizations to the accounts that are identified in the transactions." Velde (2013: 3) puts this in another way as follows: "The many ingenious features of bitcoin try to emulate ... properties of cash, but do so at some costs. One prominent cost is the loss of anonymity. Possession of the virtual currency must be linked to the unique identifier of the wallet. Admittedly, there ... are ways to make the wallet hard to trace back to its owner, but these require additional efforts."

Will Bitcoin Become a Major Medium of Exchange?

Here the object is to consider the possibility that, while quantitatively unimportant at present, Bitcoin will in the foreseeable future become a major (and perhaps main) medium of exchange—provided it is not thwarted by legal actions of the U.S. government. A natural way to argue that Bitcoin will grow is to identify some of its major advantages. A useful (and highly positive/optimistic) viewpoint has been expressed by Andreessen (2014). Since that writing is intended to be persuasive, I will quote from it extensively in what follows.

First, Andreessen emphasizes the reduction in certain transaction costs that Bitcoin could bring about. A major example is the case of international remittance: "Every day, hundreds of millions of low-income people go to work in hard jobs in foreign countries to make money to send back to their families in their home countries—over $400 billion annually. ... Every day, banks and payment companies extract mind-boggling fees, up to 10 percent ... to send this money. ... Switching to Bitcoin, which charges no or very low fees, for these remittance payments will therefore raise the quality of life of migrant workers and their families significantly." Moreover, he says, Bitcoin can be a powerful force "to bring a much larger number of people around the world into the modern economic system" and thereby "can be a powerful catalyst to extend the benefits of the modern economic system to virtually everyone on the planet."

Also, Andreessen argues that another "fascinating use case for Bitcoin is micropayments, or ultrasmall payments" that "have never been feasible, despite 20 years of attempts, because it is not cost effective to run small payments ... through the existing credit/debit and banking systems" whose fee structure "makes that nonviable." By contrast, "Bitcoins have the nifty property of infinite divisibility: currently down to eight decimal places. ... So you can specify an arbitrarily small amount of money, like a thousandth of a penny, and send it to anyone in the world for free or near-free. ... Think of content monetization, for example. One reason media businesses such as newspapers struggle to charge for content is because they need to charge either all (pay the entire subscription fee for all the content) or nothing." But "with Bitcoin, there is an economically viable way to charge arbitrarily small amounts of money per article, or per section, or per hour, or per video play, or per archive access, or per news alert."

In this context, Andreessen states that "another potential use of Bitcoin micropayments is to fight spam. Future email systems and social networks could refuse to accept incoming messages unless they were accompanied with tiny amounts of Bitcoin—tiny enough to not matter to the sender, but large enough to deter spammers, who today can send uncounted billions of spam messages for free with impunity." This is a type of use that seems likely to appeal to economists, many of whom are (I believe) appalled by the view (evidently held by many Internet developers and guardians) that use of the Internet should be *entirely* free with respect to the sending of e-mail messages.

Bitcoin Growth Rate

As most descriptions of the Bitcoin system explain, the total stock of bitcoins outstanding is programmed to grow automatically at a rate that is currently 25 bitcoins every ten minutes but which will be halved every four years, implying that the stock will asymptotically approach 21 million bitcoins. Thus, if real economic growth continues and Bitcoin becomes a dominant currency, the bitcoin price of goods will at some point have to begin a continuous fall. This plan could be modified, if I understand correctly, by Bitcoin's five-man "development team" that could in principle alter the schedule of growth rates.[9] It is of some interest from the perspective of monetary economics, then, to consider what a desirable rate of growth

9 See, e.g., Selgin (2013: 21) and Grinberg (2011: 175–76).[9] A member of the Bitcoin development team has indicated to me that the process for changing the code is more difficult than the foregoing discussion implies. What a member (or, in fact, anyone) actually can do is to submit a proposal for changing the code. Any such proposal is then reviewed by all interested members of the Bitcoin community. If a proposed change would have the effect of changing the path of the Bitcoin supply, it would amount to a "hard fork" that would entail the existence of two different versions of the Bitcoin code. Then if all users adopted the proposal, the change would be incorporated. If they did not, then the result would be two competing versions

would be for the stock of bitcoins. Suppose that Bitcoin became the dominant medium of exchange; what then would be the socially optimal rate of growth of the bitcoin stock? Well, if there is only a negligible resource-cost difference for different rates of growth of the bitcoin stock, one could use Milton Friedman's famous argument regarding the "optimal inflation rate" in the bitcoin context.[10]

That is, one could argue that the optimal money-creation rate should be that which drives the nominal (money) rate of interest to zero, since lower rates of interest lead economic agents to hold larger money stocks in real terms thereby providing more real transaction-facilitating *services* for their holders. Since there are no tangible costs of producing these additional services, it is socially optimal to increase their magnitude to a satiation level. So, applying this line of argument to an economy with a Bitcoin medium of exchange, we get the Friedman result again: the optimal inflation rate is the negative of the real rate of interest, which makes the nominal interest rate equal to zero.

The foregoing line of argument suggests, however, that if the Bitcoin development team or others can propose altered rules for the creation of bitcoins and have them adopted by the Bitcoin community, then it is possible that the development team could lead the way into adoption of an *activist* rule or to one that would generate some inflation. So it seems that the ultimate fundamental difference between a highly developed Bitcoin system and our current Fed-based, paper-money arrangement is *political*—the tangible resource costs of creating the medium of exchange are extremely low in both cases. In this regard one might be able to argue—as in footnote 9—that a Bitcoin-type system would be less subject to political forces inimical to price level stability. But, on the other hand, one might be impressed by Velde's statement that "it is hard to imagine a world where the main currency is based on an extremely complex code understood by only a few and controlled by even fewer, without accountability, arbitration, or recourse" (Velde 2013: 3).

In this context it is pertinent to remember that the U.S. Constitution clearly intends, as specified in Article I, Sections 8 and 10, for the nation's monetary system to be based on gold and/or silver.[11] Since there is nothing in the existing Amendments that suggests any change in this arrangement, it is clear that the inconsistency of today's reality with the Constitution's specification is severe—and that it can be traced to Supreme Court rulings

---

of Bitcoin—in which case its market value might be endangered. Accordingly, all Bitcoin holders would have, he suggests, a strong incentive not to adopt the proposal.

10 The usual reference is Friedman (1969) but that article's basic argument was developed much earlier, in Friedman (1960: 73). Selgin (1995) has suggested that that Friedman's analysis "superficially resembles arguments for the productivity norm" which Selgin has championed.

11 More precisely, it put constraints on monetary arrangements made by Congress and the states, evidently presuming that the main monetary institutions would be provided by Congress.

in the 1871 cases of *Knox v. Lee* and *Parker v. Davis*. I have written a short paper (McCallum 2010) discussing this astonishing episode, drawing heavily on several earlier writings by Richard Timberlake that are beautifully and extensively developed in *Constitutional Money: A Review of The Suptreme Court's Monetary Decisions*.[12]

Will Bitcoin Prosper?

In thinking about the future of Bitcoin, a major question is whether the U.S. government will, or will not, take legal steps to prevent its growth and possible dominance. A substantial discussion of this matter has been provided by Grinberg (2011: 181–206). He observes that the U.S. Constitution "has nothing to say about private parties creating money," and that the relevant existing federal statutes are the Stamp Payments Act of 1862 and an assortment of federal statutes concerning counterfeiting. Regarding the first of these, he concludes that it is unlikely that this act would form the basis for a federal attack on Bitcoin: "It is a 150-year-old statute that has outlived its usefulness." Specifically, "there has been no published court opinion interpreting the Act since 1899." In addition, "the availability of more fitting statutes under which to attack Bitcoin" is "likely to dissuade prosecutors from trying to breathe new life into the Stamp Payments Act" (Grinberg 2011: 190–91).

What, then, about the statutes regarding counterfeiting? Grinberg's discussion is highly informative, but does not leave one with much confidence regarding the major issue at hand—namely, whether the U.S. government would permit control of monetary management to pass from the Federal Reserve to a system not under its dominance. In this regard, Selgin (2013: 23–24) states:

> Although I have suggested that a synthetic commodity monetary regime might perform better than either existing fiat money regimes or than potential commodity money alternatives, I have deliberately avoided suggesting that any government is likely to take steps to establish such a regime. Indeed, rather than make that suggestion, I'm inclined to argue that, while it is possible to conceive of a government-sponsored synthetic commodity monetary regime, it is difficult to imagine a government actually embracing the idea, and more difficult still to imagine one that would not be tempted to interfere with, and ultimately to undermine, an established synthetic commodity standard by

12 Timberlake (2013) argues that not only was the majority Supreme Court reasoning in these cases faulty, but also that there exists a possibility of reversing the *Knox v. Lee*, *Parker v. Davis*, and *Juilliard v. Greenman* decisions, these themselves being startling and fascinating reversals of the *Hepburn v. Griswold* decision of 1870.

> means of its ability to introduce and to confer legal tender status upon some new fiat currency.

I find it difficult to argue with Selgin's conclusion. Yet, I would like to believe that it might be possible for Bitcoin to survive and succeed in providing the useful services identified by Andreessen.[13] In this context, it is interesting that an outcome of this type could be possible, should be welcomed, and seems reasonably likely, as St. Louis Fed economist David Andolfatto (2014) has recently argued.

An Intriguing Possibility

In conclusion, I would like to mention an unlikely but intriguing possibility that could arise from the existing situation. It is, that there exists a rather prominent possibility that the U.S. government will take legal steps to constrain or banish the Bitcoin system. In that case, it would seem that any legal attack by the federal branch of government on Bitcoin would have to begin by establishing the government's responsibility for management of the U.S. monetary system.[14] But, given the explicit provisions of the Constitution, doing so would apparently need to rely on the Supreme Court decisions in the "Legal Tender Cases" of *Knox v. Lee* (1871) and *Parker v. Davis* (1871), plus *Juilliard v. Greenman* (1884), which served to overturn the post–Civil War decision in *Hepburn v. Griswold* (1870). But, given the illogical nature of the decisions in these three cases, as richly detailed by Timberlake (2013), a competently developed counter-argument should be able to yield a reversal of their rulings, which permitted the development of today's arrangements—ones that appear to be (whether one likes them or not) fundamentally inconsistent with the Constitution.

References

Andolfatto, D. (2014) "Bitcoin and Beyond: The Possibility of Virtual Currencies." Federal Reserve Bank of St. Louis *Dialogue with the Fed* (31 March).

---

13 It might be asked what one could reasonably believe would be the case if it were not for the likelihood of government resistance to Bitcoin. To me it would nevertheless seem unlikely that Bitcoin would replace government currencies to a large extent. If, however, I think back to the early 1990s, I would have myself never believed that e-mail and the Internet would have taken over as large a part of my daily activities as, in fact, they have.

14 There will be regulations at the state level—New York, for example, has been holding hearings in preparation for the design of its version—but these will be of a different nature than ones that would entail a challenge to the Federal Reserve as the nation's monetary authority.

Andreessen, M. (2014) "Why Bitcoin Matters." dealbook.nytimes.com/2014/01/21/why bitcoin Matters.

Clower, R. W. (1967) "A Reconsideration of the Microfoundations of Monetary Theory." *Western Economic Journal* 6: 1–9.

Friedman, M. (1960) *A Program for Monetary Stability*. New York: Fordham University Press.

__________ (1969) "The Optimum Quantity of Money." In Friedman, *The Optimum Quantity of Money and Other Essays*. Chicago: Aldine.

Grinberg, R. (2011) "Bitcoin: An Innovative Alternative Digital Currency." *Hastings Science and Technology Law Journal* 4 (1): 159–207.

Jevons, W. S. (1875) *Money and the Mechanism of Exchange*. London: H.S. King.

Luther, W. J., and White, L. H. (2014) "Can Bitcoin Become a Major Currency? George Mason University, Department of Economics Working Paper No. 14–17.

McCallum, B. T. (1989) *Monetary Economies: Theory and Policy*. New York: Macmillan.

__________ (2010) "The Future of Central Banking: A Lesson from United States History." Bank of Japan *Monetary and Economic Studies* 28: 27–34.

Selgin, G. (1995) "The 'Productivity Norm' Versus Zero Inflation in the History of Economic Thought." *History of Political Economy* 27 (4): 705–35.

__________ (2013) "Synthetic Commodity Money." University of Georgia Working Paper.

Spear, S. E. (2014) "Electronic Payment Systems, Digital Currencies, and the Bitcoin Phenomenon." Unpublished Slide Show, Carnegie Mellon University.

Timberlake, R. H. (2013) *Constitutional Money: A Review of the Supreme Court's Monetary Decisions*. New York: Cambridge University Press; a Cato Institute book.

Velde, F. R. (2013) "Bitcoin: A Primer." Federal Reserve Bank of Chicago *Letter*, No. 317.

White, L. H. (1999) *The Theory of Monetary Institutions*. Oxford: Blackwell Publishers.

Wicksell, K. (1935) *Lectures on Political Economy*, Vol. 2. London: Routledge & Kegan Paul.

Reading 9

The Market for Cryptocurrencies

Lawrence H. White

CRYPTOCURRENCIES LIKE BITCOIN ARE TRANSFERABLE DIGITAL assets, secured by cryptography. To date, all of them have been created by private individuals, organizations, or firms. Unlike bank account balances, they are not anyone's liability. They are not redeemable for any government fiat money such as Federal Reserve Notes or for any commodity money such as silver or gold coins. The cryptocurrency market is thus a market of *competing private irredeemable* monies (or would-be monies). Friedrich A. Hayek (1978a) and other economists over the last 40 years could only imagine how market competition among issuers of private irredeemable monies would work. Today we have an actual market to study. In what follows I will discuss the main economic features of the market. I also discuss whether the market is purely a bubble.

As an introduction to the topic, I offer the following comic verse about the contrast between Bitcoin and the physical gold coins of the past:

> In the past, money's value was judged with our teeth;
> We *bit coins* to confirm they were real.
> Now a Bitcoin's just data, no gold underneath.
> That's okay if it buys you a meal.[1]

The Size and Composition of the Cryptocurrency Market

Bitcoin rightly gets the lion's share of media attention, but it is not alone in the market for cryptocurrencies. The authoritative website CoinMarketCap.com tracks the U.S. dollar price and total "market cap" (price per unit multiplied by number of units outstanding) for each of more than 500 traded cryptocurrencies. Bitcoin is the largest by far. On a recent day (March 9, 2015), the

1 The fourth line is mine. It refers to the news that Washington, D.C. now has a food truck that accepts Bitcoin payments. The first three lines are by Gary Crockett (2014). His original fourth line was: "Bitten bits don't make much of a meal."

Lawrence H. White, "The Market for Cryptocurrencies," *Cato Journal*, vol. 35, no. 2, pp. 383-402.

site showed Bitcoin trading at $291 per unit, with a market cap of $4.05 billion. The second and third largest cryptocurrencies, Ripple and Litecoin, had market caps respectively 8.5 percent and 1.8 percent as large. The entire set of non-Bitcoin cryptocurrencies (known as "altcoins") had a market cap of roughly $619 million, or 15 percent of Bitcoin's. Stated differently, Bitcoin had roughly 87 percent of the market, altcoins 13 percent. In percentage terms, altcoins do a higher share of Bitcoin's business than Bitcoin does of the Federal Reserve Note's business (currently $1.35 trillion in circulation). In trading volume the percentage share of altcoins (led by Litecoin and Ripple) has been similar.

The cryptocurrency market has grown about fourfold in market cap over the last 22 months, with altcoins growing faster than Bitcoin. This is seen by comparing recent data to the oldest snapshot of the CoinMarketCap site available via the Internet Archive "Wayback Machine," which reports data for May 9, 2013. On that date, Bitcoin had a price of $112 per unit, and a market cap of $1.2 billion. The two largest altcoins at that time, Litecoin and Peercoin (aka PPCoin), had market caps respectively 4.7 percent and 0.4 percent as large. Only 13 altcoins were listed. Jointly their market cap was about 6 percent of Bitcoin's, giving Bitcoin 95 percent of the market. Since then, the market share of altcoins has doubled, and their market cap has grown ninefold. Trading volumes then were not reported.

At $4.05 billion, the market cap of Bitcoin, as of March 2015, was slightly smaller than the dollar value of the September 2014 monetary bases of the Lithuanian litas ($5.8 billion) and the Guatemalan quetzal ($5.5 billion), but larger than those of the Costa Rican colon ($3.3 billion) and the Serbia dinar ($3.3 billion).[2] The August 2014 figures from the Central Bank of the Bahamas do not provide the monetary base, but count Bahamian dollar currency in circulation at $210 million, less than two-thirds of Ripple's recent market cap of around $344 million.

Medium of Exchange, Store of Value, and Medium of Remittance Functions

The retail use of Bitcoin as a medium of exchange for goods and services is small to date, but is growing. In December 2014, Microsoft began accepting bitcoin payments "to buy content such as games and videos on Xbox game consoles, add apps and services to Windows phones or to buy Microsoft software" (BBC 2014). In doing so it joined prominent online retailers Overstock, Dell, Expedia, TigerDirect, and Newegg, and the payment processors Paypal and Square. The list grows weekly. Payments processing firms Bitpay, Coinbase,

2 All figures to follow come from official central bank websites, converted to U.S. dollars using the xe.com rates for September 30, 2014.

Coinkite, and others are enabling (and recruiting) brick-and-mortar retail shops to accept Bitcoin from any consumer whose smartphone "Bitcoin wallet" application can display a QR code. On its website Bitpay claims a clientele of "44,000 businesses and organizations"; Coinbase claims 37,000. These processors offer to purchase the consumer's bitcoin as it is spent, paying the equivalent (minus a fee) in dollars or other preferred currency to the merchant. The merchant avoids all exchange rate risk of holding bitcoin. For the retailer on the front end of the transaction, "accepting bitcoin" via these services actually means receiving dollars (or euros, etc.), just like accepting a credit card or debit card does. Bitpay and Coinbase thereby remove the barrier against transacting in cryptocurrency posed by the incumbency advantage of the established domestic currency unit (Luther and White 2014), just as Visa and Mastercard enable merchants to accept credit and debit cards from a customers whose accounts are denominated in a foreign currency.

A potentially vast market for bitcoin and altcoin use is international remittances. For example, workers abroad send an estimated $25 billion per year to the Philippines, where remittances contribute a remarkable 10 percent of national income. The established remittance services Western Union and MoneyGram commonly charge more than 10 percent in fees. Bitcoin remitters, by contrast, are charging only 1 percent. As the CEO of a recently launched bit-coin remittance service remarked to a reporter: "We thought: with Bitcoin we can do it cheaper." A Filipino working in Singapore or Hong Kong (say) doesn't need to have online access or a Bitcoin wallet. The worker can purchase bitcoins at a BTM (bitcoin teller machine), bring the QR code printout to the local "rebittance" provider's office, and the service delivers Philippine pesos as a direct deposit into a designated recipient's account at a participating bank back home or (for an addition fee but still much less than the legacy firms) as cash (Ferraz 2014, Buenaventura 2014).

Market Competition

The market for cryptocurrencies has always been characterized by free entry. A new development in the past two years is competition from profit-seeking enterprises. Free entry is exhibited by the remarkable growth in the number of altcoins, from the 13 listed in May 2013 to the 500_listed in March 2015. Profit-seeking by new entrants is especially conspicuous in systems like Ripple (2nd behind Bitcoin in market cap as of March 9, 2015), BitShares (4th), Nxt (6th), and MaidSafeCoin (8th). In each of these systems a substantial share of "premined" coins was initially held by their developer-entrepreneurs. The entrepreneurs hope to profit by raising the coin's market price through efforts to promote wider use of the coin and its associated proprietary payment network or trading platform, such that they can eventually realize a market value for their coin holdings greater than their expenditures on development and promotion.

Bitcoin, by contrast, was launched by a pseudonymous programmer (or set of programmers) apparently as a public-spirited experiment. Revenue from producing ("mining") new coins, the reward for validating peer-to-peer transfers, is open to anyone with the computing power to participate successfully. While Federal Reserve Bank of Chicago economist François Velde (2013) is thus right to contrast the nonprofit Bitcoin system to the profit-seeking firms that Hayek (1978a) foresaw, the contrast does not apply to the new enterprises that are launching altcoins for profit.[3] In these new altcoin enterprises we see a working embodiment of competitive issue of irredeemable money by profit-seeking private firms. It is no longer correct—if it ever was—to say that Bitcoin is not "operating in a competitive environment." Bitcoin competes with altcoins in the same way that the giant nonprofit YMCA competes with smaller nonprofit and for-profit health clubs, or a large nonprofit hospital competes with smaller nonprofit and for-profit immediate-care clinics.

The Novel Implementation of Quantity Commitments

We should not be too surprised that the features of competing irredeemable privately issued currencies are different from what Hayek (and other economists) imagined, for two reasons. First, market competition is a discovery procedure as Hayek (1978b) elsewhere emphasized, in which successful entrepreneurs discover profit in overlooked or unforeseen ways of producing products and reconfiguring product features. Secondly and more specifically, Hayek imagined that the issuer of a successful irredeemable private currency issuer would retain discretion to vary its quantity. The issuer would promise (but not make any contractual commitment) to maintain a stable purchasing power per unit.[4] A naked promise of that sort unfortunately appears to be time-inconsistent (Taub 1985; White 1989: 382–83; White 1999: ch. 12). An issuer whose promise was believed could reap a large one-time payoff by spending a massive batch of new money into circulation until the public caught on. The one-time profit would exceed the normal rate of return from staying in business. By assumption, there would be no legal recourse against the decline of the money's value.

---

3 Velde also writes that Bitcoin does not "truly embody what Hayek and others in the 'Austrian School of Economics' proposed." But I would distinguish Hayek's *proposal*—to allow free choice and private competition in currency—from his *prediction* about what type of money would then dominate the field.

4 Benjamin Klein (1974), in a more formal model, supposed perfect competition among issuers on "rental price"—that is, the risk-adjusted rate of return to holding money—in an environment of perfect foresight or the equivalent (see White 1999: ch. 12).

Aware of the problem, the public would not believe the promise to begin with, giving the money zero value in equilibrium.

The traditional solution to the problem of giving a privately issued money a reliably positive value is a redemption contract, an enforceable money-back guarantee or *price commitment* (White 1989). Under the gold standard, a banknote was worth $20 when the bank of issue was bound to pay a $20 gold coin for it. Today a bank deposit is worth $100 when the bank is bound to pay $100 in Federal Reserve Notes for it. A suitable medium of redemption has a value that is known and independent of actions by any particular bank of issue.

Ronald Coase (1972) identified an alternative solution to the problem—how an issuer is to bind himself not to run down the price of the thing issued—in the context of a monopolist selling a durable good priced above marginal cost. To get customers to pay $200 for an art print when the marginal cost of producing a duplicate copy is $1, the artist must convince them that she will not run off and sell lower-priced duplicates in the future. To commit herself, the artist produces the print in a numbered edition with a stated maximum ("this print is #45/200"), providing an enforceable *quantity commitment* that she will issue no more than a fixed number of prints. Despite discussing this solution years ago (White 1989), I did not foresee that a quantity commitment could be used in practice to launch a successful irredeemable private currency.[5]

It is this second solution that Bitcoin has creatively introduced to the field of private currency. The implementation uses an entirely new technology: the limit on the number of Bitcoin units in the market is not guaranteed by a contractual promise that can (with some probability) be enforced on an issuing firm, but rather by a limit having been *programmed* into the Bitcoin system's observable source code and being continuously verifiable through a public ledger (the "block chain") that is shared among all "miners" who participate in bitcoin transactions processing.[6] Altcoins employ the same basic idea of a programmed quantity commitment verified through a public ledger, though sometimes implemented in a different way.

Altcoin Innovations

In order to compete with the market leader Bitcoin, the developers of altcoins have understandably emulated its best features (decentralized peer-to-peer exchange, quantity commitment embedded in an open source code, and shared public ledger), while introducing various

5 I believed that redeemable claims to a commodity money would be preferred over any IOU-nothing as a medium of exchange. And perhaps they would be even today, if not for government suppression of the former. For recent examples of suppression, see Dowd (2014: 1–37) and White (2014b).

6 On the mechanics of the Bitcoin system see King, Williams, and Yanofsky (2013), Velde (2013), and Dowd and Hutchinson (2015).

general improvements and customizations. Most of the emphasis has been on improving speed, robustness, and privacy. A few altcoins aim to serve niche constituencies.[7]

The first generation of altcoins are nonprofit projects like Bitcoin, but tweak the Bitcoin code. Litecoin was introduced in October 2011 to provide faster transaction confirmation times (2.5 minutes versus 10 minutes). Peercoin, launched in August 2012, increases the speed even more by using a newer protocol ("proof of stake" rather than Bitcoin's "proof of work") that is less computationally demanding. This protocol also promises to allow participants to share in the rewards from mining without joining mining pools or buying the expensive specialized equipment that it now takes, as the result of competition, to succeed at Bitcoin mining. Because Peercoin's protocol, unlike Bitcoin's, does not promote the merger of miners into ever-larger pools, it is said to be less vulnerable to a possible collusive attack by 51 percent of miners.[8] Primecoin, a later project from Peercoin's main developer, implements a newer proof-of-work protocol (finding prime numbers) to reduce confirmation times to 1 minute.

Darkcoin, a nonprofit project launched in April 2014, and recently renamed Dash, has introduced payment confirmation "within seconds." Dash alters the Bitcoin code to provide greater anonymity to users. Whereas the Bitcoin ledger puts every transaction and transactor address on public view, Dash transactions are "obfuscated." BlackCoin, supported by an active nonprofit foundation and first listed in February 2014, uses a "proof of stake" protocol for speedy verification. It is connected to a proprietary trading platform, BlackHalo, that promises greater user anonymity than other systems. Blackcoin can now be spent (along with Bitcoin and Litecoin) at participating retail shops using the Coinkite debit card.

Ripple, first traded in August 2013, is a cryptocurrency issued by the for-profit enterprise Ripple Labs. It does not rely on a mining protocol. A fixed stock of Ripples was "premined," though the developers have not released them all yet. To make the fixity of the Ripple stock credible, the system follows Bitcoin's lead in having a shared public ledger. The Ripple payment network confirms transactions through a "consensus" protocol that works *much* faster than mining protocols (5 seconds versus 1 to 10 minutes), so has a much better prospect of competing with ordinary credit and debit cards for point-of-sale transactions. The coin is

---

7 While CoinMarketCap.com tracks market caps, the site CoinGecko.com ranks altcoins on a combination of market cap, trading volume, ongoing development activity, and social media buzz. In December 2014 it had Dogecoin at #2 and Darkcoin at #6, each four steps above its market cap ranking, based on their buzz factors. By March 2015 Darkcoin (Dash) had risen to #5 in market cap.

8 On this problem with the Bitcoin protocol, see Dowd and Hutchinson (2015), who predict that it will bring Bitcoin's demise. Whether or not they are right about that, many altcoin developers have recognized the problem and have made deliberate design changes to avoid what Dowd and Hutchinson call "inherent tendencies toward centralization, takeover, and collapse."

only one part of the parent firm's efforts, which include building a wholesale remittance system for "real-time, cross-border payments" between banks, cheaper and faster than the legacy Automated Clearing House system (Liu 2014). Stellar is a non-profit project that emulates Ripple.

BitShares also promises greater anonymity and ease of use. Like Ripple, it is part of a larger for-profit enterprise funded by venture capital. In this case the larger project, according to the BitShares Wiki (http://wiki.bitshares.org/index.php/BitShares), is an "experiment," based on "a business model similar to existing banks or brokerages," to enable the creation and trading of "BitAssets," digital derivative contracts on "the value of anything from dollars, to gold," to exchange-traded equities, bonds, and commodities. The project exemplifies what two *Wall Street Journal* writers (Vigna and Case 2014) describe as "so-called Bitcoin 2.0 technologies—those bitcoin-inspired software applications that bypass financial middlemen and allow almost any asset to be digitized and traded over a decentralized computer network."

The niche-market strategy of CannabisCoin is to offer a payment service for medical marijuana dispensaries and other cannabis retailers whose access to bank accounts and credit cards is currently being blocked by the federal government even where their business has been legalized at the state level. In October 2014, the coin's promoters were seeking retailers willing to provide a specific type of cannabis to patients at one gram per one CannabisCoin. Whether this will lead to the institution of a new commodity money standard remains to be seen, however, as the number of participating retailers and their supplies were quite limited. The promotional effort appears to have helped the market cap of CannabisCoin to surge ahead of other cannabis-themed cryptocoins, such as the earlier-launched Potcoin and the more recent MaryJaneCoin.

Auroracoin is an Iceland-only altcoin introduced in February 2014 for the purpose of helping Icelanders evade the country's exchange controls. (The controls, which included a ban on Bitcoin purchases, were imposed during the financial crisis in October 2008 and are still in place.) Scotcoin, launched by an Edinburgh venture capitalist in May 2014, in advance of Scotland's independence referendum, is likewise a nationally specific enterprise. Its backer has expressed the hope (Hern 2014) that "introducing a voluntary cryptocurrency, which may in the future act as a medium of exchange for the Scottish people, can only benefit them should there be major disruption." A recent entry is CzechCrownCoin, launched October 2014, at least half of which is being distributed to Czech citizens. None of these national coins had a March 2015 market cap above $55,000.

But Aren't They All Just Bubbles?

A quantity commitment solves the problem of making a credible commitment not to overissue. But it has a major shortcoming when applied to currency. Unlike a price commitment, it leaves the market price of the currency to vary with demand. This explains how it is possible for the prices of Bitcoin and other cryptocurrencies to be as volatile as they have recently been (Luther and White 2014). And it explains how it was possible for several altcoins, when enthusiasm for them evaporated, to decline to near-zero market cap.

The collapse of several altcoins is readily evident on CoinMarketCap.com. Three of the earliest thirteen altcoins have declined substantially in market cap. Terracoin, which at its peak had a market cap of $7.1 million, is now (March 2015) down to around $23,000, a decline of more than 99 percent. Freicoin, which peaked at $16.1 million, has fallen to around $61,000, also a decline of more than 99 percent. The whimsically named BBQCoin, having peaked at $7 million, now trades around $21,000, another 99+ percent decline. All three had very sharp run-ups to their peaks in early December 2013, mostly reversed by month's end. Megacoin, first listed in July 2013, experienced the same December 2013 pattern, soaring from $1.2 million on November 23, 2013, to a peak of $47.5 million on December 1, then sliding to around $328,000 today, a decline of more than 99 percent. Later-peaking examples of altcoins suffering 98 percent or greater peak-to-present declines have included Mooncoin, CryptCoin, Scotcoin, Bitgem, and CrtCoin.

Looking only at the market cap charts, the most remarkable case appears to be Auroracoin, which quickly climbed to chart a recorded market cap of $953 million, but is valued today at around $46,000, a drop of more than 99.99 percent. The incredible valuation of nearly $1 billion was, even at the time, a misstatement. The Auroracoin launch plan (Hern 2014) was to jump-start enthusiasm by giving away about 30 premined coins to every Icelandic citizen, for a total of 10 million units. (Such a giveaway is known, in honor of Milton Friedman's famous thought experiment, as a "helicopter drop" or "airdrop.") Dividing the CoinMarketCap.com peak valuation by the price on that day (March 4, 2014) indicates 10 million units in the market, when the number of coins actually available was one-hundredth of that figure (Torpey 2014), the airdrop having yet to be made. Multiplying the price by the actual number of coins, the true market cap was one-hundredth of the reported value, around $9.53 million. A drop from $9.53 million down to the current $46,000, however, is still a 99+ percent drop.

The repeated experience of crashing altcoins, in which the market valuation of a once-popular cryptocurrency all but evaporates, suggests in retrospect that the prices of *those* coins, at least, were simply bubbles. That is, such a coin's demand was unsupported by any price-independent usefulness that would put a floor under its equilibrium market price. (By contrast, industrial and ornamental uses support gold's market value.) To understand the argument, consider again the example of an artist's print. Some print buyers are presumably not just speculators who will put the print in storage and hope for its price to rise, but art-lovers planning to hang it on the wall and enjoy the real aesthetic pleasure it provides. That enjoyment is independent of its price. An irredeemable currency, by contrast, is presumed in standard monetary theory to be held only in order to be later spent or sold. It provides no service that is independent of its market value. People thus presumably have a positive demand price for any irredeemable currency, giving it a positive market value, only to the extent that they expect it to have a future market value. A market valuation anchored by *nothing* but expectations of market valuation is the definition of a bubble.[9]

Does this logic show that the prices of all cryptocurrencies are pure bubbles? No. We cannot rule out that the flourishing cryptocurrencies have some fundamental support.

As several economists have proposed, owning Bitcoin (or other cryptocurrency) may provide a kind of real pleasure to at least some of its holders, say anti-statists who like what it stands for,[10] tech enthusiasts who admire its ingenuity, or its own developers who gladly stake some wealth to help their project succeed (Luther 2013, Murphy 2013, Selgin 2014). For such an individual we can determine his affinity-based demand curve for Bitcoin by positing that he wants to own Bitcoin worth not just any old amount, but rather a specific amount of purchasing power, say 100 real U.S. dollars. (A "real dollar" here means the equivalent in purchasing power to the dollar of a specified base year.) We can plot the individual's demand curve against the real price, i.e. the U.S. dollar price of Bitcoin divided by the dollar price level. The individual's demand curve will be a rectangular hyperbola, a familiar construct in the basic theory of a fiat money's value. The market demand curve sums all the individual demand curves. At a given U.S. dollar price level, if ten thousand individuals want to hold an average of $100 worth of Bitcoin each, just because Bitcoin is cool, then the market cap of Bitcoin must be at least $1 million.

This account does not explain day-to-day variations in the market price of Bitcoin, but it does potentially explain why the price is above zero. In this way real affinity demand provides an answer to economist-blogger Brad DeLong's (2013) rhetorical question: "Placing a floor on the value of bitcoins is ... what, exactly?" Of course, if Bitcoin were to become completely uncool to *everyone*, the floor would vanish.[11]

---

9 The same argument applies to any fiat money, to the extent that its market value exceeds whatever floor value it has due to exclusive tax receivability or other government compulsion. No cryptocurrency has *that* kind of support.

10 A pseudonymous commenter on the reddit CryptoMarket page (Pogeymanz 2014) writes about Darkcoin: "I have some DRK because I like what it stands for."

11 DeLong (2013) also writes: "Placing a ceiling on the value of bitcoins is computer technology and the form of the hash function ... until the limit of 21 million bitcoins is reached." Actually, of course, Bitcoin's source

I previously (White 2014a) too hastily rejected this argument as an explanation of how Bitcoin first achieved a positive market price, on the grounds that it "does not deliver what the argument requires, namely, an account of how Bitcoins initially had a positive value *apart from their actual or prospective use as medium of exchange*. The value at every point in this scenario derives entirely from use or prospective use as a medium of exchange (only such use as a dollar competitor is what might [provide aesthetic pleasure], not the existence of untraded digital character strings)." I was mistaken to think that the argument has such a requirement. A positive affinity valuation of a cryptocurrency may well require the *possibility* of its taking off as a nonstate money, but that does not imply a chicken-or-egg problem. Affinity demand and hence market value can be positive before actual medium-of-exchange use begins.

The affinity account has the additional merit of being consistent with the great market cap of Bitcoin, esteemed for being the first mover, the middling market cap of altcoins that embody valuable technical improvements and have active support communities, and the low market cap of me-too altcoins. Five hundred altcoins are not all making a statement or breaking new technical ground. They have positive market caps, but most of them are slight.

A second grounding for fundamental value lies in the real demand for the sorts of payment services offered by a cryptocurrency. Ownership of a particular brand of cryptocurrency units is needed to make use of the brand's payment system, which may offer advantages over other systems (Tucker 2014).

With regard to the "bubble" element in cryptocurrency valuation, economist-blogger Stephen Williamson (2011) reminds us that official fiat money or a commodity money likewise trades well above its fundamental value. In a case where the surplus of a currency asset's market value over its fundamental value results from its solving a medium-of-exchange coordination problem, that surplus is a good thing because it represents value-added:

> Bubbles can be good things, as any asset which is used widely in exchange will trade at a price higher than its "fundamental," and the asset's liquidity premium—the difference between the actual price and the fundamental—is a measure of the asset's social contribution as a medium of exchange.

---

code does not put a ceiling on the market cap or *value* of bitcoins, only a limit on the *quantity*. The conceptual ceiling on *value* is Bitcoin achieving a 100 percent share of the real value of all money balances in the world (Luther and White 2014).

I would, however, qualify this claim by saying that the difference is a reliable measure of social contribution only insofar as it arises through voluntary trade rather than legal compulsion, and only after we subtract the costs of generating and maintaining the asset in question. It is from by adding such value that Ripple's entrepreneurs hope to profit. Unlike an official fiat currency, no part of Ripple's valuation is based on legal compulsion.

Is There a Problem of Monopoly? Is There Too Much Competition?

Milton Friedman (1960: 8) wrote of "the technical monopoly character of a pure fiduciary currency which makes essential the setting of some external limit on its amount." By "pure fiduciary currency" he meant an irredeemable or fiat currency. By "technical monopoly character" he meant that open entry into counterfeiting would drive the value of an irredeemable paper currency note down to the cost of paper and ink,[12] and all the way down to zero if ever-higher denominations could be introduced at no higher cost. Therefore, a single authorized issuer was needed to preserve the currency's value. As Benjamin Klein (1974) pointed out, however, Friedman here conflated monopoly with enforcement of trademarks. To ban the selling of knock-off perfume in bottles bearing a counterfeit Chanel trademark does not imply giving Chanel a monopoly except in the sale of Chanel-branded perfume. It does not require any restriction on the production of competing perfumes under different trademarks. Enforcing a ban on the counterfeiting of Federal Reserve Notes, or in other words having the Secret Service protect the Federal Reserve's trademark, does not require giving the Fed a monopoly on currency issue.

The counterfeiting of bitcoins (also known as the problem of "double spending") is prevented not through police work and legal prosecution by any central authority, but quite elegantly by the decentralized verification process that prevents the transfer of any coin of unattested provenance from being accepted onto the public ledger. With such effective de facto counterfeiting protection, the quantity of bitcoins remains on its programmed path.

Velde (2013) states that Bitcoin has "a status of quasi-monopoly in the realm of digital currencies by virtue of its first-mover advantage." By "quasi-monopoly status" he may mean only that Bitcoin has a large market share, derived from its being the first mover into (that is, creating) the market. But such a status is distinct from the usual concept of natural monopoly (or quasi-monopoly) status due to economies of scale, which denotes the ability

12 For a real-world example of this happening, see Luther (2012).

to serve every (or nearly every) part of the market at lower marginal cost than competitors. The main static danger of a monopoly in the usual sense, whether natural or state-granted, is that the monopolist firm may restrict output to raise price above marginal cost, thwarting efficiency by sacrificing potential gains from trade. Because the quantity of bitcoin is predetermined by a program and not manipulable by a discretionary issuer, it poses no danger of any such monopolistic output restriction.

Competition from new entrants surrounds Bitcoin. The new entrants have the advantage of being able to introduce altcoins with improved features while the Bitcoin code was written five-plus years ago. The Bitcoin community can at most agree to patch the code, not to fundamentally revise it. Bitcoin does have the largest established network, but a dominant proprietary network does not imply monopoly pricing (in this context, transaction fees above marginal cost) when the market is contestable. Ripple, Litecoin, BitShares, and others entrants are vigorously contesting the market. The cryptocurrency market exhibits Schumpeterian competition from new business models rather than only static price competition.

DeLong (2013) raises an issue that is the opposite of monopolistic restriction. He worries that competition from more and more altcoins may expand the total quantity of cryptocoins without limit, and thereby—unless Bitcoin "can somehow successfully differentiate itself from the latecomers"—drive the market value of Bitcoin and all other cryptocurrencies to zero. He writes: "the money supply of BitCoin-like things is infinite because the cost of production of them is infinitesimal." To consider this possibility let us suppose, for the sake of argument, that the cost of introducing a me-too altcoin is indeed infinitesimal. The economic implication is that in a fully arbitraged equilibrium the marginal altcoin will have an infinitesimal real value (which is an approximate description of the marginal altcoins we do in fact observe). But this is not to say that the value of bitcoins (or of established altcoins) will tend toward zero. Infinitesimally valued altcoins do not eat into Bitcoin's market share in real terms. Only valued altcoins can do that, as they have since May 2013 (reducing Bitcoin's share to 87 percent from 95 percent as noted; but at the same time Bitcoin's market cap in U.S. dollars grew more than three-fold).

In the foreign exchange market for government fiat monies with flexible exchange rates, hyper-expansion in the nominal supply of dollar-like things, say Zimbabwe dollars or Venezuelan bolivars, does not drag down the purchasing power of the U.S. dollar. Likewise, in the existing altcoin market with its completely flexible exchange rates, cheap altcoins simply have low exchange value against Bitcoin and do not drag down Bitcoin's real market value.

Cryptocurrency and Fiat Currency: Comparisons and Contrasts

DeLong likens Bitcoin to government fiat money in the following way: "Bitcoin is like fiat money, and unlike 18th and 19th century Yap stone money, in that its cost of production is zero." In fact, although Bitcoin is similar to a government fiat money (and unlike gold) on the demand side, in that nothing supports its price if transaction and other money-related demand for it goes to zero, it is absolutely *unlike* a government fiat money on the supply side. It does not have an indefinitely expandable supply but the opposite. Just as monopolistic under-supply is ruled out (see above), so too is hyper-expansion. Bitcoin has a verifiably programmed commitment to a pre-specified quantity path.[13] In light of that commitment, the cost of production beyond the scheduled quantity is extremely high, not zero.[14]

Noting that "improvements, bug fixes, and repairs" to the Bitcoin code have been "carried out by the community of bitcoin users, dominated by a small set of programmers," Velde (2013) downplays the prospects for Bitcoin to rival the fiat U.S. dollar:

> Although some of the enthusiasm for bitcoin is driven by a distrust of state-issued currency, it is hard to imagine a world where the main currency is based on an extremely complex code understood by only a few, and controlled by even fewer, without accountability, arbitration, or recourse.

Substitute the phrase "bureaucratic agency" for the word "code" in this statement, however, and the hard-to-imagine world becomes a fair description of our current world of Federal Reserve currency. This fact completely overturns Velde's argument. If the prospects for Bitcoin against the dollar depended only on the public's choice between trusting an open source code with a public ledger and trusting a byzantine central bank, the prospects would look extremely good.

Bitcoin as a Vehicle Currency and Unit of Account

Finally, Bitcoin has an interesting role that is often overlooked or denied. A recent paper by a team of Bank of England economists (Ali et al. 2014), for example, declares that

---

13 Blogger Charlie Stross (2014) colorfully comments that Bitcoin "wears a gimp suit and a ball gag, padlocked into permanent deflation and with the rate of issue of new 'notes' governed by the law of algorithmic complexity." That padlocked "gimp suit and ball gag" is Bitcoin's binding quantity commitment. It is a feature, not a bug.

14 In light of its programmed production limit, Selgin (2013) calls Bitcoin a "synthetic commodity money." He helpfully likens Bitcoin's quantity commitment to the quantity commitment of an artist who publicly destroys the engraved plates from which a known number of lithographic prints have been made.

cryptocurrencies "are not typically used as media of exchange" and "there is little evidence of digital currencies being used as units of account." In fact Bitcoin is the vehicle currency (commonly accepted medium of exchange), and consequently is the unit of account, in most altcoin markets. With a few exceptions (Litecoin against U.S. dollar, Chinese yuan, and euro; Chinese exchanges where altcoins trade against yuan; Peercoin against dollar), the vast majority of altcoin exchanges trade and quote prices in bitcoins, not in dollars, euros, or yuan.[15]

The altcoin market is structured this way for the same reason that the U.S. dollar is the vehicle currency for foreign exchange transactions (Kreuger 2012). To trade (say) Australian dollars for British pounds, the standard route is AUD for USD, then USD for GBP. Thicker markets enjoy lower bid-ask spreads. The U.S. dollar currency markets are so much larger than others that for most almost all currency pairs that do not include the U.S. dollar (euro-yen is an exception) the sum of bid-ask spreads is less for indirect exchange via the U.S. dollar than for direct exchange. This pattern is self-reinforcing by bringing more volume to the U.S. dollar markets.[16] Most non-USD to non-USD foreign exchange markets are missing.

The Bitcoin-U.S. dollar market has much more volume and thus much lower spreads than any altcoin-U.S. dollar market. To trade U.S. dollars for an altcoin, often the *only* route in practice is to trade U.S. dollars for Bitcoin, and then Bitcoin for the altcoin. Most altcoin-dollar markets are missing because volume would be too low to have attractive bid-ask spreads. With by far the thickest potential markets against any altcoin, even compared to U.S. dollars, Bitcoin is naturally the vehicle currency and thus the unit of account in altcoin markets.

Policy Implications

The market for cryptocurrencies is still evolving, and (to most economists) is full of surprises. Policymakers should therefore be very humble about the prospects for improving economic welfare by restricting the market. Israel Kirzner's (1985) warning about the perils of regulation strongly applies here: Interventions that block or divert the path of entrepreneurial discovery will prevent the realization of potential breakthroughs such that we will never know what we are missing.

15 See http://www.cryptocoincharts.info/main/priceBoxes.

16 The positive network effect that makes the U.S. dollar the common medium for inter-currency exchange echoes the self-reinforcing Mengerian process by which a common medium for inter-commodity exchange (money) emerged out of barter.

References

Ali, R.; Barrdear, J.; Clews, R.; and Southgate, J. (2014) "The Economics of Digital Currencies." Bank of England *Quarterly Bulletin* (Q3): 1–11.

BBC (2014) "Microsoft to Accept Payments made in Bitcoins" (11 December): www.bbc.com/news/technology-30377654.

Buenaventura, L. (2014) "The Rise of Rebittance: Reinventing Money Transfers in the Philippines with Bitcoin." *The Next Web* weblog (28 September): http://thenextweb.com/insider/2014/09/28/rise-rebittance-reinventing-money-transfers-philippines-bitcoin.

Coase, R. (1972) "Durability and Monopoly." *Journal of Law and Economics* 25 (April): 143–49.

Crockett, G. (2014) "Bitcoin Is Seen as an Ephemeral Currency." *Washington Post* Style Invitational Contest, Week 1062: Poems from the headlines (27 April): www.washingtonpost.com/entertainment/style-invitational-week-1069-big-thoughts-little-words-plus-more-from-recent-contests/2014/04/16/f556bf74-c331-11e3-b574-f87488871856a_story.html.

DeLong, B. (2013) "Watching Bitcoin, Dogecoin, Etc." *Equitable Growth* weblog (28 December): http://equitablegrowth.org/2013/12/28/watching-bitcoin-dogecoin-etc.

Dowd, K. (2014) *New Private Monies: A Bit-Part Player?* London: Institute of Economic Affairs.

Dowd, K., and Hutchinson, M. (2015) "Bitcoin Will Bite the Dust." *Cato Journal* 35 (2): 357–382.

Ferraz, E. (2014) "Send Home Your Wages Using Bitcoin and Avoid Hefty Money Transfer Fees? That's Now a Reality." *Tech in Asia* (3 July): www.techinasia.com/send-home-wages-bitcoin-avoid-hefty-money-transfer-fees-reality.

Friedman, M. (1960) *A Program for Monetary Stability*. New York: Fordham University Press.

Hayek, F. A. (1978a) *The Denationalisation of Money*, 2nd ed. London: Institute of Economic Affairs.

__________ (1978b) "Competition as a Discovery Procedure." In Hayek, *New Studies in Philosophy, Politics, Economics, and the History of Ideas*. London: Routledge.

Hern, A. (2014) "Bitcoin Goes National with Scotcoin and Auroracoin." *The Guardian* (25 March): www.theguardian.com/technology/2014/mar/25/bitcoin-goes-national-with-scotcoin-auroracoin.

King, R. S.; Williams, S.; and Yanofsky, D. (2013) "By Reading This Article, You're Mining Bitcoins." *Quartz* webzine (17 December); http://qz.com/154877/by-reading-this-page-you-are-mining-bit-coins.

Kirzner, I. M. (1985) "The Perils of Regulation: A Market-Process Approach." In Kirzner, *Discovery and the Capitalist Process*, 119–49. Chicago: University of Chicago Press.

Klein, B. (1974) "The Competitive Supply of Money." *Journal of Money, Credit, and Banking* 6 (November): 423–53.

Krueger, M. (2012) "Money: A Market Microstructure Approach." *Journal of Money, Credit and Banking* 44 (September): 1245–58.

Liu, A. (2014) "Ripple Labs Signs First Two US Banks." *Rippleblog* weblog (24 September): https://ripple.com/blog/ripple-labs-signs-first-two-us-banks.

Luther, W. J. (2012) "The Monetary Mechanism of Stateless Somalia." Kenyon College Working Paper, http://papers.ssrn.com/sol3/papers.cfm?abstract_id=2047494.

———— (2013) "Cryptocurrencies, Network Effects, and Switching Costs." Mercatus Center Working Paper No. 13–17, http://papers.ssrn.com/sol3/papers.cfm?abstract_id=2295134.

Luther, W. J., and White, L. H. (2014) "Can Bitcoin Become a Major Currency?" *Cayman Financial Review* (August): www.compass-cayman.com/cfr/2014/08/08/Can-bitcoin-become-a-major-currency.

Murphy, R. P. (2013) "The Economics of Bitcoin." *Library of Economics and Liberty* (3 June): www.econlib.org/library /Columns/y2013/Murphybitcoin.html.

Pogeymanz (2014) Comment in the Thread "Darkcoin Is Going to Be a Behemoth," www.reddit.com/r/CryptoMarkets/comments/20t9nc/darkcoin_is_going_to_be_a_behemoth.

Selgin, G. (2013) "Synthetic Commodity Money." University of Georgia Working Paper, http://papers.ssrn.com/sol3/papers.cfm?abstract_id=2000118.

———— (2014) "Mises Was Lukewarm on Free Banking." *Liberty Matters* (January): http://oll.libertyfund.org/pages/misestmc.

Stross, C. (2014) "Schadenfreude." *Charlie's Diary* weblog (25 February): http://www.antipope.org/charlie/blog-static/2014/02 /schadenfreude-1.html.

Taub, B. (1985) "Private Fiat Money with Many Suppliers." *Journal of Monetary Economics* 16 (September): 195–208.

Torpey, K. (2014) "Auroracoin's Market Cap Is Highly Inflated." *Cryptocoins News* (4 March): www.cryptocoinsnews.com/aurora-coins-market-cap-highly-inflated.

Tucker, J. (2014) "What Gave Bitcoin Its Value?" *The Freeman* (27 August): http://fee.org/the_freeman/detail/what-gave-bitcoin-its-value.

Velde, F. R. (2013) "Bitcoin: A Primer." *Chicago Fed Letter* 317 (December): www.chicagofed.org/digital_assets/publications/chicago_fed_letter/2013/cfldecember2013_317.pdf.

Vigna, P., and Case, M. J. (2014) "BitBeat: Ratings Firm Coinist Tackles Trust Problem with Bitcoin 2.0 Projects." *Wall Street Journal MoneyBeat* weblog (12 August): http://blogs.wsj.com/moneybeat/2014/08/12/bitbeat-ratings-firm-coinist-tackles-trust-problem-with-bitcoin-2-0-projects.

White, L. H. (1989) "What Kinds of Monetary Institutions Would a Free Market Deliver?" *Cato Journal* 9 (Fall): 367–91.

———— (1999) *The Theory of Monetary Institutions*. Oxford: Basil Blackwell.

(2014a) "Ludwig von Mises's The Theory of Money and Credit at 101." *Liberty Matters* (January): http://oll.libertyfund.org/pages/misestmc.

———— (2014b) "The Troubling Suppression of Competition from Alternative Monies." *Cato Journal* 34 (Spring/Summer): 181–201.

Williamson, S. (2011) "Bitcoin." *New Monetarist Economics* weblog (24 June): http://newmonetarism.blogspot.com/2011/06/bitcoin.html.

Reading 10

An Introduction to Blockchain

George (Yiorgos) Allayannis and Aaron Fernstrom

I love this stuff—Bitcoin, blockchain technology—and what the future holds ... huge new markets and products will be built on these platforms.

Abby Johnson, CEO of Fidelity[1]

Introduction

For more than 7,000 years, humankind has used ledgers (see Exhibit 1 for a glossary) to record economic transactions.[2] Clay tablets in ancient Mesopotamia recorded simple purchases and sales of basic goods, growth of herd sizes, and so on.[3] Even the concept of counting was impacted[4] by developments of ledger keeping in antiquity. Maintaining a record of transactions appears to be a common denominator of all human life.

The world has come a long way since clay tablets. Modern computing has transformed basic financial ledgers into lightning-fast, highly automated, and precisely accurate relational databases (Exhibit 1). Today, as cybersecurity and transparency emerge as paramount priorities during a digital transaction, blockchain has the potential to be the next generational improvement in how parties record the exchange of value.

However, while commercial enterprise has moved from pen-and-ink ledger keeping to digital databases, it appears unclear whether there will be widespread adoption of blockchain technology.[5] This may be in part due to a lack of understanding of the technology and an opaque regulatory

---

1 Joe Morris, "Abby Johnson: 'I Love Bitcoin'," *Ignites*, May 24, 2017.

2 George T. Friedlob and Franklin J. Plewa, *Understanding Balance Sheets*, New York: John Wiley, 1996; Beverley Milton-Edwards, "Iraq, Past, Present and Future: A Thoroughly-Modern Mandate?" History & Policy, May 8, 2003.

3 Friedlob and Plewa, *Understanding Balance Sheets*.

4 Keith Robson, "Accounting Numbers as 'Inscription': Action at a Distance and the Development of Accounting," *Accounting, Organizations and Society* 17, no. 7 (1992): 685–708.

5 "Blockchain Reaches beyond Financial Services with Some Industries Moving Faster," Deloitte, December 13, 2016.

environment.[6] Recent qualitative surveys across senior executives in different industries revealed that, while many believe the impact of blockchain will be profound, nearly 40% have little or no knowledge of what it is.[7]

This note introduces blockchain, its potential uses and limitations, and includes additional considerations for current and future leaders in financial services.

What is Blockchain?

In its most abstract sense, blockchain is a new platform technology enabling an improved ability to verify and record the exchange of value among an interconnected set of users; it is a secure and transparent way to track the ownership of assets before, during, and after any transaction. Each transaction between parties in the network is a "block," and the cumulative set of transactions across the entire network is the "chain:" blockchain.

> Blockchain technology enables any network of users to track and trade virtually anything of value.

Broadly speaking, there are currently two types of blockchains: public and private. The Bitcoin blockchain is an example of a public—or "permissionless"—blockchain (**Exhibit 1**). These networks—these blockchains—are open to anyone, and each use their own digital, native currencies (**Exhibit 1**), for example, Bitcoin and Ethereum. These native currencies are the required mediums of exchange for using public blockchains to exchange value. Public blockchains allow for unlimited, anonymous or pseudonymous participation. On public blockchains, native currencies are needed for two reasons: (1) to compensate network members who verify their transactions (called "miners"), and (2) given the anonymous or pseudonymous nature of network members, it is the medium required to claim an underlying asset from its issuer.

Exhibit 2 represents a simple example of trading assets using a digital currency on a public blockchain: using bitcoin to pay monthly rent for an apartment. To trade and claim the underlying assets, in this example, rent in U.S. dollars and an apartment to live in for one month, the property owner and tenant both exchange their assets using Bitcoin as the common currency. From the perspective of the tenant, the benefits include permanence

---

6 "Blockchain Reaches beyond Financial Services;" Stan Higgins, "New York Reveals BitLicense Framework for Bitcoin Businesses," CoinDesk, July 17, 2014.

7 "Blockchain Reaches beyond Financial Services."

and tamper-resistance of the record of transaction (i.e., it is auditable), increased security (e.g., checks can be lost in the mail, destroyed or counterfeited), and increased privacy (e.g., a stranger would not be able to see the routing number and account number on the checks). See the bulleted list below for a more complete list of blockchain transaction benefits. From the perspective of the property owner, though, the **Exhibit 2** transaction may bring unwanted exchange rate risk. The price of Bitcoin is highly volatile (**Exhibit 3**), and it may decrease in value versus the U.S. dollar in the time it takes to exchange Bitcoins for dollars, which has also been historically volatile (**Exhibit 4**). Additionally, there is a fee miners require to verify transactions, which is also volatile (**Exhibit 5**). It is worthwhile to consider whether these benefits and challenges will benefit certain types of digital currency transactions and hinder others.

A private—or "enterprise" or "permissioned"—blockchain (**Exhibit 1**) also records the exchange of value between parties in a network, but access to the network is permissioned because not everyone can join it. Private (i.e., enterprise) and public blockchains are not mutually exclusive either. In practice, and in general, organizations that are piloting proof-of-concept blockchain projects can build on public blockchain infrastructure and design additional bespoke, internally developed technology in order to use it for their own private network's purposes. JPMorgan Chase's Quorum is an archetypical example of this for financial institutions.[8]

In general, while specific applications of blockchain technology are still developing, there appears to be consensus[9] that enterprise blockchains have the following benefits versus legacy ledger technologies:

- Consistent. A blockchain records a history of all transactions within it, and all users in the network have an identical copy of the record/ledger.

---

8 As of August 13, 2017, JP Morgan Chase offered an enterprise blockchain platform called Quorum, specifically for and marketed to financial institutions.

9 Morris; "Blockchain Reaches beyond Financial Services;" "Simple Introduction to Smart Contracts on a Blockchain," YouTube video, 5:07, uploaded by "Chainthat," December 6, 2015, https://www.youtube.com/watch?v=FkeLDPZ-v8g (accessed Aug. 31, 2017); Matthew Hancock and Ed Vaizey, "Distributed Ledger Technology: Beyond Block Chain. A Report by the UK Government Chief Scientific Adviser," UK Government Chief Scientific Adviser, January 19, 2016; "The Blockchain Practice," Deloitte UK, 2017; Christian Cachin, "Blockchain, Cryptography, and Consensus," IBM (Zurich), October 2016; "Blockchain Innovation in Wealth and Asset Management," EY, 2017; Accenture Digital, "Blockchain Technology. How Banks Are Building a Real Time Global Payment Network;" Accenture, 2016; Matt Higginson, "How Blockchain Could Disrupt Cross-Border Payments," The Clearing House, 2017; "Leading Global Transaction Banks Kick off Blockchain Proof of Concept with SWIFT Gpi," SWIFT, April 25, 2017; He Dong, "Fintech and Financial Services: Initial Considerations. Staff Discussion Notes," IMF, June 19, 2017; and Lucy Burton, "Bank of England Trials Artificial Intelligence and Blockchain in Bid to Stay Ahead of the Pack," *Telegraph*, March 17, 2017.

- Democratic. The network using the blockchain agrees on and governs the rules for its use.
- Secure and accurate. Cryptography (ref. Glossary) protects all data and information, and the use of digital keys and digital signatures is required to access data in the ledger.
- Segmented and private. Based on pre-defined rules, users' digital keys and digital signatures (**Exhibit 1**) can access the entire ledger, a particular transaction, a set of transactions, and so forth.
- Permanent and tamper resistant. The ledger does not require a centralized point of control (**Exhibit 1**), and the details of all recorded transactions cannot be altered retroactively without the full agreement of the network.
- Quickly updated. The ledger reflects any changes (e.g., a new transaction) in near real time, every user's copy within the network reflects these changes in the same time frame, and records of transactions can be maintained and updated securely by the users themselves.
- Intelligent. Blockchain enables the creation of "smart contracts" (**Exhibit 1**).

These benefits enable the development of many potential products and applications for industry.

What Blockchain Can Do

With an understanding of the potential benefits of blockchain, we can now begin to develop visibility into possible ways to deploy blockchain technology. In practice today, it appears that most current blockchain products and applications fall into three buckets: (1) the clearing, payments, and settlement functions in financial services companies (e.g., banks, asset managers), (2) creation and use of a digital identity within an enterprise, and (3) smart contracts. Before exploring applications, though, we need to understand digital identities and smart contracts.

Blockchain enables the creation of a secure, private and tamper-resistant "single source of truth" for each customer within an enterprise—a customer's digital identity. Digital identities have the potential to affect the customer onboarding process, which can be cumbersome and time consuming. Recall the last time you bought insurance, opened a checking or savings account, opened an account at a brokerage or investment firm, or applied for a mortgage or a bank loan. We refer to this broadly as customer onboarding. The purpose of customer onboarding is to provide personal information and verify your identity to an enterprise, and for the enterprise to meet compliance requirements for onboarding new customers (e.g., know your customer [KYC] and antimony laundering [AML]). Customer onboarding has the potential to be a cumbersome process for both the customer and the enterprise and can include waiting in line, holding on the phone, meeting face-to-face with an agent or salesperson, signing many documents, filling out long forms, sending documents back and forth, making deposits, or paying premiums, and so forth. Using a diversified financial institution as an example, a customer who has checking and savings products, investment management products, and a mortgage all within that same enterprise more than likely had to do an onboarding process for each one of these products even though these products exist within the same enterprise ... and even though the individual was already a customer.

Referencing the benefits of blockchain from the previous section, the digital identity is:

- Consistent: the record is the same across the organization(s);
- Secure, accurate, and private: only those with the necessary digital keys can access the record;
- Tamper-resistant: others in the network cannot alter the record; and
- Quickly updated: everyone that has access to a customer's digital identity receives any updates the customer makes to their record immediately (e.g., mortgage broker, consumer banker, investment manager, insurance agent).

Smart contracts[10] are a type of blockchain transaction that can be thought of as event-triggered automated pieces of computer code. They can be as simple as "ship the product when we receive the payment" or "distribute dividends to shareholders upon their declaration." All smart contract transactions are stored on a blockchain, which provides both an audit trail (ref. Glossary) of events and assurance of fulfillment of contract terms. Further, if any party/user fails or does not fulfill their obligation, the blockchain continues to function with no loss of data or integrity.[11]

Including digital identity and smart contract applications, the following are examples of possible ways for asset managers to use blockchain technology in a product or application:[12]

---

10 https://www.youtube.com/watch?v=FkeLDPZ-v8g.

11 Hancock and Vaziey.

12 Morris; "Blockchain Reaches beyond Financial Services;" https://www.youtube.com/watch?v=FkeLDPZ-v8g; Hancock and Vaizey; "Distributed Ledger Technology;" "The Blockchain Practice;" Cachin; "Blockchain Innovation in Wealth and Asset Management;" Accenture Digital; Higginson; "Blockchain Proof of Concept with SWIFT Gpi;" Dong; and Burton.

- Client onboarding
- Management of model portfolios
- Trade order generation
- Voting of any kind (e.g., proxy)
- Regulatory reporting
- Dividend distribution
- Clearing and settling securities transactions
- Real asset transactions (e.g., property)
- Cross border payments
- Data storage
- Compliance reporting (e.g., KYC)
- Contracts (e.g., rollovers, estates)

Potential blockchain applications touch other industries, too. There are also potential applications across enterprises in CPG, government, and technology industries:[13]

- Customer loyalty programs
- Tax collection/payment
- Medical recordkeeping
- Customer payments
- Supply chain management
- Government benefit distribution
- Passport and customs controls
- Inventory controls

Many of the applications listed above are expected to reduce many forms of operational waste. While the quantifiable impacts remain unproven given the stage of implementation of blockchain technology industry-wide, financial services institutions specifically expect blockchain to yield benefits in the following areas in the short term:[14]

- Intrabank cross border payments
- Cross border remittances
- Interbank cross border transactions
- Corporate payments
- Cross border payments

---

13 "Blockchain Reaches beyond Financial Services;" Cachin; "Blockchain Innovation in Wealth and Asset Management."

14 Accenture Digital.

- Person-to-person transactions

Financial services institutions expect these benefits to accrue due to:[15]

- Lower transaction costs
- Fewer errors and exceptions
- Lower administrative costs
- Lower capital costs
- Shorter settlement times

Blockchain has the potential to deliver cost savings to financial services institutions, better customer experiences, and more seamless interactions between enterprises and customers—as well as capturing the benefits of blockchain listed in the previous section.

Use Case Example: Cross Border Payments

Whether it is at the household level or between *Fortune* 100 enterprises, sending payments across a border is, at present, a highly intermediated, cumbersome, somewhat opaque, costly, and slow process. Global financial services institutions with retail bank businesses appear particularly interested in using blockchain to simplify, hasten, and reduce the cost of cross border payments.[16] For the sake of illustration, **Exhibit 6** is a simplified description of how blockchain can potentially improve a straightforward cross border payment.

Sender wants to send money to receiver, and sender and receiver are in different countries using different currencies. Sender goes to their bank (or the bank's website) and initiates the transfer. Sender and receiver's banks then work with networks of domestic and cross border banks, each of which add incremental cost and additional processing time. Fees that sender's bank are charged during the transfer are not always known at its initiation, and it is not always clear when costs will also be charged to receiver.[17] Fees are high, too, running an average of 2% to 3% when volumes of payments and payment values are high, and can exceed 10% if they are low. Sender and receiver are not typically able to track the transfer while it is taking place, either, creating additional uncertainty regarding delivery and final payment amount; as of 2015, the average time to complete a cross border payment was from three to five business days. Finally, total pricing, fees, and foreign exchange rates for the cross border payment are not actually finalized until the funds arrive in the receiver's account.

---

15 Accenture Digital.

16 Hancock and Vaizey; "The Blockchain Practice;" Cachin; Accenture Digital; Higginson; "Blockchain Proof of Concept with SWIFT Gpi."

17 The remainder of this paragraph is drawn from Higginson.

In this case, if global financial services companies with retail and/or commercial banking businesses set up an enterprise blockchain, this cross border payment could occur in near real time, require no additional intermediaries other than the sender and receiver's banks (i.e., no third parties are needed to verify transactions), and cost a negligible fee (**Exhibit 7**). Additionally, in this case, foreign exchange providers could compete to offer the lowest rate to these global financial institutions for these transactions, and banks in the network could search for and select the best rate offered in the market. Additionally, the transaction would be secure, private, and verifiable. This could potentially both drive cost savings for the banks as well as the customers and immediately improve the customer experience.

There is evidence that global financial services companies have come to the realization that blockchain technology can be applied to cross border payments. Some of the largest banks in the world, including the Bank of England,[18] are currently piloting applications like this,[19] and the IMF is evaluating it independently for this purpose as well.[20]

But ... Is What We Have Already Good Enough?

There appears to be a lot of interest in blockchain across diverse industries,[21] and industry-leading technology companies and financial institutions have deployed teams of experts to work on how to use it.[22] There also appears to be a consensus that blockchain offers a host of new features and benefits versus legacy methods for exchanging value.[23]

Does this mean companies should invest in developing blockchain-driven products or applications? Some experts are skeptical that blockchain technology will find a broader home in industry.[24] The basic argument against investing in a blockchain project appears to be that financial ledgers can be easily expressed as tables (i.e., relational databases), and current best-in-class database tools are more proven tools that are typically sufficient for many needs. More precisely, as Gideon Greenspan argues:

> If your requirements are fulfilled by today's relational databases, you'd be insane to use a blockchain. Why? Because products like Oracle have decades

18 Burton.
19 "Blockchain Proof of Concept with SWIFT Gpi."
20 Dong.
21 "Blockchain Reaches beyond Financial Services."
22 "Linux Foundation Unites Industry Leaders to Advance Blockchain Technology," Linux Foundation, December 17, 2015.
23 "Blockchain Reaches beyond Financial Services;" Cachin; Accenture Digital; "Linux Foundation Unites Industry Leaders."
24 Gideon Greenspan, "Avoiding the Pointless Blockchain Project," LinkedIn, November 24, 2015.

> of development behind them. They have been deployed on millions of servers running trillions of queries. They contain some of the most thoroughly tested, debugged and optimized code on the planet, processing thousands of transactions per second without breaking a sweat ... [Blockchain] is still in its diapers.[25]

Bill Gates wrote in his 1995 book *The Road Ahead*, "We always overestimate the change that will occur in the next two years and underestimate the change that will occur in the next ten."[26] Applying that concept to blockchain invites reflection regarding whether or not relational databases will be sufficient today but blockchain might be preferred tomorrow.

An Introduction to Network Effects[27]

All other things being equal, blockchain technology becomes more valuable as more people use it to do different things. However, while many large, multinational organizations have carefully studied blockchain and its possible uses, there does not appear to be unified agreement regarding blockchain usage and deployment. Why? The answer may be in that blockchain is a "network effect" technology. A network effect describes anything that becomes more valuable to its users as more users use it.

There are several types of networks, and each has a corresponding valuation concept that help explain their value relative to one another. The most straightforward example of the most basic network type is the broadcast, for example, when a group of people consumes the same material at the same time broadcast from a single source. In a broadcast network, none of the viewers are connected with one another and the connection is unidirectional (i.e., information flows in one direction). From a valuation perspective, it has been suggested that the value of a broadcast network is described by Sarnoff's Law,[28] which says that the value of this type of network is proportional to the number of viewers, or N.

A step beyond the broadcast network is the homogenous network, in which the same type of user uses a platform or product for a similar purpose. A good example of this type of network is Skype (**Exhibit 8**). To illustrate the value of a network effect within a homogenous network, Skype has more limited value if only two people use it to call each other, but

---

25 Greenspan.

26 Bill Gates, Nathan Myhrvold, and Peter Rinearson, *The Road Ahead* (New York: Viking, 1995).

27 Richard Johnson, Paul Farris, and Paul Pfeifer, "The Value of Networks," UVA-M-0645 (Charlottesville, VA: Darden Business Publishing, 2001); Anu Hariharan, et al., "All about Network Effects," Andreessen Horowitz, March 26, 2017, https://a16z.com/2016/03/07/all-about-network-effects/ (accessed Aug. 10, 2017).

28 Johnson, Ferris, and Pfeifer.

becomes more valuable with tens of millions of users using it for calls, texts, videoconferencing, and so on. From a valuation perspective, the value of networks in which users are connected is described by Metcalfe's Law,[29] which says that the value of this type of network is proportional to the square of number of connected users, or N^2.

A step beyond the homogenous network is the heterogeneous network, in which diverse sets of users use a platform or product for varying purposes. A simple example of this type of network is OpenTable, in which two distinct categories of participants—diners and restaurants—interact with one another (**Exhibit 9**). The value of OpenTable, though, would still be described by Metcalfe's Law. However, one of the features that makes heterogeneous networks so valuable is that groups can form within it. In this case, Facebook may be the ultimate example of a heterogeneous network, as it has a large user base and a large number of self-forming groups. From a valuation perspective, the value of networks capable of generating user groups is explained by Reed's Law,[30] which says that value grows exponentially with the size of the network, or 2^N.

However, as Peter Thiel wrote in 2015, "Network effects can be powerful, but you will never reap them unless your product is valuable to its very first users when the network is small."[31] If blockchain technology attracts diverse users doing different things with it, its value will be described by Reed's Law, and it will become increasingly more valuable as engagement increases (measured by an increasing number of transactions across an increasing number of users occurring at an increased frequency).[32]

Regulatory and Governance Considerations

When novel technologies in the financial services industry gather—or appear to gather—critical mass, regulation follows. Blockchain does not appear to be an exception to this rule. Legislators and central banks started publically talking and wondering about blockchain in 2015 and 2016, and most of the focus appears around payments, clearing, and settlements—"a core element of the financial infrastructure at the national and international level."[33]

The U.S. House of Representatives is exploring the regulatory and legislative implications of blockchain on payments, clearing, and settlement systems, specifically the irreversibility

---

29 Johnson, Ferris, and Pfeifer.

30 Johnson, Ferris, and Pfeifer.

31 Peter A. Thiel and Blake Masters, *Zero to One: Notes on Startups, or How to Build the Future* (London: Virgin Books, 2015).

32 Hariharan et al.

33 "Payment, Clearing and Settlement Statistics," Bank for International Settlements, December 11, 2015.

of a transaction on a blockchain, and that criminals are able to transfer assets and extract Bitcoin-denominated ransoms.[34] The Federal Reserve System in the United States is also focusing on payments, clearing, and settlements, believing that "[blockchain] may represent the most significant development in many years in payments, clearing, and settlement."[35] This focus appears to makes sense, too: U.S. payment, clearing, and settlement systems process approximately 600 million transactions per day, valued at over $12.6 trillion.[36] While the Federal Reserve and the U.S. legislature have provided some indication on their respective foci, as of 2017 it is unclear what plans the SEC has to address the regulatory implications of blockchain within the financial services industry.

There is also the question of whether or how digital currency regulations will trickle down to affect blockchain use, and there appears to be regulatory interest connected to how people will ultimately use digital currencies.[37] For example, if people use digital currencies to pay for goods and services, then it is important to remember that Bitcoin transactions on the blockchain are permanent and tamper-resistant; transactions cannot be altered retroactively without the full agreement of the network. This presents a possible challenge for merchants and retail customers, for example, in refunding a purchase. If digital currencies are issued to raise money for an enterprise (e.g., an initial coin offering or ICO), the SEC has indicated that it will regulate digital currencies as securities, making them subject to federal securities law.[38] Additionally, product developers are trying to create marketable securities (e.g., exchange-traded funds [ETFs]) that track the value of digital currencies; in March 2017, the SEC denied a bid to list a Bitcoin-tied ETF (though this decision appears to be an ETF structure–related decision rather than a blockchain-related one).[39]

From a governance standpoint, public blockchains are decentralized, open-source technologies with no single set of leaders or owners. Industry observers have commented that, for public blockchains and digital currencies, establishing a governance structure—establishing

---

34 "Disrupter Series: Digital Currency and Blockchain Technology," Public Hearing before the Energy and Commerce Committee of the U.S. House of Representatives, March 16, 2016.

35 "Speech by Governor Brainard on Distributed Ledger Technology: Implications for Payments, Clearing, and Settlement," Board of Governors of the Federal Reserve System, October 7, 2016.

36 David Mills, "Distributed Ledger Technology in Payments, Clearing, and Settlement," Federal Reserve Board Divisions of Research & Statistics and Monetary Affairs Finance and Economics Discussion Series, 2016.

37 Higgins; "Digital Currency and Blockchain Technology;" "Speech by Governor Brainard."

38 Connie Loizos, "In the Murky World of ICOs, this Young Founder Aims to Lead the Way," TechCrunch, July 26, 2017.

39 Stan Higgins, "SEC Rejects Winklevoss Bitcoin ETF Bid," CoinDesk, March 10, 2017.

underlying reliability and accountability of public blockchains—will be critical to their continued development and adoption.[40]

Considerations for the Future

At present, blockchain is a relatively nascent technology that appears to offer possibly valuable product and service applications. All practitioners whose businesses might evolve from technological advances need to decide: should they determine how to use this and pursue those opportunities, or should they wait until others try it, see how they do, and learn from their mistakes. The urgency of this decision will vary depending on industry; the financial services industry may undergo a greater degree of evolution sooner than other industries. Industries that feature complicated global supply chains, have high degrees of intermediated global payments, require high levels of data security, and whose transactions face strong degrees of regulatory scrutiny may be motivated to adopt and deploy blockchain within individual enterprises.

For example, blockchain has the potential to improve investment and asset managers' operating businesses, as each one uses retail and wholesale payment systems, trading platforms, clearinghouses, and settlement systems for securities. However, at present, there is less clarity surrounding financial services industry regulators and what regulations will ultimately govern blockchain use.[41] Will blockchain be the underlying technology that transforms how an asset manager runs core parts of its business? In a vacuum, one could make a strong argument that this is at least possible. Yet as a network effect technology, the ultimate utility in any industry will be a function of who uses it and how.

JPMorgan Chase perhaps offers some directional guidance for financial services; it invested in and built an enterprise blockchain specifically for the financial services industry and are giving it away for free. It believes that its blockchain platform, Quorum, balances data privacy with regulatory transparency, and offers high speed and high throughput processing. Further, JPMorgan Chase is piloting Quorum as an underpinning of the global payments function of their enterprise.

If blockchain can deliver products and services that improve the customer experience and the profitability of an enterprise, the organizations that use it may capture a larger, more profitable share of a competitive marketplace moving forward.

---

40 Nathaniel Popper, "Some Bitcoin Backers are Defecting to Create a Rival Currency," New York Times, July 25, 2017.

41 Higgins, "Bitlicense Framework for Bitcoin Business;" "Digital Currency and Blockchain Technology;" "Speech by Governor Brainard;" and Mills.

Exhibit 1
An Introduction to Blockchain
Glossary of Terms

Audit trail: A chronological record, set of records, and/or destination and source of records that provide documentary evidence of the sequence of activities that have affected at any time a specific operation, procedure, or event.[42]

Centralized point of control: The single storage and maintenance location of a database.[43]

Cryptography: The computerized encoding and decoding of information.[44]

Digital identity: Information used by a computer system to represent an external agent.[45]

Digital key/signature: Cryptographic technique used to validate the authenticity and integrity of an identity, message, software, or digital document.[46]

Ledger: A complete record of financial transactions over the life of the company.[47]

Native currency: The "currency" (e.g., Bitcoin) required to claim an underlying asset traded on a blockchain from its issuer. This currency is also the form of compensation network members receive that verify public blockchain transactions (called miners).

Permissioned blockchain: Restricts the actors who can contribute to the consensus of the system state. In a permissioned blockchain, only a restricted set of users have the rights to validate transactions and create smart contracts.[48]

Permissionless blockchain: Anyone can join the network, trade assets, validate transactions, and/or create smart contracts.[49]

---

42 Merriam Webster Unabridged Online, s.v. "audit trail," http://unabridged.merriam-webster.com/unabridged/audit%20trail (accessed Aug. 31, 2017).
43 "Centralised Database," Internet Archive, https://web.archive.org/web/20140827182930/http://ict.stmargaretsacademy.org.uk/isint2/infosystems/centraldb.html (accessed Sept. 27, 2017).
44 Merriam Webster Unabridged Online, s.v., "cryptography," http://unabridged.merriam-webster.com/unabridged/cryptography (accessed Aug. 31, 2017).
45 "ISO/IEC 24760-1:2011—Information Technology—Security Techniques—A Framework for Identity Management—Part 1: Terminology and Concepts." International Organization for Standardization, 2011–2012, http://standards.iso.org/ittf/PubliclyAvailableStandards/c057914_ISO_IEC_24760-1_2011.zip (accessed July 19, 2017).
46 "Digital Signature," TechTarget, http://searchsecurity.techtarget.com/definition/digital-signature (accessed July 19, 2017).
47 "General Ledger," Investopedia, http://www.investopedia.com/terms/g/generalledger.asp?ad=dirN&qo=investopediaSiteSearch&qsrc=0&o=40186 (accessed Sept. 27, 2017).
48 Deva Annamalai, "Blockchain—What Is Permissioned vs Permissionless?" LinkedIn, January 11, 2017.
49 Annamalai, "Blockchain—What Is Permissioned vs Permissionless?"

Relational database: A database that presents information in tables with rows and columns, with the ability to retrieve data from the table based on searchable keys and concepts or commands.[50]

Smart contract: Event-triggered, automated pieces of computer code intended to facilitate, verify, or enforce the negotiation or performance of a contract.[51]

Exhibit 2

An Introduction to Blockchain

The Lifecycle of Paying Apartment Rent Using Bitcoin

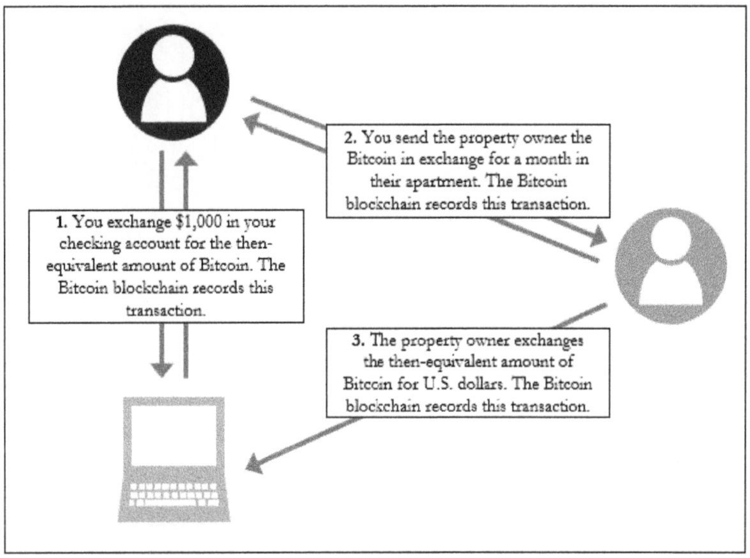

Source: Created by authors.

50 "A Relational Database Overview," Oracle https://docs.oracle.com/javase/tutorial/jdbc/overview/database.html (accessed Sept. 27, 2017).

51 Nick Szabo, "Formalizing and Securing Relationships on Public Networks," *First Monday*, September 1, 1997.

Exhibit 3
An Introduction to Blockchain
Historical (30-Day) Rolling Volatility (Annualized) for Bitcoin (BTC) and Ethereum (ETH) Since Inception

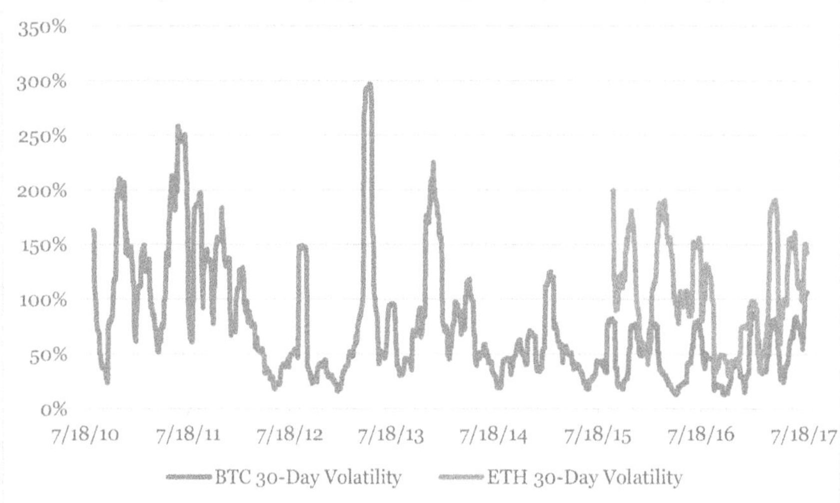

Data source: BraveNewCoin.

Exhibit 4
An Introduction to Blockchain
Median Bitcoin Transaction Confirmation Times Since Inception

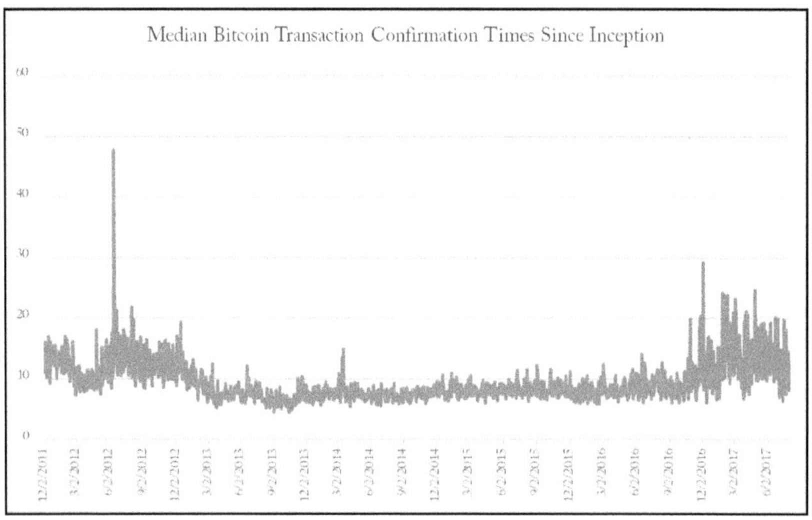

Data source: SpreadStreet.

Exhibit 5
An Introduction to Blockchain
Cost per Bitcoin Transaction Since Inception

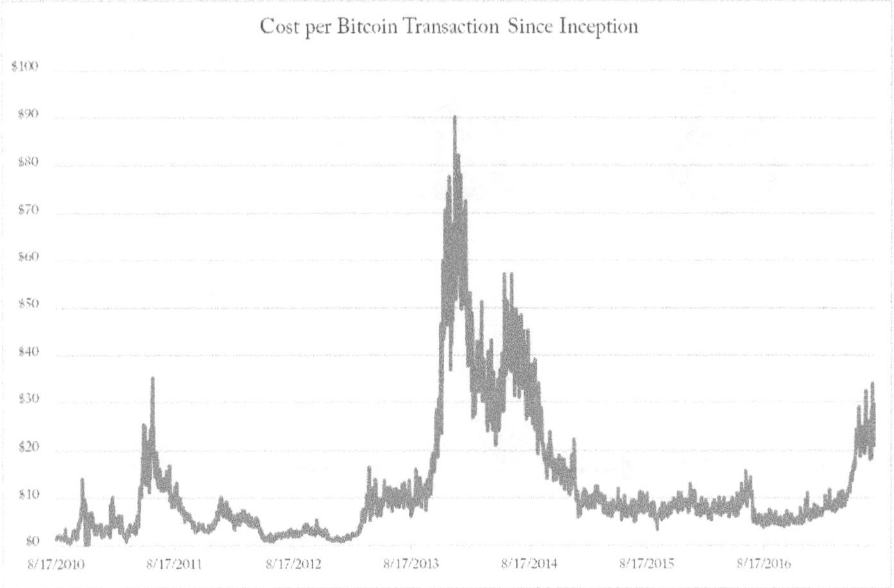

Data source: SpreadStreet.

Exhibit 6
An Introduction to Blockchain
Current Example of a Simple Cross Border Payment

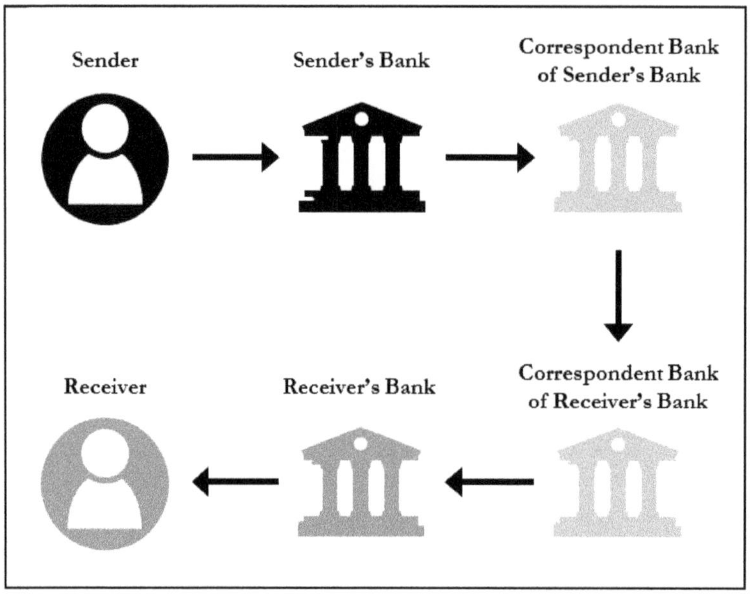

A sender in the United States needs to send money to a receiver in another country in another currency. Sender requests its bank in the United States, sender's bank, send a payment to receiver. Sender's bank requests its correspondent bank facilitate the transfer. Correspondent bank of sender's bank sends the funds to correspondent bank of recipient's bank, which then sends the funds to recipient's bank. At each step, fees and time accumulate. The sender and receiver only know the total amount of fees and the incremental exchange rates once the funds are in receiver's account.

Source: Created by authors.

Exhibit 7
An Introduction to Blockchain
Example of a Simple Cross Border Payment Using an Enterprise Blockchain

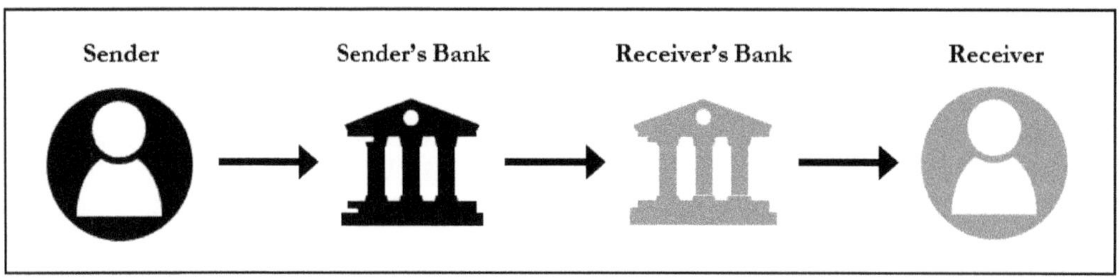

Sender in the United States needs to send money to receiver in another country in another currency. Sender requests its bank in the United States to send a payment to receiver. Sender's bank transfers the funds to receiver's bank.

Source: Created by authors.

Exhibit 8

An Introduction to Blockchain

Example of Homogenous Network

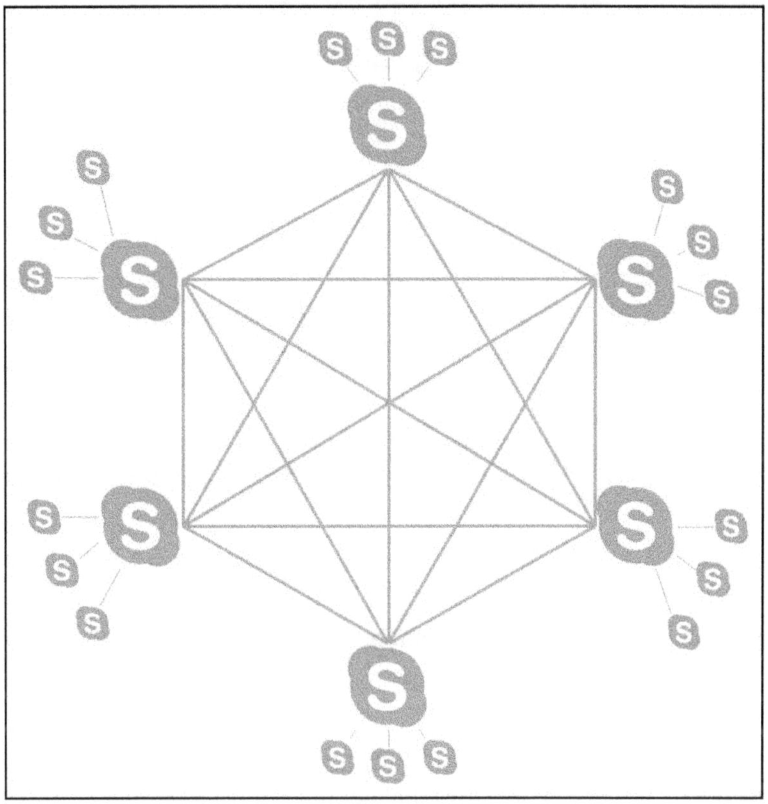

Source: Created by authors. The Skype Color Icon is a trademark or other intellectual property of the Microsoft group of companies, and this technical note is not affiliated, sponsored, authorized or otherwise associated by/with the Microsoft group of companies.

Exhibit 9

An Introduction to Blockchain

Example of Heterogeneous Network

Source: Created by authors. The OpenTable Logo is the intellectual property of OpenTable, Inc. and is used in accord with the branding guidelines provided by the company. This technical note is not affiliated, sponsored, authorized or otherwise associated by/with OpenTable, Inc. or any of its affiliates.

Reading 11

Blockchain Economies

The Crowd as the Market Maker

Arun Sundararajan

> Think about gambling without a casino, think about stock trading without an exchange, think about real estate transactions without deeds, and think about transactions without clearing houses—that is the world we are heading into. We have just barely scratched the surface today.
>
> —Fred Wilson, from a talk at the Collaborative-Peer-Sharing Economy Summit, New York University, May 30, 2014

In June 2015, the New York City venture capital firm Union Square Ventures (USV), well known as an early lead investor in the social media giant Twitter and the microblogging platform Tumblr, announced a $3.4 million seed investment in a new company called OB1.[1]

When the investment was announced, there was little public information about OB1. Internet searches for the company were more likely to yield discussion groups about spelling the name of the *Star Wars* character Obi-Wan Kenobi. The company's own website, a serene, detail-free, Zen-white page, offered no additional details, simply stating a promise: "Helping make trade free for everyone, everywhere."

Brad Burnham, the USV partner who led the investment, explained in a blog post that OB1 was formed to further the development of OpenBazaar, an open-source decentralized marketplace protocol. To the otherwise uninformed, a visit to the OpenBazaar website leaves one with a feeling the effort is subversive, almost sinister. "Even though the Internet is global, governments and corporations are restricting free trade," says a disembodied voice on an OpenBazaar promotional video.[2] "They collect your data and violate your privacy. They censor your transactions and take their own cut. It's time to take control back."

A look at OpenBazaar's history is hardly reassuring. It evolved from a prototype peer-to-peer market called DarkMarket developed in April 2014 by Amir Taaki, the founder of the Internet anarchist group unSYSTEM. Taaki created DarkMarket following the shuttering of a market called the Silk Road, best known for facilitating the sales of illegal drugs, and whose founder Ross Ulbricht is currently serving a life sentence in a US prison.[3] "Like a hydra, those of us in the community that push for individual empowerment are in an arms race to equip the people with the tools needed for the next generation of digital black markets," Taaki explained to *Wired* reporter Andy Greenberg in 2014.[4]

On its website, OpenBazaar commits to "zero fees," indicating that because there are no parties in the middle of the transactions, there are no fees to pay. As Burnham further clarifies about OpenBazaar in his blog post, "There is no way for a central authority to leverage network effect market power to extract rents from the participants."[5]

At a time when most venture capitalists seem to be plowing money into sharing economy platforms that are able to do precisely what Burn-ham claimed OpenBazaar made impossible (i.e., "leverage network effect market power to extract rents from the participants"), why would a visible and successful venture capitalist like USV want to invest in a company aimed at furthering a technology that is not only, in a sense, "off the grid," but is also open-source and committed to "zero fees." Burnham explains further:

> This begs the question of how OB1 can be a for profit business that will generate a return on the investment we are announcing today. How can a business that is consciously architected to undo network effect defensibility, one that is tearing down the walls and filling in the moats that every paper on market based competition has insisted are necessary for success ... succeed.
>
> OB1 will offer a set of value added services to buyers and sellers on the OpenBazaar market. They expect others to provide services to the participants on OpenBazaar, and they don't expect to have any proprietary advantage over those competitors. As investors, we hope that their familiarity with the marketplace and the goodwill they generate as early sponsors of the open source project will give them an advantage but we understand they must execute very well or be left behind.[6]

Time will tell whether USV counts OB1 as a success story or not. But it's a more promising investment than it might seem. OB1 is part of a new generation of peer-to-peer systems that promise to expand the potential of crowd-based capitalism significantly over the coming years, transitioning the role of the crowd from being the source of capital and labor to actually owning and running the marketplace in a decentralized fashion. Many of these nascent systems are based on the ideas and "blockchain" technologies that power the popular digital currency Bitcoin.

And USV is hardly alone in its interest in this technology. Adam Ludwin, a partner at RRE Ventures, currently runs a startup called Chain that is also funded by the famed Silicon Valley investor Vinod Khosla. RRE, along with the venture capital firm Andreessen Horowitz, has also invested in Ripple Labs, which is building a blockchain-based market for interbank settlement. Andreessen Horowitz partners Marc Andreessen and Chris Dixon frequently express significant levels of excitement about the commercial promise of the blockchain.

These are just a few examples of a new marketplace technology paradigm that may power the next generation of crowd-based capitalism, To better appreciate the economic and social impacts of these marketplaces, we first need to understand how some of them work. The right place to start is by understanding Bitcoin.

Understanding Decentralized Peer-to-Peer Exchange

In the simplest possible terms, bitcoin is a digital currency. (I refer to the currency using lowercase "b," and the platform, technology, or ecosystem using uppercase "B.") You can acquire bitcoin by exchanging it for your dollars, euros, or yen, by providing someone with a product or service that they pay you for in bitcoin, or by "mining" bitcoin (more on this later). Your acquisition and subsequent possession of this bitcoin exists as one or more entries in a public ledger (the blockchain) in which you are identified by a secure anonymized "key." Each time you use your bitcoin, the new transaction is recorded as yet another entry in the ledger.

A lot of the attention paid to Bitcoin has focused on its success in creating currency without a government backer, about how bitcoin value measured in traditional money fluctuates a lot over time (although its exchange rate has stabilized considerably in 2015), and perhaps also about the use of bitcoin for commerce that many governments consider illegal. Instead of rehashing those topics, I focus here on thinking about Bitcoin as one of many applications of a new set of enabling technologies. I also discuss two other related applications: OpenBazaar and La'Zooz. Through this discussion, some of the key elements of the economics and technology of decentralized peer-to-peer marketplaces will become more transparent.

Bitcoin

Many of the critical pieces of a decentralized peer-to-peer market are part of Bitcoin. Let's say that you want to send your friend Clay digital money. You would ideally say something like this: "I possess at least one currency unit from prior transaction Q, and I am giving Clay one unit." This establishes that you have the money, commits you to the transaction, and gives Clay access to the money. The physical-world equivalent would be if you were to give Clay a banknote.

Establishing a digital equivalent first requires the use of a "digital signature." Let's say that there are two unique numbers (called "keys," analogous to what goes into a lock) associated with you. One of these is known only to you, or is stored on a device you own, and is called your private key. Another, available for anyone to look up, is called your public key. If someone "locks" a message (or encodes it using a cryptography algorithm) with your public key, this encrypted message can only be "unlocked" with your private key. And vice versa—if a message is encrypted with your private key, it can only be decrypted with your public key. This allows for a simple way to create a "signature": since you are the only person who has your private key, then a message encrypted with it could only have come from you. And since your public key is public, anyone can verify that this is your signature.

Next there must be a way to prevent you from arbitrarily spending money you don't have. In the physical world, this is accomplished by making bank notes hard to counterfeit. In a system like PayPal, on the other hand, a trusted third-party (i.e., a centralized entity, or PayPal itself)—keeps track of who has how much, and updates a *private* digital "ledger" of some sort every time someone sends money to someone else.[7] Bitcoin, in contrast, uses a *public* ledger, the *blockchain*. Every user of Bitcoin has a copy of this blockchain, and it contains every single bitcoin transaction since the currency was created. When you say, "I possess at least one currency unit from prior transaction Q, and I am giving Clay one unit," Clay can verify that the message is from you by checking your signature, and he can then check his copy of the blockchain to be assured that you in fact have bitcoin to spend.

But this approach leads to a problem. Suppose you only have one currency unit to spend. Now, let's say you simultaneously send a signed message to both Clay and Emily giving them each one unit. If they both checked their current copy of the blockchain, they would find the prior transaction, it would seem like you have the money, and both of them would update their ledgers, leading to a problem down the line.

A possible solution might be to delegate maintaining the integrity of the ledger to the "crowd," as I illustrate here with this simple scenario: After both Clay and Emily receive your message and check their copies of the blockchain to see if you have the money to spend, they then broadcast the transaction to the entire network of users. This transaction then joins a list of "pending transactions," each of which will "clear" only when enough people on the network match the transaction against their copy of the blockchain and indicate that it is OK. During this waiting period it will likely be discovered that you have (perhaps mistakenly) tried to spend your unit twice.

This is sort of like writing a check in the physical world. If you hand over a personal check to someone, they now have it in their possession, but until the bank has "cleared" the check, they don't actually receive the money. In the example above, the user network (possessing individual copies of the blockchain) serves collectively as the bank.

But what's to prevent you from creating millions of identities online and "taking over" the network by controlling a majority of the user accounts? If you managed to insert fake transactions suggesting you have money to spend into a majority of the copies of the block-chain, wouldn't this allow you in effect to create "counterfeit" money?

Bitcoin solves this problem in an ingenious way: continuing to rely on a crowd-based method of clearing transactions, but artificially adding complexity to the validation process. How is this accomplished, and why does it work? Well, when a user, let's say Clay, checks the list of pending transactions and confirms their validity, Clay also has to solve an intensely challenging computational problem (the "challenge"). Solving a challenge is sort of like factorizing a big number—generating the two factors is difficult, but once you do that, verifying that their product yields the original number is easy. A Bitcoin challenge is significantly harder, but once solved, checking that the answer is correct is relatively simple.[8]

Meanwhile, Emily and others might have also validated the list of pending bitcoin transactions and, in parallel with Clay, would be trying to solve the challenge as well. If Clay happens to win (solve the challenge first), others will verify that his answer is correct, then update their block-chains with his list of validated transactions. (It actually takes a little longer than that for a set of transactions to be accepted by the block-chain, but this is a detail that is less relevant to our discussion.)

As a consequence, Clay can't simply or arbitrarily generate fake identities to take over the network and insert fake ledger entries. He'd need a large amount of computational power, and meanwhile, others are busy solving the same challenge to validate the transactions. And there's enough randomness in the challenge so that the person with the most computational power doesn't necessarily win (although having that power does have an advantage, on average.) So, while there is a risk that someone will invest way more than everyone else in computational power and start to take over the network, this is far more difficult and expensive than setting up millions of fake identities.

This leads to yet another problem, though. Computational power isn't free. What incentive do Clay and Emily have to invest their resources into solving the challenge repeatedly? Well, the "winner" of the challenge gets issued new bitcoin! (As of 2015, this reward is 25 bitcoin, worth a few thousand US dollars.) This process of validating transactions, solving the challenge, and collecting the reward is referred to as "mining" new bit-coin. Since there's a new list of transactions (or "block") to verify every 10 minutes or so, mining can translate into pretty good returns on one's investment in computational power.

Put differently, the blockchain facilitates "permissionless innovation," much like the TCP/IP protocol does for the Internet. In an early and influential 2013 blog post about the blockchain, Albert Wenger, a partner at New York's Union Square Ventures, explains the importance of such protocols:

> Policy makers, however, need to understand the importance of protocols for enabling distributed permission-less innovation—that is, innovation by many individuals and startups. For instance, the hypertext transport protocol (http) is what lets a browser talk to a web server—as long as the server implements the protocol it can deliver innovative content or services to any browser. HTTP itself builds on many other lower level protocols, such as DNA and TCP/IP. Historically, protocols have emerged from either research projects or from individuals/small groups simply throwing something out that sticks. In the debate about bitcoin it is critical to understand that bitcoin has the potential to be such a protocol that enables a lot of new innovation to take place.[9]

Although the exact details of how Bitcoin works are a little more complicated than my short description in this section, a few key ideas come across: digital signatures that facilitate identity; the distributed ledger (the blockchain) that is stored on every client's device; the crowd collectively clearing each transaction; the need to make clearing transactions challenging to avoid a potential takeover of the blockchain; and the need for an incentive (some equivalent of money, typically called the "coin" that is generated from within the system) to get the crowd interested in performing the challenging work that accompanies verifying transactions.

Now, if you think about it, peer-to-peer payment is actually a fairly simple commercial application. Once you establish identity, build a system to clear transactions, and convince people that they won't lose their money, you've got enough trust to make things work. What's being transferred is uniform (money). There's no product variety to contend with. There are no physical assets involved. There's no need to discover what's available or compare prices. There's no imperative to think about how to get the physical asset from seller to buyer. There's no quality uncertainty—money is money. No complicated contracts are needed about delivery and quality. There's no business need to reveal your physical world presence or location. There's no risk associated with meeting someone unsavory.

Not surprisingly, therefore, much of the initial focus of blockchain marketplace development has been on creating new systems for trading assets that are non-physical: digital and financial assets. In a 2015 conversation I had with Adam Ludwin, the CEO of the blockchain startup Chain I mentioned earlier in the chapter, he described the blockchain as a "new database technology, purpose-built for trading assets," and sees immense potential in new blockchain based marketplaces for loyalty points, mobile minutes, gift cards, and of course, a range of financial assets. Ludwin described how many current systems for trading such assets could benefit significantly from a new decentralized marketplace. "Not that there's anything wrong with a centralized institution, but it increases costs, freezes innovation potential, and needs layers of reconciliation," he noted, further pointing out how innovation can be spurred simply by the threat of a decentralized marketplace, much like illegal peer-to-peer filesharing networks may have led to the emergence of iTunes, Pandora, and Spotify.

If one considers the history of electronic marketplaces, this initial focus on financial marketplaces is not surprising. Many stock exchanges were the early adopters of digital technologies, a decade or more before the emergence of eBay or Amazon. However, to move beyond marketplaces for digital assets and toward broader real-world marketplaces for goods and services, each of the (familiar) issues I allude to above—regarding non-uniformity, logistics, and uncertainty, among others—comes up and needs to be addressed if we hope to move toward creating serious decentralized alternatives for more complex marketplace interaction.

OpenBazaar and Smart Contracts

The OpenBazaar platform takes a first step toward creating a decentralized peer-to-peer marketplace. If you have an item for sale, you list it on the OpenBazaar client (a program or app you download to your device), along with a product description, and a price (in bitcoin). Once you confirm listing the item, this listing is broadcast to all the other clients on OpenBazaar.

So, how do you find what's available? Beyond the first critical "infrastructure" element of a distributed marketplace (i.e., the *shared ledger*), there is a second: a *distributed hash table*. For context, let's go back to the discussion in chapter 2 about the difference between Napster and Gnutella—Napster had one central index of music stored on a centralized Napster computer. In contrast, Gnutella distributed that index across the different peers on the network. While Gnutella pioneered the distributed index, the trouble with its approach was that it took users a long time to find what they were looking for; further, every time someone conducted a search, the activity would "flood" the network. And since not every peer knew about every other peer, there was no guarantee that this approach would actually find a song that was available.

A distributed hash table, the result of efforts to improve on the Gnutella method, is a more sophisticated way of indexing what's available on a distributed network. It is smarter about dividing up the index, replicating it, and distributing the information across peers, in a way that makes discovery more reliable. Today's most popular peer-to-peer file-sharing technology, BitTorrent, uses this approach. So does Facebook when retrieving your friend's photos from one of its millions of database servers.

But, getting back to OpenBazaar: if you find a product that you like you can pay for it with bitcoin. Much like PayPal, which was a critical part of making eBay work early in the evolution of peer-to-peer markets, Bitcoin provides the necessary payment infrastructure for OpenBazaar. And analogous to eBay's auction system, if the OpenBazaar price is too high for you, you can propose a new, lower price to the seller.

Once you (as the buyer) agree with the seller on a price, you arrive at another challenge. How do you ensure that you'll actually get the product you bought? This is where a third critical infrastructure element of distributed peer-to-peer markets comes in: *contracts*. On OpenBazaar, the contracts are relatively simple, using a notary as the trusted third party—and on OpenBazaar, this notary can be any other client. Once the contract is set up, you send your bitcoin payment, and these are held "in escrow." You, as the buyer, notify the seller, saying, "I've sent the funds." The seller then ships the product (and handles all the logistics). When the product arrives, you acknowledge receipt. The funds are then released to the seller. If there's a dispute, the notary acts as the mediator. (A decision by any two of the three parties—buyer, seller, or notary—releases the funds. So, for example, the buyer and seller could resolve their dispute themselves.) There's a rating system to help choose sellers, buyers, and notaries. It's a little different from what's used in a centralized marketplace, and is not completely immune to manipulation.[10]

There is a more sophisticated class of contracts (called *smart contracts*) emerging for blockchain-based transactions. In *Blockchain: Blueprint for a New Economy*, Melanie Swan explains that while a traditional contract is an agreement between two or more parties to do something, in the case of a smart contract, the same terms exist, but with one exception—trust that comes from having a third-party is less important.[11] This is because the smart contract protocol can specify, as computer code, terms under which certain obligations are fulfilled, and can execute actions like sending a payment or deactivating a file once there is evidence of the contract's terms being fulfilled. (A precursor to a smart contract is the method implemented in the digital rights management system of a media store and player like iTunes, where a movie you rent is automatically deactivated after 24 hours.)

How does a "smart contract" manage to accomplish this? As Primavera De Fillipi explained in her influential 2014 talk at Harvard University's Berkman Center, the risks associated with peer-to-peer contracting can be reduced by the introduction of three new provisions: autonomy, self-sufficiency, and decentralization.[12]

Smart contracts are autonomous if after they are finalized, the initiating agents theoretically never need to have contact again. Smart contracts are also self-sufficient to the extent that they are able to marshal their own resources. Finally, smart contracts are decentralized; they are distributed across network nodes rather than residing in a centralized location, and are self-executing. This means that smart contracts will be applicable across jurisdictions or, in a sense, will be borderless. We may thus be inching even closer toward the realization of Stanford University professor Lawrence Lessig's memorable mantra, "code is law."[13] In this respect, smart contracts would solve a dilemma that we've faced since the Internet's initial spread in the 1990s—transcending jurisprudence's reliance on political borders. The answer in the end, not surprisingly, is code itself.

There is reason to be cautious, however. To date, regulation through code has yielded mixed results. With the Internet came spam. Over time, we have attempted to stop spam using various different automated methods, but, as Lessig himself points out, efforts to block spam have also blocked other types of information from circulating on the Internet. Code has failed, in a sense, to regulate without compromising one of the very principles upon which the Internet was founded—free speech. It remains unclear whether similar human limitations will restrict the scope of usefulness of smart contracts.

Decentralized Service Platforms

A currency like bitcoin or a marketplace like OpenBazaar gets stronger as it has more users. If you think about it, however, the early users of Bitcoin participated in the enterprise with no guarantee that their contributions of time, support or computing power would yield anything of real value. Of course, some have now been compensated handsomely, as the bitcoin they mined is worth millions of dollars. In a way, as the physicist Matan Field, a serial entrepreneur and thinker about the blockchain, explained to me in the summer of 2015, these early users added a tremendous amount of value to the system—at the margin, much more than a new user today might add—and, correspondingly, many were well compensated. Analogous to the way a venture capitalist gets compensated for risking financial capital on an early-stage company, the early users took a huge risk—but with human capital and processing power investments—and realized a big return.

But beyond the users and the folks who verify transactions, there are many other parts of the Bitcoin system that have added to its value today. People contributed to the writing of the underlying open-source computer code. Others publicized it. Others wrote user guides. Arguably, many of these stakeholders also contributed to the eventual success; but the system, although perhaps more equitable than a privately owned company, was engineered in a way that only gave the "miners" a big financial return.

This highlights another challenge facing a decentralized peer-to-peer market. In the absence of any central, third-party owning the network, how do you make sure that different peers have the right incentives to contribute appropriately, how do you make sure that the rewards match the effort and the risk, and how do you keep people motivated to sustain contributions, in effort and resources, needed to continue clearing the transactions? The presence of some sort of internally generated "coin" clearly seems integral, but how do you make it valuable, and how do you spread this value?

Co-founded in 2013 by Matan Field, Oren Sokolowsky, and Shay Zluf, La'Zooz is (as of 2015) a decentralized peer-to-peer ridesharing marketplace that takes a novel approach to this problem. (The platform is based in Israel, and the word "lazuz" means "to move" in Hebrew.) Think about a service like Uber. Sure, there's value in the technology, but eventually, the system is more valuable to passengers when there are more drivers; and the system is valuable to drivers when there are more passengers. So a critical "input" into such a ridesharing system is user participation. Correspondingly, the users who "seed" the system with early participation are likely to be more valuable, at the margin, than those who join later.

La'Zooz has created what seems to be a familiar-looking mobile device app for ridesharing, but with a key difference: embedded in each app is a "mining app" as well, designed to encourage early participation. Here's how it works. You download and install the app. You turn it on when you are driving, and earn "zooz," the La'Zooz currency, simply by driving around with the app on. The more you drive, the more zooz you earn. You also earn zooz by inviting others to download the app. (The project leaders also sold some zooz to raise money.) Once the level of adoption in any neighborhood is sufficiently high, the ridesharing portion of the app gets activated. You can then use your accumulated zooz to buy rides, much like you'd use currency to buy an Uber or Lyft ride.

As Vitalik Buterin, an influential writer about decentralized peer-to-peer systems and the founder of Ethereum, a decentralized platform that runs smart contracts, noted in a blog post, "the idea of releasing a new currency as a mechanism for funding protocol development is perhaps one of the most interesting economic innovations to come out of the cryptocurrency space."[14] But a critical determinant of success is architecting this distribution of value right. [15] It also seems important for the manifestation of this value, the "coin," to be of continuing value as the platform grows and matures. And what's also important here is to think of the coin as not just currency, but as a store of value, like shares in a private company. The coin provides returns to early contributors—of human capital, of risky early participation, of effort publicizing the marketplace and facilitating critical mass—a new breed of purpose-driven investors.

Value Creation and Capture in Decentralized Exchange

There are a number of new forms of economic activity that new decentralized peer-to-peer marketplaces will facilitate simply because they lower transaction costs. Other decentralized systems, either independent or embedded in traditional privately owned corporations or markets, may emerge in contexts where there was previously insufficient trust for digital exchange, where the potential market was too small to attract private capital in the past, or where the blockchain lowers operating costs. Toward the end of the chapter, I'll discuss some current examples.

First, however, let's consider the broader future of decentralized peer-to-peer markets. Will the democratic promise sustain over time? Or will we see the emergence of "layers" of intermediation that represent private capital? Should we expect a trajectory resembling what followed the commercialization of the permissionless Internet, where the initial decentralized promise was followed by extensive re-aggregation and the subsequent capture of massive market value as manifested by the emergence of companies like Amazon, Google, and Facebook?

We have already witnessed the emergence of Bitcoin, a widely used peer-to-peer decentralized payment system with many users. It is instructive here to look at other fundamental capabilities that create value in any system of exchange, whether digital or not, whether decentralized or otherwise, and see what we can learn from some recent historical examples.

Attention, Search, and Discovery

As the World Wide Web blossomed in 1994, anyone with an Internet connection could publish content accessible to anyone else with an Internet connection. This massive influx of decentralized content almost immediately led to the emergence of a set of search engines and directories that facilitated *discovery*—among them, Yahoo (initially a hand-curated directory), Lycos, Infoseek, and Altavista. These search engines were able to index and organize the Web's information with a reasonable level of comprehensiveness, but were unable to provide any reliable "quality" information in an automated way. It took until 1998 and the emergence of Google before we had a good search engine for not just finding what we wanted, but for focusing us on what might be pertinent—a reliable system for both discovery and for ranking. And over the next decade—as digital information was created in smaller, more numerous, and more focused units as social media posts and microblogs—another centralized intermediary, Facebook, emerged as the dominant, human-network-mediated arbiter of discovery.

Google and Facebook have shown that immense market value can be captured from guiding discovery in a decentralized information-publishing world. Both continue to be valuable in part because what they are enabling us to discover—information on websites, information shared by other humans—is a complex "product." (In comparison, a product listing on a marketplace is relatively simple. The information about a typical product is fairly easy to describe, and prices and shipping costs are just numbers.) Besides, value placed on the same piece of information varies significantly across different end-users. Your friends' Facebook updates are far more valuable to you that those of a random person. News your friends like is more likely to be of interest to you.

It is very likely that as decentralized peer-to-peer marketplaces for the exchange of goods and services become popular, different discovery layers will follow. There are a number of search engines that specialize in finding content distributed across BitTorrent clients. BazaarBay is a search service for listings on OpenBazaar. What the first 20 years of the commercial Internet have taught us is that as *offers* proliferate—whether they are offers of information or of commercial opportunities—the critical constraint is human attention. Any service that is able to direct our attention in a manner that lets us discover what we want, quickly and reliably, is likely to be a source of value creation.

Of course, every online retailer or peer-to-peer platform today with product variety—from Amazon to Airbnb to specialized retailers—has its own search capability as well. The distributed hash tables that index the offers across OpenBazaar facilitate this form of search on a distributed peer-to-peer marketplace. But, unless all of the world's consumer commerce aggregates into a handful of such marketplaces, perhaps a worldwide, decentralized version of Alibaba's Taobao marketplace in China, it seems reasonable to anticipate that new equivalents to Facebook and Google will emerge.

Trust and Reputation

While Google was being built in Stanford's computer science department, a little-known and somewhat different search engine was being developed there as well. Called Junglee, it was a search engine for comparing the *prices* of products being listed across the tens (and sometimes hundreds) of online retailers who were springing up. In 1998, Amazon bought Junglee from its co-founders Venky Harinarayan and Anand Rajaram (both graduates from my alma mater, the Indian Institute of Technology, Madras) for a little under $200 million, and quietly retired the service, perhaps to ensure that it would not encourage too much attention being redirected to the Amazon competitors who frequently charged lower prices at the time.

Many of you may no doubt remember the other marketplace search and price comparison services that followed, most notably one called mySimon that was quite popular in 1999. However, they did little to stop the progress and eventual dominance of Amazon. Why? In part, because while people valued lower prices, they also valued other dimensions of the transaction—reliable promises of delivery, speedy delivery, and the assurance that any credit card numbers they provided were safe. And by 1999, Amazon emerged as a trusted intermediary on this front. (The company also invested heavily in logistics, something I get to shortly.) This led to the birth of the Amazon brand, and coupled with operational excellence, the dominance of Amazon in online retailing.

[...] We discussed the central role trust plays in peer-to-peer exchange. It is hard to overstate the importance of this role. Perhaps new third-party systems that facilitate a greater level of peer-to-peer trust in decentralized marketplaces will emerge, much like the different layers of the trust infrastructures from Airbnb and BlaBlaCar facilitate high-stakes intermediated peer-to-peer exchange today. For example, as of 2015, Traity, the reputation service [...], has already created a version of its service that facilitates the use of one's trust profile in a blockchain-enabled transaction. As Carlos Herrera-Yague, a former MIT computer scientist and Traity's chief scientist explained to me, this involves a set of "cards" one keeps in something akin to a Traity wallet, and which can be accessed during a transaction while preserving one's anonymity. Rather than being a completely decentralized trust system, however, this trust profile service is centralized to the extent that its use involves, in its origins, a third-party—Traity.

In the near future, however, I expect a majority of customers to continue using "brand" as the basis for their choices. [...] we are reminded that today's successful platforms have invested very heavily in layering a familiar, centralized, hierarchical branded experience on top of their crowd-based marketplaces. Perhaps new brands will emerge associated with specific decentralized peer-to-peer marketplaces—and be built the way brand should be built—by creating a consistently high-quality end-user experience. But even in a decentralized peer-to-peer world, it is also likely that the trust from brand will be layered in a less organic, more capital-induced manner.

Logistics

In 1998, the retailing giant Walmart sued Amazon for infringing on its trade secrets. The charge: over the previous year, Amazon had hired about 15 of Walmart's employees, including Amazon's CIO in 1998, Richard Dalzell, who joined the company in 1997 after serving as a Walmart vice president. Walmart claimed that these former employees had leaked proprietary information about Walmart's famed supply chain management systems.

The suit was settled in 1999, but it underscored the fact that Amazon wasn't merely investing in product variety or search and discovery innovations like user reviews and recommendations. They were making massive investments into inventing an entirely new infrastructure for inventory management, warehousing, and delivery, one that was optimized for a retail world in which goods had to be moved not in bulk to outlets or stores, but one-by-one to individual consumers.

Amazon's current dominance of online retailing in the United States owes much to these early investments, and to the capabilities it has built to move physical goods faster and cheaper than any of its competitors. (Thousands of other sellers now sell through the Amazon platform, leveraging its logistics expertise and giving Amazon a slice of their profits.) Although Chinese ecommerce giant Alibaba's business model may seem more decentralized than Amazon's (at least through its primary consumer site Taobao), Alibaba has a significant ownership stake in and control over a number of its highly efficient logistics partners. Similarly, Uber and Lyft rely on systems that optimize their current pool of available drivers in real time.

Thus, although additive-manufacturing technologies such as 3-D printers will continue to increase the fraction of physical products sold as pure digital information (as we discussed in chapter 2), the need for reliable and low-cost logistics is unlikely to go away any time soon. It seems quite likely that as peer-to-peer logistics get more sophisticated, a platform like Instacart may do to local commerce what Amazon did to mail-order, aggressively capturing the merchandizing and customer-relationship dimensions of local commerce while reducing neighborhood stores to little more than a distributed network of small, glorified warehouses located close to where consumers live. It is also possible that decentralized alternatives to the centrally coordinated peer-to-peer delivery service Deliv could emerge, adding a logistics layer to the blockchain economy. History suggests that when moving either people or products in real time, a balance between centralized control and decentralized information trumps a system built on just one or the other.

Some Challenges and Opportunities

In many ways, this new generation of decentralized peer-to-peer technologies mirrors the P2P vision of Michel Bauwens [...], and promises to create immense economic value over the coming decades. As the venture capitalist Chris Dixon wrote on his blog in 2014, Bitcoin makes activities like international microfinance, markets for computing capacity, incentivized social software, and other micropayments possible—not because we haven't considered the value of these before, but because the transaction costs were too high.[16]

There are signs that traditional businesses will embrace many of the new capabilities of decentralized peer-to-peer technologies, much like Facebook actively uses BitTorrent within its privately owned server farms. In spring 2015, NASDAQ announced plans to leverage blockchain technology to support the development of a distributed ledger function for securities trading that will provide enhanced integrity, audit capabilities, governance, and transfer of ownership capabilities. The startup R3CEV has assembled a consortium of 25 of the world's largest banks that are creating a framework for using blockchain technology in world financial markets.[17] The startup Provenance provides a blockchain-based authentication service, where, for example, you can credibly establish the provenance of a high-value item by keeping track of and being able to access every trade associated with its ownership. At the 2015 Consumer Electronic Show, IBM and Samsung demonstrated a blockchain- and smart-contract-based system that allowed an autonomous washing machine to order detergent when it ran low, and make a smart-contract-based payment when it sensed that the detergent had been replaced. A simple task, no doubt, but something that points to the promise of blockchain-based marketplaces for an Internet of (Autonomous) Things.

However, many challenges remain before we can reliably conclude that the blockchain and other distributed peer-to-peer technologies can take on significant fractions of the world's economic activity. Security concerns remain. Furthermore, a ledger that has to be distributed across every client can grow awfully large over time, and scalability of blockchain-based applications remains an open question. Payment systems like Bitcoin, because of the way they delay settlement, may need to be rebuilt to handle the real-time payments that credit cards and mobile payment systems like PayPal manage with ease today. Part of the solution to both of these challenges will come from the creation of a greater fraction of "off-the-book" transactions, but this creates a new layer of inter-mediation. Off-the-book transactions also create new risks. Some of you may recall Mt.Gox, the exchange that held its users' bitcoin in its own centralized Bitcoin accounts while maintaining a parallel off-the-block-chain system of keeping track of which users had how much bitcoin. Mt.Gox ceased operations in 2014 following the 2013 loss of the equivalent of $450 million of its users' bitcoin because of what appeared to be a hacker having gained access to its Bitcoin accounts.

There are also concerns that someone who controls significantly more than 51% of the computing power being used to clear transactions (in Bitcoin's case, for example, for mining bitcoin) has the ability to alter ledger entries by "building their own chain," which, over time, will replace the true blockchain as the one that is associated with consensus. In 2014, ghash.io, a bitcoin mining pool, did attain this dominance in computing power being spent on mining bitcoin, and were in a position to launch a "51% attack" of this kind, although they were quick to reassure the community that they had no intention of doing so.

Any decentralized marketplace must also generate enough value to make the "coin" awarded for transaction-clearing activity sufficiently attractive. An alternative might be for each transaction to have a small, voluntary "commission" associated with it, and for this to be added to the payment the customer sends the provider, then shared as a reward to the "miner."[18] This would also suggest that there will be "attention" economies of scale associated with decentralized peer-to-peer marketplaces—the crowd has to notice the blockchain and care enough about it to verify its transactions and maintain the integrity of the ledger. Otherwise, what begins as a decentralized system may simply evolve into a traditional third-party platform that merely uses a glorified blockchain database.

Perhaps some of the greatest opportunity from decentralized peer-to-peer systems will come from the emerging decentralized autonomous organizations (DAOs) and decentralized collaborative organizations (DCOs) such as those that are being architected by Buterik's Ethereum and by Field and DeFillipi's Backfeed. Such organizations posit a holistic model for organizing economic activity in a decentralized manner. Perhaps these will allow the kind of decentralized, distributed ownership and control of the "platform cooperatives" [...].

One might wonder what realistic possibilities exist for organizations that seemingly exist embedded only in computer code. However, as Buterik points out about decentralized protocols in general, "On the one hand, much like Bitcoin itself, they are in a very clear way 'backed by nothing.' On the other hand, they actually have quite a powerful backing underneath, and one that is difficult to unseat."

What is this backing that Buterik refers to? As he notes in an *Ethereum Blog* post in April 2014, "It is important to first understand that, in the space of tech companies and especially social networking startups, a large number of them are literally backed by almost nothing but social consensus." He then goes on to explain:

Theoretically, it is entirely possible for all of the employees at Snapchat, Tinder, Twitter or any other such startup to all suddenly agree to quit and start their own business, completely rebuild all of the software from scratch within months, and then immediately proceed to build a superior product. The only reason why such companies have any valuation at all is a set of two coordination problems: the problem of getting all employees to quit at the same time, and the problem of getting all of the customers to simultaneously move over onto the new network.

In the abstract, this may seem like a flimsy justification for why tech companies are valuable; when thinking about something that represents billions of dollars of value, one naturally expects that value to be backed up by something tangible like physical resources or government force, not just some ethereal instantiation of the fact that it's hard for large groups of people to suddenly move from one social configuration to another.[19]

"Fortunately," concludes Buterik in the blog post, "we still have many decades to go in seeing exactly how the decentralized protocol ecosystem is going to play out." It looks like an interesting future indeed.

End Notes

1. See the link to OB1 at https://www.usv.com/portfolio#2015.
2. The video is posted on YouTube and available at https://youtu.be/nuRgHbTU9pk.
3. Benjamin Weiser, "Ross Ulbricht, Creator of Silk Road Website, Is Sentenced to Life in Prison," *New York Times*, May 29, 2015. http://www.nytimes.com/2015/05/30/nyregion/ross-ulbricht-creator-of-silk-road-website-is-sentenced-to-life-in-prison.html.

4. Andy Greenberg, "Inside the 'DarkMarket' Prototype, a Silk Road the FRI Can Never Seize," *Wired*, April 24, 2014. http://www.wired.com/2014/04/darkmarket.

5. Brad Burnham, "Introducing OB1," *USV Blog*, June 11, 2015. https://www.usv.com/blog/introducing-ob1.

6. Ibid.

7. For example, let's consider what happens when you swipe your credit or debit card. Data about the transaction is communicated via networks built by companies like VISA and MasterCard. Your account is then debited and the merchant's account is in turn credited. The bank that issued the credit or debit card is the trusted third party that verifies and clears the transaction.

8. The details of the problem are not important for what follows here. Briefly, Clay has to generate a number (called the *nonce*) that, when appended to the identifier number associated with the list of transactions (the "block"), and then "hashed" using the SHA-256 hash function, yields an output that satisfies a particular mathematical property (e.g., has a value less than some minimum, or has a bunch of zeroes at the beginning). It is very computationally intensive to actually find this nonce-identifier combination, but once the combination has been found, it is very easy to verify that the combination satisfies the mathematical property.

9. Albert Wenger, "Bitcoin as Protocol," *USV Blog*, October 31, 2013. https://www.usv.com/blog/bitcoin-as-protocol.

10. Dionysis Zindros, "A Pseudonymous Trust System for a Decentralized Anonymous Marketplace," *GitHub Gist*, 2015, https://gist.github.com/dionyziz/e3b296861175e0ebea4b.

11. Melanie Swan, *Blockchain: Blueprint for a New Economy* (Sebastopol, CA: O'Reilly Media, Inc., 2015).

12. Primavera De Fillipi, "Ethereum: Freenet or Skynet?," Talk presented at the Berkman Center for Internet & Society, Harvard University, Cambridge, MA, April 15, 2014.

13. Lawrence Lessig, *Code and Other Laws of Cyberspace* (New York: Basic Books, 1999).

14. Vitalik Buterin, "Decentralized Protocol Monetization and Forks," *Ethereum Blog*, April 30, 2014. https://blog.ethereum.org/2014/04/30/decentralized-protocol-monetization-and-forks.

15. It is likely that architecting it "optimally" is impossible, based on a set of results from a branch of economics called *mechanism design*.

16. Chris Dixon, "Some Ideas for Native Bitcoin Apps." *CDixon Blog*, October 4, 2014. http://cdixon.org/2014/10/04/some-ideas-for-native-bitcoin-apps.

17. Jemima Kelley, "Nine of the World's Biggest Bank Join to Form Blockchain Partnership," *Reuters*, September 15, 2015, http://www.reuters.com/article/2015/09/15/banks-blockchain-idUSL1N11L1K720150915#k5rPvtF0 AteX3fFK.97 ; Jemima Kelly, "Three Banks Join #3 Blockchain Consortium Taking Total to 25," *Reuters*, October 28, 2015, http://www.reuters.com/article/2015/10/28/us-global-banks-blockchain-idUSKCN0SM1U120151028#2rAUwQDFjkKbPeS1.97.

18. Bitcoin has this feature, although, as of 2015, this was just a couple of percent of the total miner revenue.

19. Buterin, "Decentralized Protocol Monetization and Forks."

Post-Reading Questions

1. How does Bitcoin produce value in the economy?
2. What is the connection between blockchain and cryptocurrency?
3. Are decentralized digital assets a value or detriment to the global economy?

www.ingramcontent.com/pod-product-compliance
Ingram Content Group UK Ltd.
Pitfield, Milton Keynes, MK11 3LW, UK
UKHW051453290926
15471UKWH00008B/1176

9 781516 540693